THE VICTIM'S CRY

DISCOVERING HOPE & HEALING THROUGH FORGIVENESS

STEVEN D GRIFFIN

According to the Scriptures the name of the one true God is YHVH, which is often written as *Yahweh* (pronounced Yah-way) or *Yahuvah* (pronounced Yah-hoo-vah) or *Yah* for short as is used in the phrase HalleluYah (praise be to YHVH). Some older English translations also used the name Jehovah (pronounced Je-ho-vah). In *The Victim's Cry,* YHVH is most often referred to by the titles: Lord, God, and Father. The name of His only begotten Son, God in the flesh, is *Yeshua* or *Y'shua* (meaning "YHVH saves" or "God is salvation") and He is referred to using the widely accepted Greek/Anglican name "Jesus" or by the title, "Lord."

www.xulonpress.com

Dedication and Acknowledgements

This book is dedicated to my beautiful wife, Angel, and our children: Brent, Eric, William, Sarah, and Mary—all of whom God has used to teach me about forgiveness and about trusting Him with my whole heart.

As we homeschooled our children, Angel and I would teach them something about life or academics nearly every day, and I would routinely share with them what God was teaching me at the time about forgiveness and other things.

Having my wife and children as my initial audience significantly helped me to better organize my thoughts before I typed them out, and without their assistance and encouragement, I probably would not have completed this book.

I especially want to thank Angel for putting up with me all these years and for serving as my chief editor and cover artist. She is talented in many areas, and I thank God for bringing us together and for keeping us together all these many years.

I also want to thank my father, Doug Griffin, late mother, Sandra Griffin, and my wife's parents, Thomas and Mary Spikes, who have taught me a great deal about God and life and have encouraged me in many ways.

Thank you all for putting up with me, encouraging me, and loving me all these years.

TABLE OF CONTENTS

INTRODUCTION

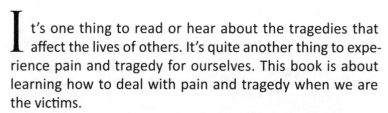

I t's one thing to read or hear about the tragedies that affect the lives of others. It's quite another thing to experience pain and tragedy for ourselves. This book is about learning how to deal with pain and tragedy when we are the victims.

There are many harassed and hurting people in the world who desperately need real and lasting help but cannot find it. I was once one of those desperate people from an emotional perspective. After my wife and I separated in 2001, I was emotionally devastated, but I turned to God for help, and He rescued me.

I've personally experienced the awesome, miraculous, healing power of God by applying His plan for restoration to my own life, and I believe the Lord has directed me to write this book in order to teach and encourage other people the truths that I have learned so they too can find true healing and hope through forgiveness and the power available through Jesus Christ.

One particular day after God rescued me, my heart was moved with compassion for hurting people, and I prayed and asked God what I could do to help. He immediately impressed upon my heart, "I want you to write a book about My plan of rescue for people who have been hurt. Many of

My people are bound up, and I will use this book to help set them free."

Wow, I thought to myself, somewhat surprised to have heard so clearly. *That sounds good, but I've never written a book. I can't possibly do that without a lot of help.*

The Lord answered, "That's just the way I want it. I will help you."

A few weeks later, I was inspired to title the book, *The Victim's Cry*, and I was encouraged. Thereafter, every time I again felt overwhelmed and unqualified to write this book, I felt the encouraging presence of God spurring me onward.

The cry of a victim's heart is to be heard, understood, and to find relief from their pain. This book exposes what I understand to be the truth about offenses, pain, and forgiveness and describes the steps that are usually needed to identify and release even deeply buried offenses in order to bring lasting freedom.

Do you ever find it difficult to forgive the offenses of people who have hurt you time and time again? Do you find yourself judging them for hurting you repeatedly and wishing God would punish them for their wrongful deeds? If so, then this book is for you.

I believe anyone can forgive offenses and judgments, but in this book, I explain the motives and mechanics of forgiveness from a Christian's perspective.

I believe the Bible contains God's inspired words written down by ordinary people who encountered an extraordinary God in ways similar to what we can experience today. In this book, I include true stories from the Bible as well as personal testimonies in order to illustrate various concepts through real life applications.

My hope is that nothing in this book has been misguided by my own or any other man's opinion and that every concept aligns with Scripture and helps others as God intends. I encourage every reader to check my statements against

God's written words and depend upon the Spirit of God to reveal and teach them the specific truth to apply to their own lives.

I've learned that the path to healing and restoration involves taking a few steps that lead to victory in every situation. The steps are few in number, but they require us to humble ourselves, to seek after the living God, and to follow His fresh and specific instructions for each moment – not just a prescribed set of rules.

God wants us to spend time with Him and develop a close relationship with Him, so we will learn to trust and follow Him instead of simply following rules or copying what worked for someone else. He wants us to open our hearts to Him and communicate our hopes, dreams, doubts, fears, and pain so He can know us intimately and help us dramatically.

We all have unique talents and personalities, and we all have various experiences and come from different backgrounds. Therefore, God's specific remedies for our individual situations also vary.

Being physically or emotionally mistreated causes us to become victims as we live in this world, but we do not have to let that victimization dictate our direction in life, or let it hinder us emotionally or spiritually. We can overcome every obstacle as we walk out the realization that we are more than conquerors through Jesus Christ who strengthens us and provides everything we need for a fulfilling life.

I don't claim to be an expert on healing or forgiveness. I only know that walking out His plan of forgiveness turned my world around and has resulted in many blessings for me and my family.

The final chapter in the book describes several possible reasons why bad things happen to us. I debated about whether I should include it in the main section of the book or not at all. In the end, I decided to include it as an Appendix because understanding why people suffer in this world and why I've suffered helped me quite a bit. So my hope is that you and other readers will be helped as well.

My hope and prayer is also that as you read this book, you will soften your heart and allow God to teach you exactly what He wants you to know and you will quickly apply that instruction to your own life so that you will soon move from victim to victory as you experience the healing, restoration, joy, and fulfillment already made available through God's finished work.

1

ARE YOU A VICTIM?

Do you consider yourself a victim? According to Dictionary.com, if you've been mistreated by someone or hurt by circumstances beyond your control, then, by definition, you are a victim.[1]

You may think calling yourself a victim displays weakness, so you hesitate to label yourself as one. That's understandable, but feeling pain or loss is common to all of humanity, and having been a victim is not something about which to feel guilty or ashamed.

I would guess that you and nearly everyone else on the planet has been hurt or suffered loss at some time or another either by a natural disaster (like a tornado, hurricane, flood, or earthquake) or by the words or actions of other people. We've likely all been a victim at some point in our lives.

After being hurt, a victim needs to know that someone understands and cares. Unfortunately, we often find that we are misunderstood more often than we are understood, and that can discourage us tremendously.

---

[1] Dictionary.com

Sometimes, friends and family members appear to be unable to hear, much less understand, the cries of our wounded hearts. Even if they do understand, they may not be able to help us because they're struggling with their own issues.

That's why it's essential to remember that God can always be trusted to understand our pain, and we can always turn to Him for help. God loves each of us, and He compassionately reaches out to us and meets us where we are without finding fault.[2]

Life can be challenging at times, but we must not believe the lie that there is no way out. The chains of bondage can be broken. If we learn to view things from God's perspective and quickly turn to Him for help with every aspect of our lives, then our lives will be much less stressful, less complicated, and more fulfilling.

Unfortunately, for various reasons, we don't always turn to God for help. When our pain comes to the surface, we often turn to temporary pleasures or vain exercises in an effort to cover up the pain and cope with our aching hearts. These coping tactics often give temporary relief, but when the distractions or numbness fade away, the pain returns, and the self-destructive cycle repeats itself.

This pattern is a common and frustrating routine for many victims, and after repeatedly riding this roller coaster, it's all too easy to lose heart and give up hope of ever being free from the emotional pain and heartache that you might feel right now—that dull ache or sharp pain that's always just beneath the surface that can be triggered at almost any time by a word, thought, or memory.

If you find yourself in this category, remember that your life does not have to be defined by your past experiences. God has provided a Way to help us all move past our painful

---

[2] James 1:2-12

experiences, but we need to begin by acknowledging that we need God's help.

Harassed But Not Helpless

Many of us suffer from the effects of being mistreated by others, and we get stuck. We walk through life constantly seeking relief from the pain that fills our hearts, and as much as we want to forget the pain and cover it up, we can't make any lasting progress.

Thankfully, God has an amazing plan to bring complete restoration to every heart that has been wounded or broken, and He wants victims to be healed from the inside out. We simply have to humble ourselves before God and cry out to Him for help like King David did many times when he was in distress.[3]

If you ever wonder whether God sees or cares about the troubles you're going through, then read what King David wrote about how God treats victims:

> But You, O God, do see trouble and grief; You consider it and take it in hand. The victim commits himself to You; You are the helper of the fatherless...You hear, O Lord, the desire of the afflicted; You encourage them, and You listen to their cry, defending the fatherless and the oppressed, in order that man, who is of the earth, may terrify no more.[4]

Do you understand what this means? God listens, and He answers the victim's cry. God, who created you and loves you,

---

[3] Psalm 8:5-7
[4] Psalm 10:14,17-18

really cares about you.[5] He listens to you when you humbly call out to Him in the midst of your suffering. God is available, and He wants to help you.

According to the Bible, during the time that Jesus walked the earth, He saw the people as "harassed and helpless, like sheep without a shepherd," and He had compassion and helped them.[6]

In my opinion, people haven't changed that much over the years. Our living conditions, clothing, hobbies, and modern conveniences are certainly different, but people are the same. We all require food, shelter, and sleep to survive, and we all want to be free to pursue our own happiness.

Therefore, like people who lived thousands of years ago, we too are often harassed by outside influences and feel helpless at times, and we can easily slip into feeling depressed and hopeless as we face the various challenges of this life.

I consider a person who has been harassed and feels helpless to be a victim of the troubles we all face to varying degrees as we live in this world. Some people refuse to consider themselves victims in order not to appear weak or vulnerable, but we should remember that God's strength is perfected through our weakness.[7]

From God's perspective, we are all weak and vulnerable and in need of His assistance. So when we humble ourselves and agree with God that we are weak, and we turn to Him for help, He has compassion on us and empowers us to overcome obstacles that we would otherwise be unable to overcome.[8]

Being a victim does not mean our value is somehow reduced, and having been victimized certainly does not

5 1 Peter 5:7
6 Matthew 9:36
7 2 Corinthians 12:9
8 Romans 8:26, 2 Corinthians 12:10

mean we have to allow our lives to be defined by that victimization. With God's help, we can overcome any setback.

It's normal and totally right to feel hurt and ask for help when we are wounded. It's even good to cry and accept sympathetic charity for a while.

A problem arises, however, when we choose to pridefully refuse help and passively let the wounds go untreated. When we choose to complain about our issues, embrace the victim mentality, and selfishly take advantage of others to take care of our needs, we get into trouble.

The old saying, "the less said, the sooner mended" does not apply when we're hurting and dealing with emotional abuse or mistreatment. We need to talk with someone and ask for help to overcome the lingering effects of the troubles we've had in our lives.

Therefore, instead of isolating ourselves and aimlessly wandering through life where we can be more easily lured into various traps, it's a good exercise to open our hearts and confide in caring family members or friends while trusting God to help us.

Many times, our outlook can be improved simply by changing our minds to stop complaining and accept the circumstances that we cannot change while giving thanks for the good things we have. At other times, however, we must work to identify hurts, disappointments, or worries that we are carrying that first need to be released before healing can begin.

If you see yourself as strong and in control, then you probably don't think you need help, and you will remain stuck. If, however, you feel like a victim who is trapped in a life full of trouble and disappointment, and you are ready for something better out of life, then be encouraged. You can always turn to God who will have compassion on you and help you.[9]

---

[9] Matthew 14:14, 15:32

Jesus, who knows everything about every person, has compassion on us because He knows that in this world we all have been harassed and sometimes feel helpless like sheep without a shepherd.[10] We have all been vulnerable to attack and been injured in various ways, and God has provided a path to healing and restoration for each of us. We simply have to trust God to help us and follow His steps.

Time to Make a Change

We are all born into this world at a specific time and place, and we each have a specific purpose to accomplish while here on earth. We cannot change the people responsible for bringing us into this world or the time or place in which we were born, but we can control how we conduct ourselves and relate to the people around us while in this world. Our choices matter, and many of them have eternal consequences.

As we move along our various paths in life, we inevitably face circumstantial challenges and we cross paths with others who either intentionally or unintentionally cause us pain. We all play the part of the victim at some point. And how we respond to being hurt and how we treat those who hurt us is critical in determining whether we walk in misery or blessing.

For every victim, I believe that there's a time to remember the pain, there's a time to cry, there's a time to ask for help, a time to be healed, and a time to embrace the freedom and the full life for which God created them.[11]

In my opinion, life on this earth is too precious and short for us to waste time weighed down with offenses, disappointments, and judgments. There are already enough

---

[10] Matthew 9:35-36
[11] John 10:10

economic, political, and weather-related troubles and challenges in our lives without having to unnecessarily suffer through bruised and broken relationships. Our Creator has mapped out a better plan for us.

Sometimes only God knows why things happen the way they do and why we find ourselves hurting. Thankfully, God always has a plan to rescue us. We just have to humble ourselves, turn to God, do what He says, and wait patiently for Him to work things out.

God Himself loves you and wants you to trust Him to help you out of whatever painful circumstance in which you find yourself. If you have been led to believe God doesn't play an active part in the lives of people anymore, then you have been misled.

God reveals Himself only to those who earnestly seek Him.[12] So if you find yourself in a mess and feeling alone, then perhaps now is the time to make a change and rethink what you believe about yourself and God. With God's help, people can always change their ways and overcome the impossible.

Our past experiences have brought us to where we are today, but they do not define the path that takes us into the future. With God's help we can change that path.

God is For Us

It's always good to remind ourselves that God is for us and not against us. He knows the challenges that we face here on earth, and He meets us where we are. He wants only what's best for us, and He doesn't judge and condemn us as we struggle through life on this earth.[13]

---

[12] 2 Chronicles 15:2, Jeremiah 29:13
[13] John 3:17-18, 8:10-11, Romans 8:1

Certainly, we make choices today that sometimes bring about challenging circumstances for ourselves, but God does not condemn us when we find ourselves in a mess for which we can't see a way out. He actually wants to help us as it is written:

"I have chosen you and have not rejected you. So do not fear for I am with you; do not be dismayed for I am your God. I will strengthen you and help you; I will uphold you with my righteous right hand."[14]

As Christians, we are included in this promise to the people of Israel. Also, God strengthens those whose hearts are loyal and fully committed to Him.[15] So if God has chosen us, and He is for us, then as we honor Him and do what is right, we should have nothing to fear because no challenge can overcome us when we are standing with God.

He also knows that you and I are often misguided by other people and our own selfish tendencies and that we often find ourselves caught in the traps that Satan and his messengers set for us.

Thankfully, He doesn't condemn us for stumbling around in the dark. Instead, He offers His light to shine into our hearts and lives so that we can see the direction that our paths are taking us. Plus, when we repent, He empowers us to change, and He rescues us when we humbly ask for help.

Therefore, let's choose to believe that we are lovable because our Creator says we are.[16] And let's believe that we don't have to live with emotional pain and the chains of unforgiven sin anymore because God will help us.[17]

---

[14] Isaiah 41:9-10
[15] 2 Chronicles 16:9
[16] John 3:16, 15:12, 16:27, 17:23, Romans 1:7, 5:5-8, 8:35-39
[17] Matthew 11:28, 1 Peter 5:7

God, our Creator who lives today, truly cares about us, and He has a great plan to bring complete restoration to every single heart that has been wounded or broken.

A Fresh Plan

One of the keys to walking in victory is knowing that God wants us to depend on Him daily for guidance. Do you remember reading about when the Israelites were thirsty in the desert? At one time God told Moses to strike a rock and water gushed out.[18] Then later when they needed water again, God told Moses to speak to the rock, but Moses struck it again like he did the first time.[19]

Instead of following God's clear and simple instructions the second time, he decided to do what he had previously done that had worked. As a consequence of his disobedient act and for setting a bad example in front of others, he later missed out on the blessing of entering the Promised Land.[20]

As Moses once explained and Jesus reiterated,

> "Man shall not live on bread alone, but on every word that comes from the mouth of God."[21]

We obtain much needed spiritual nourishment by hearing the fresh words of God. We need our "daily bread," as Jesus called it.[22]

God gives us the "bread" of His guiding words every day through His Spirit who indwells all believers, and when He

---

[18] Exodus 17:5-6
[19] Numbers 20:5-12
[20] Deuteronomy 34:4
[21] Deuteronomy 8:3, Matthew 4:4, Luke 4:4
[22] Matthew 6:11, Luke 11:3

speaks to us, we have to choose whether or not we will listen and respond to Him.

Remember, "the word of God is living and active,"[23] and Jesus, who is the "Word [who] became flesh"[24] and the "Bread of life,"[25] is alive today, and the Spirit of Jesus continues to speak to us daily.

We obtain nourishment and life in this world by following the voice of the living God, so if we want to overcome our own troubles as well as the impoverished and malnourished state of our world, we all must train our ears to hear the voice of God.

Jesus said that He only did what the Father showed Him to do for each situation,[26] and He maintained this commitment perfectly. I envision Jesus pausing to check with the Father prior to responding to requests, but not much is written about how often Jesus paused to check with the Father before responding to situations.

Sometimes He prayed, and sometimes He looked up to heaven before acting.[27] On one occasion we read that after being asked a challenging question, Jesus stooped down to write on the ground before answering.[28] It's not clear what he wrote, but it seems He may have purposefully delayed His response while He quietly checked with the Father for guidance.

One time, when Jesus came across a blind man who wanted to see, He spit on the ground and made mud to put on the man's eyes and told him to go wash it off to restore his sight.[29] At another time, Jesus touched a man's eyes, and

---

23 Hebrews 4:12
24 John 1:1-14
25 John 6:35
26 John 5:19
27 Mark 7:34, John 17:1, 11:41-44
28 John 8:6-8
29 John 9:1-7

they were healed.[30] Jesus did not just repeat past actions that resulted in success; He waited for fresh instructions.[31]

Similarly, if we want to experience the many blessings of walking with God, then we too must learn to listen and follow the voice of God daily for each specific situation and not just do what worked last time.[32] We must not dwell on the past.[33] God wants us to wait on Him and listen for His guiding voice every hour of each new day like a butler waits on his master to give him instructions.[34]

God cares about you, and He has an awesome plan to bring you out of your misery if you would turn to Him and trust Him to help you. You don't have to hide from your pain and suppress your feelings anymore. Just replace any lies that you've believed with the truth and follow God's fresh plan for you.

---

[30] Matthew 9:27-30, 20:29-34
[31] John 14:31
[32] Deuteronomy 8:3, Matthew 4:4
[33] Isaiah 43:18
[34] Psalm 27:14, Isaiah 40:31

2

MY FRACTURED MARRIAGE

I n this chapter, I share some of my marriage struggles in an effort to help you understand my perspective, to help you avoid making the same mistakes I made, and to give you hope and encouragement if you are facing similar challenges.

After Angel and I became engaged, we were excited about life and full of happy expectations. Not long after we were married, however, I became disappointed with various things, and I started holding those disappointments against my wife and started growing bitter.

At first, I was only slightly irritated by what appeared to be minor selfish habits that I thought would change over time. I tried to be the tough, good guy and forget about the minor infractions, but over time, the minor irritations accumulated in my heart so that each new irritation was magnified in my mind and ballooned into major offenses that I continued to silently hold against her.

After a while, I didn't even want to be around her. When she no longer felt loved or cherished by me, she began withdrawing from me and showing me less respect. It felt like the more time I spent with her, the worse I felt, and vice versa (according to my chief editor).

Consequently, I became even more disappointed in her, and I became tired of all of the arguing and disappointments. My home was no longer a haven for me, so I began pouring more time and energy into my work. At least I could work hard and earn respect on that front.

Of course, one of her criticisms was that I didn't appear to care about her needs and spent too little time with her while expecting her to take care of the children by herself. So my spending more time at work made things worse at home. She needed me to love and cherish her as her husband, and when I repeatedly let her down, she became more disappointed and critical of me.

I did not know Jesus at this point, and I didn't know how to lead my family in the right direction, so I struggled as a husband and father. I constantly let my wife down, and I felt more and more inadequate, but I was too ashamed and prideful to admit it. At the time, I knew almost nothing about the importance of good communication and forgiveness.

After struggling with each other for a year or so, we agreed to seek marriage counseling to try to fix what was wrong with our relationship. Every time we went to a Christian counselor or pastor, however, I was told that most of our troubles were my fault. I owned up to some of the blame, but at the time, I couldn't see or accept that our failed marriage was mostly my fault.

I thought everyone else was blind to the real flaws with my wife, so I repeatedly tried to expose her faults to the counselor. Consequently, the counseling didn't work out well, and the hope we once had for a happy life together had faded away.

After several years of holding things against her, I had also become completely blind to her beauty. Others would tell me how fortunate I was to have such a beautiful wife, but I could only see her through my eyes, which were full of bitterness.

Regretfully, I spent those years degrading her and not appreciating the value that God had placed in her, and she responded similarly by having a disrespectful attitude toward me.

In our fourth year of marriage, I received Jesus as my Lord and Savior, which was the best decision I've ever made. I wish I could say our marriage was instantly repaired, but it wasn't. Most of the destructive patterns continued, and our situation felt hopeless.

By our ninth year of marriage, we had five children. I worked nine hours a day, six days a week, and at some point we started ignoring each other. It was like a wall had grown up between us, and we stopped caring.

I often felt alone and rejected, and I blamed her. At times, I thought that if she got a taste of her own medicine, then her blind eyes would be opened and she would change and start being the wife I wanted her to be. So I began purposefully doing things to try to make her feel alone and rejected as well.

What a bad idea that was! I was just adding even more bricks to the wall that was between us and more branches to our trees of bitterness.

Not only did my rejecting her not cause her to wake up and start respecting me, but it made matters even worse. She began emotionally withdrawing from me even more, so I felt even more alone and rejected. I remained bitter and resentful, and this bitterness oozed out in my attitude and actions toward her to the point that I didn't want to meet any of her needs anymore.

Instead of really loving her, I occasionally tried to do nice things for her so she might return the favor and do nice things for me, but Angel could see through my manipulating tactics. She has always been a survivor, but it was only a matter of time before I had nearly suffocated her to death. Near the end of our eleventh summer together, she announced that she had rented a small house and was leaving me.

After unsuccessfully trying to convince her that she should stay, I lost all hope of ever being close again. We had irreversible, irreconcilable differences, or so we both thought at the time. We were headed toward divorce, and I was miserable. I felt alone, rejected, and abandoned like the victim of some wicked plot to destroy my life as well as the lives of our five children.

Our family was broken up, and I had every reason to believe that our children would be scarred for life. I was a wreck, our children were confused, and from my perspective it was all her fault.

I became even more bitter, and I was in so much emotional pain that nothing I did brought me any real relief or comfort for my aching heart. On more than one occasion, I entertained the temptation to end my misery by committing suicide.

I told my dad years later that I had felt more devastated when Angel left than I did when my mother died of cancer because Angel left me on purpose, which added a great sense of rejection to the loss. I felt no rejection when my mom passed away too early in life.

The best friend that I've ever known had seen the real me, and then she rejected me and left me. I wanted somehow to get back control of my life, to protect myself and my children from getting hurt further, and to retaliate against the ones who were hurting me. I desperately needed help.

Someone Had to Die

After weeks went by and Angel still refused to come home, I desperately cried out to God for help. Every time I wanted to give up, He spoke to my heart, saying, "This marriage will not end in divorce."

Hearing God's words encouraged me and strengthened my heart, but since we appeared so far from reconciling, I concluded that one of us must be going to die.

Thankfully, neither of us physically died. After a couple of months of struggling to see and understand what had happened, I slowly began to see and hear what God wanted to teach me. I finally began to see that our family's breakup was ultimately my fault. It was I who needed to die to my selfish and destructive ways. That was another shocker.

Just like Jimmy Buffet's song lyric, "Some people claim that there's a woman to blame, but I know it's my own damn fault," I finally accepted the truth that our family's tragic breakup was mostly my own fault. God had established my position as the head of my home, and I had been a very selfish leader.

As it turned out, I learned that the walls I had built around my heart for my own protection had also cut me off from God, who wanted to teach me and guide me to be the leader of my home. It was like my own jail cell. I felt protected from the pain of the outside world, but in reality I was trapped and isolating myself from God and everyone else.

One day I had a vision of myself as a dam that was holding back God's love from my wife and family. That was a convicting and sobering picture. I felt so stressed and under so much pressure because I was not letting God's love flow through me to provide for my family.

How could I have been so blind?

For many frustrating years, I had lived with a beautiful wife who refused to allow herself to get close to me because I had crushed her heart repeatedly. I was finally able to see how cruel and hateful I had been to her, and I was finally ready to change.

Now that I was alone most of the time, I spent a lot of time searching for answers. As I contemplated what had happened with our marriage, I realized I had been looking for security and fulfillment in all the wrong places. I had idolized my wife and depended on her to meet my needs instead of God, and of course, she let me down.

When I was ready to listen and opened my heart, God showed me the error of my ways and opened my eyes to see the truth that my holding on to the many little offenses and disappointments had caused me to build blinding, bitter, and destructive walls of resentment all around my heart.

I realized I was the one who had been blind and manipulative, and I had allowed every little disappointment to add branches to my tree of bitterness. My heart was calloused, and any love that I had tried to show was mixed with the hatred that kept oozing out of my bitter heart. I didn't know anything about forgiveness or the importance of good communication.

Through prayer, reading the Bible, and opening my heart to God, I was able to listen and learn how to receive His love and to release all of the disappointments, offenses, and judgments that I had been needlessly carrying.

Every time I knocked on God's door, He was there for me, and He welcomed me in. In fact, Jesus became such a real friend to me that I felt like I couldn't live without Him. He was always available to listen to me with my troubles, and He always made me feel good about myself and gave me comfort when I needed it. He certainly didn't approve of my selfish actions, but when I repented, He always made me feel accepted.

God became so real to me during these times that I realized I had found a real friend I could always count on to listen and help me whenever I was in trouble. Jesus was no longer just a man who lived 2,000 years ago and cared about people back then. He became the true friend who I had always wanted who truly cares about me and carries my pain when I'm hurting.

During that desperate time of my feeling hopeless and helpless, I often turned to Him for help. He taught me how to humble myself and trust Him so I could openly receive His help, see things from His perspective, and hear His voice. His Spirit also empowered me to do right, which I especially needed when I felt like giving in to my old selfish ways.

When I listened and followed His instructions to do the right things, which often included releasing offenses and judgments from those who had hurt me as well as serving them, God gave me a real sense of peace, joy, acceptance, and fulfillment inside.

The feelings of rejection that I had felt from my wife faded away. I felt more accepted than I ever had. God turned what I thought was my darkest hour into one of my brightest. I fought hard to do what was right, and I felt completely accepted and protected by God. In a real way I was able to feel the joy and security of being in His presence.

I learned I could trust God to provide everything that I needed to survive the pain. Whenever my pain became overwhelming, I would get alone and cry out to God, and unload my aches and pains at His feet. Then I would feel His peace and comforting presence and hear His loving words of encouragement and affirmation.

I was dying to my old ways and experiencing an amazing transformation! My heart was being healed, and my friends and family could hardly believe that just during the few months after my wife had left me, my countenance had turned from suicidal misery to steady joy and happiness.

Our Fight for Reconciliation

It took me a long time to identify and correct all of the mistakes I had made. One of the biggest mistakes was carrying disappointments, offenses, and judgments against Angel, and I had learned how to trust God and release them. It also took a long time for me to identify and release all the mistakes that I had held against myself and to identify and reject all of the lies I had believed.

I had to soften my heart to become teachable and open my eyes to see what I was doing and open my ears to listen to instruction. The next thing I had to do was learn how to trust God, and I mean truly trust God. Only then was I able to move forward to receive God's love and pass it on to help restore my bruised family.

After turning to God for help and learning about true forgiveness, He empowered me to take each of the necessary steps to identify and release all of the offenses, judgments, disappointments, and pain that I had held on to for so many years. As I began trusting God to execute justice and work everything out, I was able to change my mind and align my expectations with reality and find contentment.

After several months of digging through my heart and identifying and releasing the petty disappointments that I had let grow into major offenses and cause what felt like irreconcilable differences between us, I began to see my wife as the beautiful woman she truly is. Then I began to love her unconditionally, seemingly for the first time, without any of the former bitterness or manipulation mixed in.

At that time we still didn't live together, but we saw each other frequently, and she noticed the change in me. During those two years of separation and rehabilitation, God changed a few things in my wife's heart as well, and soon she also began to forgive me and my offenses toward her.

We started dating again, and then as God would have it, after nearly two years of separation, we fell in love with each other all over again and came back together. We were reconciled and reunited at last!

I still sometimes find myself being selfishly overbearing and disconnected from my wife, but I now take a more active role in communicating with her and others, and I've learned to purposefully release offenses and disappointments as soon as I recognize them instead of passively letting them fester in my heart.

In our case, we both came to the place where we wanted reconciliation. We just needed help getting there. There were many times that we thought that nearly all of our differences were irreconcilable, but with God's help, we learned, and are still learning, how to yield and compromise to reconcile those differences.

I believe reconciliation is always possible when both parties are willing to work things out and they turn to God because He loves us and wants to heal our hearts. God always works with us to achieve reconciliation.

In fact, God desires reconciliation so much that He sent His only Son to earth to show us the way to life and to take our offenses and the punishment for those sins so that we could be reconciled to Him.[35] So God is a pro at reconciliation. You don't have to know exactly what to do, but be willing to trust God and release the offenses and judgments that you've held against others or yourself.

I tell people that our first marriage ended in separation. Then I learned how to truly forgive and our second marriage began, and now we're both again enjoying our new life together. That's good news for us, but the good news for you is that God wants to perform the same miracle in your heart and in your marriage or other bruised or broken relationships.

If you feel like your situation is hopeless, then read on and don't give up hope. There is, indeed, real help available for you. God does not show favoritism.[36] What He has done for us, He will do for you. God has a plan to bless your life in miraculous ways and bring complete restoration to your heart if you just put your trust in Him wholeheartedly and follow His steps.

[35] John 3:16-18,36, Romans 5:9-11
[36] Acts 10:34, Romans 2:11, Galatians 2:6, Ephesians 6:9, Colossians 3:25

3

FIVE OPEN AND SHUT STEPS TO FREEDOM

G od knows who you are. He created you; He knows your mistakes and your weaknesses; He knows what you are going through; and He loves you.[37] You can never disappoint God or let Him down because He never has any unrealistic expectations of you. He always knows the truth about you inside and out.[38] He knows what direction you will choose to go, and He continues to love you and has not rejected you.[39]

God also knows the pain that you have endured. It breaks His heart to see you weighed down and hurting.[40] That's why Jesus said, "Come to me, all you who are weary and burdened, and I will give you rest. Take my yoke upon you and learn from me, for I am gentle and humble in heart, and

---

[37] John 3:16
[38] Psalm 139
[39] Isaiah 41:9
[40] Matthew 9:36

you will find rest for your souls. For my yoke is easy and my burden is light."[41]

We don't have to carry the heavy burdens and insults that others send our way. If we choose to let go of the insults, emotional pain, worries, and the other concerns that weigh us down, then Jesus willingly takes up those burdens and gives us rest. When we do only what He gives us to do, then our yoke becomes easy and our burdens become light.

Much of the pain that we feel comes through no fault of our own as a result of living in this polluted world. And as long as we live on the earth, we will face challenges and hurtful situations as Jesus reminded His followers:

> "In this world you will have trouble. But take heart! I have overcome the world."[42]

We can "take heart" because God loves us more than we can understand right now, and through Jesus, He has provided us with a real way to unload all of the pain and anguish that has been dumped on us and eats away at our hearts.

Jesus still lives, and He helps us when we turn to Him for help. [43] Since Jesus overcame all of the troubles and temptations of this world, we can too if we listen to Him and let Him navigate us through life's challenges.

Remember the truth that God is faithful. He always keeps His promises. And remember what the psalmist wrote:

> "In my anguish I cried to the Lord, and He answered by setting me free."[44]

---

[41] Matthew 11:28-30
[42] John 16:33
[43] Hebrews 7:24-25
[44] Psalm 118:5

It was true for this psalmist, it's been true for many others, it's been true for me, and it will be true for you. If you humbly cry out to the Lord with a grateful heart, then He will show you the path for you to walk down and He will set you free.[45]

God has set His loving plan for man's redemption in motion by revealing the truth through His words and the way of salvation through His Son. It's up to us to open our eyes and ears, believe what God shows us and tells us, pursue understanding, and turn, so healing and restoration can take place.

God truly does care about you and me! He has outlined certain steps for us to take to experience His goodness and the healing that He wants to impart to us. To the people who were hard-hearted and struggling to be free, God explained:

> You will be ever hearing, but never understanding; you will be ever seeing but never perceiving. For this people's heart has become calloused. Otherwise, they might see with their eyes, hear with their ears, understand with their hearts and turn, and I would heal them.[46]

These statements point to a familiar path within the kingdom of God. I call them the "Open and S.H.U.T. steps." They describe the path to salvation as well as the path to recovery and healing for wounded hearts. So when we are tired of carrying the pain and want to obtain relief from all of the stress in our hearts, we must take the following five steps down the path that God has lovingly laid out for us all:

---

[45] Psalm 50:14-15, Philippians 4:6-7
[46] Isaiah 6:9-10, Matthew 13:14-15, Acts 28:26-27

Step 1–Open Our Hearts: You and I must acknowledge that we are wounded and incapable of healing ourselves. If we have allowed our hearts to become calloused, then to find healing we must open our hearts and humble ourselves and look to God for help.

Step 2 – See With Our Eyes: You and I must make the choice to reject the false beliefs and opinions that we have adopted from other people in this world and open the eyes of our hearts to earnestly seek the truth about ourselves and God as revealed to us by His Spirit and described in the Bible.

Step 3 – Hear With Our Ears: You and I must choose to open our ears and learn to hear God's voice and receive His fresh and specific words for our lives.

Step 4 – Understand with Our Hearts: You and I must choose to take the time and effort to seriously consider the teachings and truth of God to gain a real understanding of all that Christ Jesus has done and continues to do for us and to understand the truth about God's goodness and faithfulness.

Step 5–Turn: You and I must then change our minds to align our expectations with the truth, allow God to change our hearts, and make the decision to turn away from our selfish and destructive patterns of thinking and behaving and turn toward God and follow His daily instructions.

After we have taken these five steps by faith, it is God who heals our broken hearts and empowers us to walk in the fullness and joy of life that He established for each of us.

Notice that these five steps require action on our part. God has already accomplished the tasks that were impossible for us to do for ourselves. We just have to accomplish these five relatively simple steps, and God will bring about the healing.

The steps may be simple compared to what God did for us, but they can be challenging for us because they require action and change. They involve softening our hearts, gathering information, processing it, making a decision, and acting upon that decision. We can accomplish each of these five steps sitting in a chair or lying on a bed, but each step requires deliberate action.

There is no set time limit for each of these steps to occur. With practice, sometimes the process of completing all five steps for a given situation appears to take place almost simultaneously. While at other times, for various reasons, obstacles must be overcome and the process requires a slower and more time-consuming step-by-step effort.

You can be sure, however, that after earnestly taking these steps, Jesus will heal your heart, and your life will be forever changed. Once you hear, understand, and apply the various instructions you are given, you will discover that your journey to healing was well worth the cost, and you will be blessed.[47]

---

[47] John 13:17

4

STEP 1: OPEN YOUR HEART

S ome time ago while on vacation, I noticed a pair of hap-
py-looking ducks paddling along the edge of the water.
I had seen the pair several times, and I realized these two
ducks must be lifelong mates. They were quiet as they paddled along—no squabbling, no cackling—just two ducks in
harmony and seemingly at peace with one another.

As I thought about the ducks, I realized that my wife's two
miniature poodles behave similarly at times. They appear at
peace with one another sniffing various parts, resting, or
exploring together most of the time. But then they have their
squabbles where they sound ferocious and look like wild animals trying to kill each other.

Thankfully, after they calm down, they soon come back
together and play and sniff each other like best friends again.
They live together and see each other constantly, and aside
from their occasional squabbles, they appear to enjoy each
other's company most of the time.

Dogs don't appear to hold grudges. You can treat your
dog harshly at times, but he or she will still act like they are

glad to see you. People, on the other hand, aren't always quick to reconcile after being mistreated. I've also noticed that after a few years of marriage, some couples appear content and happy to be together while others appear discontent and often resent and attack each other.

I wondered why, after only a couple of years of marriage, some couples don't appear to move together with unity and peace. They no longer hold hands, and they don't appear to enjoy being with each other anymore.

Then it occurred to me that the relations between people are often strained by offenses, judgments, and disappointments that exist between them which contribute to calloused hearts, lingering resentment, bitterness, separation, and strife.

I began to ponder why ducks and dogs don't appear to be weighed down by offenses and grudges like people often are. I decided that animals are created to live by their instincts. They have some level of emotions, but they don't appear to fall into the trap of holding on to offenses or judgments as people often do.

They defend themselves and their offspring when provoked, but they don't appear to get emotionally weighed down or seek revenge, as people tend to do. Hardening their hearts and holding on to offenses and judgments does not appear to be built in to the nature of animals.

Like ducks and dogs, we were also not designed to carry offenses and grudges. Yet, because we are often motivated by our emotions and our pride, we sometimes harden our hearts and carry burdens unnecessarily. When we get hurt or disappointed, we can become weighed down and polluted by bitterness and destructive thoughts, which is why we have to purposefully soften our hearts before we can move toward healing and walk in harmony with each other and with God.

What Good Are Callouses?

I've not yet met anyone who likes being hurt, and yet we all do get hurt, and we all deal with pain the best we know how. Some people who've been hurt appear to get over their pain quickly while others struggle with the pain their entire lives.

Many people turn to drugs or alcohol or some other substance or behavior in an effort to cover up or escape the pain in their hearts. It's also quite common for people to harden their hearts or let callouses form in an effort to prevent additional heartache due to repeated abuse or disappointments.

A callous on the hand or foot forms when the skin is repeatedly bruised or hurt. Callouses usually start with a blister, and as the blister heals a harder layer of skin automatically forms to help protect the tender tissue beneath from being hurt by the same kind of treatment in the future. The more often the same place is hurt, the tougher the skin becomes.

In a similar way, a person's heart becomes calloused when he or she is repeatedly mistreated or hurt and the person holds on to the offenses. Over time the constant rubbing and remembering of those offenses and their accompanying pain naturally motivates the person to harden their heart in order to try to protect it from further damage.

Just as a callous on our hand truly protects the tender skin beneath the callous, the hardening of our hearts also effectively shields us from the damaging blows caused by others who emotionally mistreat us.

There are problems, however, when we allow callouses to form around our hearts. One problem is that callouses create a rough, insensitive outer surface. If our hands are calloused, then they are rough and insensitive in those calloused places. Similarly, if our hearts are calloused, then they are also rough and insensitive in those places, and we come across as coarse, uncaring, and insensitive toward others.

Someone would say, "I don't see a problem. If I come across rough and tough, then maybe people will stop hurting me."

Unfortunately, when we harden our hearts to "protect" ourselves, we also effectively cut ourselves off from God's love and His healing and restorative power because the callouses that "protect" our hearts also prevent God's healing power from entering and setting us free from our pain and suffering.

Callouses are like bars of a prison; they prevent things from getting in or out. Unwanted things born out of hatred cannot always get through, but good things like those born out of love often can't get through either.

When our hearts are calloused and closed, we don't expose or open ourselves to others for fear of being hurt again. Consequently, a calloused heart prevents us from being able to develop rich, meaningful relationships with God and others.

One of the most basic needs that any person has in life is to be accepted and loved. And one of the vehicles through which God pours love and acceptance into our hearts is through intimate relationships with others. So if our hearts are calloused and closed, we will often feel alone and empty. I don't think anything truly good or positive results from having a calloused heart.

Closed Hearts and Callouses

Do you sometimes find yourself getting angry over little things that appear big at the time, or do you sometimes feel like you're fighting all the time just to have your feelings validated or to be respected, especially at home?

If so, then you're not alone. Unfortunately, these feelings are common in marriages or other relationships where one or more people have hardened their hearts and are holding onto offenses, disappointments, and judgments that trigger feelings of discontent and bitterness.

People with walls around their cold hearts can be challenging and abrasive to be around because no love goes in, and no love comes out. When you try to get close, you often stub your toes and get your feelings hurt because offensive remarks often fly out of cold-hearted people's mouths like bats out of a cave after sundown.

When offenses come our way, we must deal with them carefully and strategically. If offenses are retained, they accumulate like stones to form walls of division and separation between ourselves and those around us.

Our enemy tries to convince us that these walls are good to protect us from further harm, but in truth, these walls isolate us and lead to broken relationships. Walls surrounding hearts separate people and prevent intimacy.

So what about you? Do you have any walls around your heart? Are you trying to hide or protect something inside? Is your heart so dirty and full of junk that you don't want anyone to see?

It may help you to know that God already knows the junk you have in your heart, and He wants you to spend time with Him so He can help you clean it up. Three of the primary things we often hold on to that weigh us down and pollute our hearts and lives are disappointments, offenses, and judgments.

In order to be free, we must release the pain and weight of these burdens to Jesus. To accomplish this task, we must choose to soften our hearts, open them to Jesus, ask Him to show us the root causes of our burdens, and let them go.

Whether it is through a friend, husband, wife, or another person, God loves us physically and emotionally through the people around us with whom we have close contact.

He also pours love into our hearts directly by His Spirit. If our hearts are calloused and closed, however, then we prevent the love of God from flowing into our hearts, and we remain empty and have no love to give to others.

People with calloused hearts find it more difficult if not impossible to enter into close relationships with others. Instead of allowing their hearts to feel intense emotions, they have effectively shut down their hearts so they are no longer capable of receiving and experiencing the love of God and others. Therefore, intimacy is blocked.

Furthermore, hardening our hearts in an effort to protect them reinforces our tendency to rely on ourselves for comfort and strength. In our own strength, the only resources we personally have access to are the things of this world that offer only temporary comfort and satisfaction.

Have you tried to shield your heart so you no longer feel the pain that comes with the offensive words and actions of others? If so, then you might think you're better off, but remember the same shield that you think is protecting you from getting hurt also prevents the love of God from entering and nourishing your heart. Consequently, whatever love and encouragement you are able to receive gets quickly used up, and bitterness eventually returns.

If you have been hurt and you've hardened your heart to try to prevent further damage, then you can probably remember having that empty feeling. Why not try softening your heart and trusting God to help you by filling that emptiness?

Ask God to help you identify and release any hurt or offenses that you've been carrying. Offenses are like fiery darts that if retained promote callouses and spread bitterness and resentment through a person's heart and soul which leads to emotional, spiritual, and physical problems.

According to CBN News, studies have shown that holding on to offenses and judgments adds emotional and physical stress to our lives. Clinical evidence supports the fact that stress reduces the body's ability to fight off disease.[48]

Furthermore, when people are stressed or depressed, they usually try to cope by eating comforting foods and beverages that are loaded with fats and sugars that further weaken our immune systems while creating an acidic environment in which cancer cells and pathogens thrive.

Offenses from others are like invisible bullets that can penetrate your heart if you let them. They will not go away by themselves; they must be identified and released, and the sooner the better. For if sins are carried and left alone, they will fester and poison your heart with bitterness that spreads like cancer.

Therefore, one way to help guard against sickness is to pay attention to our emotional signals and release any offenses and grudges instead of ignoring them or trying to forget about them.

Our Emotional Warning Systems

Have you ever met someone who comes across as overbearing and abrasive, and you felt intimidated in their presence? Many people carry pain from wounds that were inflicted upon them many years ago, and the anger that is rooted in that pain flares up occasionally, manifesting itself as abrasiveness or frustration.

Sometimes we are tempted to hold on to painful burdens because they are familiar like old friends, and they fuel our anger and greed. Yet, we don't have to keep following the same old patterns and give in to those temptations that lead to self-destruction. God has a better way.

---

[48] http:/www.cbn.com/cbnnews/healthscience/2015/june/
the-deadly-consequences-of-unforgiveness

God equipped us with nerves in our bodies to detect physical discomfort or pleasure and to notify our minds regarding physical issues. In a similar way, God also gave us emotional receptors to detect emotional discomfort or pleasure and to notify our minds regarding emotional issues.

Even though feelings cannot be seen or touched by anyone, they are real and usually more lasting and more influential than the physical events that preceded them. Feelings are not visible on the outside, but within our hearts, they are real and measurable.

Therefore, when our emotions signal that something is wrong, like when we get our feelings hurt or we are worried about something, we should immediately stop to process and identify the cause. Then we should take appropriate action to remedy the situation. Sometimes all we need to do is consider events from a new perspective.

In any given situation, each person sees things from their own unique perspective. Even after witnessing the same event, different conclusions can be derived, and different emotional responses can be developed because our perspective influences our minds, and our minds control our emotions.

When something happens to us or around us, we make certain conclusions based upon what we believe to be true about those events. We then choose which emotions, if any, we allow to develop. If we choose not to internalize the event and not to respond emotionally, then the event passes with no emotional result and no burden to carry.

If, on the other hand, we choose to take offense or receive an injury in some way, then our minds compel our hearts to develop feelings of being insulted, injured, or disappointed. If we continue to hold on to the offense, then our minds process the event over and over again and send multiple signals to trigger more intense emotions, like anger, to develop.

This anger can be directed outwardly and result in plotting revenge and retaliation against the offender, or the anger can be directed inwardly, which often leads to depression. Neither of these options is good.

If we predetermine to not take offense, however, then with practice we can instantly release offenses while trusting God to weigh the evidence and judge every situation. We will then be empowered to resist the temptation to develop feelings of being hurt, which will also stop the downward spiral leading to anger, condemnation, retaliation, depression, and the hardening of our hearts.

Hearts Under Warranty

Whenever something we own doesn't work right, usually the best way to get help is to contact the company or person that programmed or created it. In the same way, when we are going through difficult times, and we need help in some area, the best thing we can do is go to the Person who created us; the One who programmed us. Only our Creator knows us inside and out and is able to help us in whatever area we have need.

Think about where most of your biggest struggles exist. Is it with the people around you? Is it with your house, car, or other stuff? Does your job give you the most grief? Your finances?

More than likely, it's not your physical circumstances or people that bring you down; it's how you perceive and process those situations within your own mind.

If you feel unhappy, sad, worried, troubled, angry, or hurt, or you struggle with feelings of rejection, loneliness, abandonment, inadequacy, worthlessness, or depression, then much of your problem may be caused by your perception and what you believe about yourself and the circumstances in your life.

Our emotions and actions always follow our beliefs, and many of the struggles in our lives take place in our minds. We can't see or touch our emotional issues, so we often find it difficult to fix them. In fact, sometimes we can't even identify what it is that's causing us so much pain and frustration.

When we find ourselves feeling harassed or restless, we should make time to meet with our Creator to receive a diagnostic check-up. We may need a sophisticated tune-up that only the One who created us can perform. We simply have to do our part by humbling ourselves and turning to Him for help.

We don't have to let our circumstances or the fact that we have been harassed and sometimes feel helpless dictate our outlook on life.

God knows how we are wired and what weighs us down, and He alone can carry our burdens and take away our pain. He loves us and wants us to allow Him to help us fulfill the good purpose for which He created us.

Therefore, when we understand that our hearts are under warranty, we share with Jesus our deepest struggles and most painful secrets, and we let go of our heavy yokes that are full of pain, heartaches, and disappointments, we find that the source of our troubling emotions disappear, and we can rest. [49]

Your Feelings at Work

Sooner or later, tragedies occur in our lives or we encounter selfish people who try to hurt our feelings. As long as we live in this polluted world and interact with other selfish people, we will experience emotional injuries and heartaches.

Someone once made the claim that "time heals all wounds." This statement certainly sounds promising, but it's not often true for emotional wounds. The healing of emotional wounds that were caused by offenses has nothing to

---

[49] Matthew 11:28-30

do with time, so let's not fall into the trap of passively waiting around and hoping the pain will simply disappear. We need to take appropriate action.

Many physical wounds like minor cuts or scrapes heal naturally over time, but with more serious physical wounds like bullet wounds, rapid and intentional response is very important. The sooner someone takes action, finds the bullet, removes it, and binds up the wound, the sooner healing can begin.

Likewise, with emotional wounds the sooner the cause of the pain is identified and addressed, the sooner healing and restoration can take place. As time passes, the exact causes of emotional wounds can often become covered up and quite difficult to identify, so early and rapid response is important.

Therefore, when we feel hurt, depressed, angry, or disappointed, we should not procrastinate or allow our discomfort to be covered up with distractions. We should quickly make time to be still and ask God to search our hearts and show us the source of our disturbances. As they come to mind, we should release them to Him to enable emotional healing to take place.

This same process also holds true for worries. Whenever we feel weighed down by fearful or anxious thoughts, we should identify the cause, resist giving in to the fear, release the burden to God, and ask Him to do the opposite of whatever the fear-provoking spirit is suggesting.

We should also encourage our children to face their fears, discuss their troubles, and find real solutions based upon truth instead of teaching them to turn to pacifiers or look for escapes. We should allow them to cry, comfort them, pray with them, and encourage them to turn to God for help quickly whenever troubles arise.

Since feelings are invisible, doesn't it make sense that healing and the removal of unwanted feelings would be an invisible process? Feelings are generated in the heart at the direction of the mind in response to a real or perceived event, so they can always be extinguished by the mind once the source event is released.

It's interesting that although feelings cannot be seen, they usually make the deepest imprint on a person's memory. At any moment in time, we can identify the emotions that we are feeling such as happiness, sadness, anger, anxiety, disappointment, despair, fear, or something else. When asked why we're feeling a particular emotion, however, we sometimes have trouble remembering what triggered the emotional response in us.

Nevertheless, if the resulting emotion is there, then the trigger is still there too. We may have buried and forgotten the source, but God knows exactly what happened because He was there. So if you try to avoid certain people, or you're feeling downtrodden and you don't know why, then it's important that you make time to get alone with God and ask Him to reveal the root cause.

We learn how to cope and wait for healing regarding most of our physical injuries because physical pain usually fades away naturally. Yet, the pain that we encounter with heartfelt injuries doesn't just fade away naturally. For most heartfelt injuries, we have to purposefully take certain steps in order for the pain to disappear from our hearts and to be healed.

If we're open and honest about our struggles, then we can often find family, friends, or skilled counselors who can help motivate us to identify and release burdens so that healing can begin. Sometimes, however, the pain of heartfelt injuries can be so debilitating that only God can orchestrate events or speak directly to our hearts to bring about health and wholeness.

God can always be trusted to come to our rescue. We don't have to wait for a tragedy to occur to motivate us to choose the path of forgiveness and reconciliation. All we usually have to do is humble ourselves and depend upon God for help and follow His specific plan of rescue and restoration.

Life in this world is not always fair, and sometimes we get hurt through no fault of our own, so we should not adopt the belief that we deserve to be mistreated. On the other hand, we also need to be careful not to let a prideful attitude stir up feelings of being offended, insulted, or injured unnecessarily.

We don't have to think of ourselves so highly that every remark that another person makes prompts us to take offense. God loves us all equally without showing favoritism,[50] so let's humble ourselves and let go of any offenses and let God provide for our defenses.

We are all born with the ability to feel emotions, which naturally reflect what we believe to be true. This is good, as long as we believe and understand the truth.

Unfortunately, however, if we are not solidly grounded in the truth, then the cunning and deceptive tactics of our enemy will more easily sway us. When we fall into his traps and believe lies, then our emotional responses to the circumstances of life will be inappropriate as they are based upon lies as well.

It's bad enough to have emotions that are based upon lies, but since we tend to let our emotions influence our actions, they can motivate us to do harmful or hateful things to others and ourselves. Therefore, we should always commit ourselves to being led by God and His Spirit, and not by our emotions. Through self-control we can be angry and choose not to act in a wrong way.[51] We do not have to let our emotions dictate our actions.

When we begin to recognize an internal problem, we must learn to turn to Jesus and ask Him to show us what we can't see. Let's ask Him to reveal the root causes of our

---

[50] Acts 10:34, Romans 2:11
[51] Ephesians 4:26

emotional afflictions. When revealed, we should release any offenses, burdens, or sorrows to Him, reject any lies, and allow Him to heal our broken hearts and restore our emotional health.

If it is revealed that we are in the wrong, then we should confess and sincerely commit to turn and do only what is right. When we confess and turn, God is faithful to forgive our sins and cleanse us from all unrighteousness.[52]

If you don't feel close to God, then it may be that you have hardened your heart toward Him. In this case you will need to take a chance and open the door of your heart to Him so He can help you see the truth of His love and goodness toward you.

Ask God to reveal the events of your past through the eyes of your heart and imagination. When a painful event comes to mind, take the time to work through the issue once and for all. Through your imagination, look for Jesus as you remember the event and let Him help you and comfort you and carry your burden. Life is too short to keep a closed and calloused heart with burdens that are not ours to carry.

Understanding Anger

If we know that we've been hurt, and we're still holding on to the offenses that are causing the pain, then we will have anger and bitterness issues, and we will have no one to blame for our emotional troubles but ourselves.

Angry outbursts can cause a lot of trouble, but the anger itself is not the real problem; it's only a symptom. The real problem that needs to be addressed is the underlying pain that flares up and triggers the anger.

When people become angry over something, it's often because they have been wounded in some way and refused

---

[52] 1 John 1:5-9

to forgive so that when something happens that pokes at the wound and they are reminded of the pain, they respond with an angry tone or in an otherwise angry way.

In these cases, the old saying, "the less said, the sooner mended" applies because the angry person should be careful to say as little as possible to minimize damage to their relationships.

For many people, beneath the surface lies a wounded heart that they keep hidden in order to function and avoid being perceived as weak, vulnerable, unstable, or immature. Unfortunately, the plan to conceal always backfires because their hidden wounds will continue to affect a person's attitude and behavior. Either the pain unexpectedly rises to the surface causing seemingly irrational angry outbursts, or the anger is directed inwardly, which often leads to self-condemnation and depression.

Events of the past cannot be undone, but we can take steps to loosen the ties that bind offenses, judgments, and disappointments to our hearts, forgive, accept our current circumstances, and control our attitudes and actions before we get emotionally charged and act impulsively. When we don't restrain ourselves during times of intense anger, sadness, or even happiness, we often act or speak carelessly, which usually results in hurting others.

Have you ever noticed that some people who drink alcoholic beverages become emotional? Alcohol consumption has a way of causing people to relax and speak or act in ways that honestly reflect the condition of their hearts. This is usually a good thing when consumed in moderation because it helps foster openness, honesty, and fellowship.

Too much alcohol consumption, however, can result in trouble when a person is holding on to hurts, judgments, and disappointments because feelings of anger and hatred often come to the surface.

Abundant alcohol consumption will inhibit a person's ability to control their actions when they become emotional so that a little sadness can turn into crying, a little happiness can turn into hysterical laughter, a little physical attraction can turn into aggressive passion, and a little anger can turn into rage. Crying and laughter can produce good results, but aggression and fits of rage are usually destructive.

If a person has unhealed wounds, then drinking too much alcohol can lead to trouble because carrying hurts leads to frustration, bitterness, and anger that comes to the surface when the effects of the alcohol begin to inhibit self-control.

On a positive note, however, when a wounded person opens up or displays this behavior, a caring and discerning friend can sometimes listen and identify the root causes of the pain and guide them toward help after they are sober.

Our enemy and his agents know our weaknesses and they love to stir up trouble and motivate us to drink excessive amounts of alcohol or take mind-altering substances so we will lose control, act impulsively, and hurt each other.

Therefore, we should establish boundaries for ourselves that include limiting or refraining altogether from drinking alcoholic beverages until we unbind and release all offenses, judgments, and disappointments.

Some people claim they use their anger to improve their performance like when they engage in high energy exercise routines, play contact sports, or compete in business. They claim that harnessing and channeling their anger makes them more aggressive and physically charged so they accomplish more in life.

This sounds logical, but unfortunately, many are deceived into believing the lie that holding on to hurts and grudges makes them more successful. They may be energized to outperform others at times, but retaining hurts and grudges opens doors of darkness and leads to bitterness and hatred.

Eventually, the stress on their minds and bodies cause them much more harm than good.

Softening our hearts and releasing offenses and grudges is a much better choice as this supernatural and powerful act of forgiveness totally foils the destructive plans of the enemy in a way that is far more beneficial than what can be accomplished through channeling anger or aggression.

Sand Spurs and Disappointments

Have you ever walked barefoot through grass near a beach and stepped on a sand spur? It's a little prickly, spiny seed with barbs that stab through your skin when you step on them.

If you step on one, it's only slightly painful at first, but if you don't quickly remove it, then each time you step the barbs get pushed deeper into the skin, so it hurts more and more. The longer you leave it there, the more difficult it is to pull out.

Disappointments arising out of unmet expectations are kind of like sand spurs. They often attach themselves to our hearts as we walk through life. They're also painful, and the longer they are left alone, the more difficult they are to identify and eliminate.

We need to understand that when we carry disappointments, they weigh us down and cause our hearts to ache. If retained for long, then we often harden our hearts, which leads to irritability and bitterness. Therefore, we have to be careful how we respond to them.

We often depend on people and expect certain things out of them, and that's good as long as the expectations are based on clear communication and understanding. A problem arises, however, when the actions of those people don't fulfill our expectations, and we become disappointed.

We can also fall into the trap of considering the disappointments to be intentional acts of disrespect or carelessness that we hold against them. This also usually triggers a reduction in our level of trust.

When people make sincere promises to us, we should trust them to keep them and act according to their promises. Yet, we should not expect them to keep them perfectly since none of us is perfect. That's why we should put our hope in God instead of people.

Some promises, such as marriage vows, seem much more important than others, and they promote higher expectations. So when these types of promises are broken, we often feel extremely disappointed and disrespected and take offense. We also can take offense when others fail to meet our expectations that were based upon our own assumptions and not actual promises.

Whether the expectations are based upon promises or assumptions makes little difference. In all cases we should remind ourselves that all people, including ourselves, make mistakes. So let's work diligently to maintain hearts that are open as we effectively communicate our expectations and disappointments to each other while trusting God to work everything out.

Only God can always be trusted to keep His promises, so we should keep our hearts open toward God, give Him our disappointments, and put our hope in Him instead of people.[53]

Hiding Your Heart from God

God created us with free and independent wills, so we can open our hearts to others or we can keep them closed.

---

[53] Psalm 25:3, Lamentations 3:25, Isaiah 49:23, Romans 9:33, 10:11, 1 Peter 2:6

In order for someone to truly know you, however, you have to choose to open your heart to them.

Even though God knows everything we're going through, He chooses not to push in where He is not invited. He stands at the doors of our hearts, knocks, and waits.[54] It is then up to us to open the doors, invite Him in, and share our lives with Him.

There's no good reason for us to try to hide from God. Do you remember how Adam and Eve responded the first time they failed to follow God's instructions? They were immediately seized with remorse and full of guilt. They were ashamed of what they had done, and they were also afraid of what God would do to them, so they covered up and tried to hide.[55]

That's exactly what our enemy wanted them to do, and he also wants us to be afraid and to hide from God too. Unfortunately, we too often fall into his traps. Not only does the devil tempt us to do wrong, but he also tries to convince us to cover up our mistakes and troubles instead of confessing them to our Creator and asking for help.

Have you ever noticed that it helps to share your troubles with a caring friend or counselor? It's natural to feel a burden partially lifted when you open your heart to a caring individual. They can help you carry the burden, and this is good as long as they respond appropriately and turn the burdens over to God themselves.

You and I were not designed to carry the burdens and stress that accompany the troubles of this world. Whether we personally experienced the trouble, or we are helping carry someone else's burdens, God wants us to come to Him for refuge and to cast our cares upon Him so we can rest.

[54] Revelation 3:20
[55] Genesis 3:10

Our burdens are real, and they must be fully released in order to find true rest. Only Jesus can truly and completely carry all of our burdens, but we must choose to let them go and give them over to Him.[56]

He longs for us to open our hearts to Him and give Him everything that weighs us down. He wants to give us the rest that we long for.[57] So we should place our trust in Jesus and not hesitate to soften and expose our hearts. When we turn to Jesus and follow Him, there is no reason to be afraid.

If you have been wounded by the repeated mistreatment of others, don't accept their views of you. Instead, ask God how He feels about you and read His encouraging words as recorded in the Bible. God always speaks the truth, so you can always trust Him.

Childlike Trust

As I sit here and write on a covered porch overlooking Banks Channel in Wrightsville Beach, North Carolina, I'm hearing joyful sounds and seeing a young couple cheering as their three and four-year old boys hesitantly leave Mom and jump into the water as Dad waits to catch them.

It's a happy scene because Dad is encouraging them to leap off of the dock, and then he is indeed rescuing them when they hit the water just as he promised he would. Soon the boys can't wait to jump in again.

This reminds me of how God encourages us to place our trust in Him and directs us to step out by faith like little children knowing that He too will catch us and rescue us at just the right time.

A good example of how God rescues us occurred after Jesus told Peter to step out of the boat and come to him by

---

[56] Isaiah 53:4
[57] Matthew 11:28

walking on the water.[58] Peter obediently stepped out of the boat and successfully walked upon the surface of the water toward Jesus.

After taking a few steps, however, he took his eyes off of Jesus and noticed the wind and waves. He began to question and doubt what he was doing, and he began to sink. Quickly, he called to Jesus for help, and Jesus reached out and rescued him.

Peter was participating in a miracle until he took his focus off of Jesus and gave in to fear and doubt after considering his surroundings. We learn from this true story how we need to depend wholeheartedly upon God and know that we can do whatever God calls us to do. We need to trust God like a small child trusts his or her parents.

Unlike adults and older children, little children are almost completely dependent on their parents for everything. They trust Mommy and Daddy to help them, and when they are in trouble, they run to them for help.

In a similar way, our Creator designed us to have fellowship with Him and to run to Him for refuge and help whenever we face trouble.[59] It's interesting that Jesus said that in order to see and experience the kingdom of God, we must become like little children and be born again.[60]

A newborn is completely helpless and vulnerably dependent upon his or her caregiver. That's the way we need to approach God. Also, as they grow, most young children follow their hearts, and they are trusting, even when things may not logically make sense. This may be one reason that Jesus also told His followers,

---

[58] Matthew 14:28-31
[59] Psalm 46:1
[60] John 3:3

"I tell you the truth, unless you change and become like little children, you will never enter the kingdom of heaven."[61]

Notice that Jesus put the responsibility to change on the people. We are the ones who must choose to humble ourselves and change our ways.

I can think of four attributes that little children have that many adults are missing, which may prevent them from experiencing the blessings of heaven:

1. Little children are trusting. They believe whatever they are told.
2. Little children are good at exercising their imaginations.
3. Little children know they are weak or vulnerable and need help.
4. When they get hurt, little children cry and run off to find their parents to obtain comfort and freedom from the pain.

Children are initially trusting and long to be loved, and they have not yet built walls around their hearts. If the people around them are loving and nurturing, then they feel safe and secure, and they grow up feeling confident about themselves and trusting toward others.

Children are naturally vulnerable and dependent upon their parents or other guardians. And like children, we must see ourselves as dependent upon our Father. This means we need to turn away from our self-reliant and independent ways and choose to trust God and follow Him.

Unfortunately, changing to become like little children can be very challenging for many of us. Not everyone can remember feeling safe and secure as a child because early

---

[61] Matthew 18:3

in life they were hurt. Perhaps they felt rejected from birth because they were the result of an unwanted pregnancy, or perhaps they were abandoned by one of their parents or otherwise neglected or abused emotionally or physically. Thankfully, unlike our parents or other trusted people in our lives, God will never let us down or lead us astray. God always tells the truth and is always faithful and trustworthy,[62] so He wants us to trust Him and believe everything He tells us without doubting His words or His ability to accomplish whatever He says.[63]

Next, God wants us to exercise our imaginations and visualize ourselves going to Him whenever we're hurting or weighed down.[64] Our parents may not have always given us the comfort we needed, but God always does. When we soften our hearts and imagine ourselves humbly going to Him for help, God always welcomes us with open arms, loves us, and provides what we need.

Jesus understands our aching hearts, and He knows the path to freedom. Like children who start out trusting their mom and dad and believe everything they say, we must also return to that same level of trust toward our Heavenly Father and believe everything that He says.

We also need to know that God sees us as His children, so we can cry in His presence and He will receive and comfort us. We may have important jobs in business or in homes where we need to display confidence in front of others, but when we are alone and weighed down or hurting, we can crawl into the arms of our Father, pour out our hearts, and cry our eyes out. God understands.

[62] Psalm 34:8, John 11:40
[63] Matthew 14:31, Luke 24:38
[64] Matthew 11:28-30

The Bible says that Jesus is the only way to life and freedom.[65] If we choose to believe some of His words and reject some, then we will fall short of living in complete freedom. We must wholeheartedly trust and believe God, who is our only hope for true life, peace, and joy in this life and forever.

In order to experience new life and freedom, we must allow God to renew our minds by purposely surrendering our own will to the will of His Spirit within us. This is a choice we must make day by day and moment by moment.

Therefore, we should understand God's ways and stop relying on ourselves and stop trying to cover up our hurting hearts. To find deliverance and healing, we must choose to be like little children and open our hearts to God, believe and trust Him, and turn from our self-reliant ways. As hopeless as our situations sometimes appear, we can always take heart because God truly understands, and He cares.

Learning to Trust Again

Have you ever been hurt by someone you trusted? Have you been physically or emotionally abused? If so, then you know how it feels to be a victim, but you don't have to let the fact that you were victimized set the course for your life.

At some time or another, we all experience feelings of abandonment, rejection, or disappointment. Many people have been hurt so many times by others that they harden their hearts and choose not to trust anyone until they are convinced that the person is trustworthy. They hesitate to trust people, and they hesitate to trust God because they feel they have been treated so unfairly in life.

Often our biggest obstacles to getting back on track after being mistreated is our own lack of understanding of the truth and our lack of trust in God.

---

[65] Deuteronomy 18:18-19, John 14:6

I used to trust in myself more than anyone or anything else, including God. I decided that since I couldn't erase the pain in my heart, I just had to find ways to escape it and cover it up. I tried many things to find relief from the constant aching in my heart, but nothing ever truly satisfied me until that one day when I gave up on the things of this world and decided to turn to God.

I learned that God's desire is to comfort us in our times of trouble.[66] In His presence, we truly find safety and refuge from the aches and pains of life. Just like a hospital is a place of refuge and healing for anyone who has been physically injured, God's presence is a place of refuge and healing for anyone who has been emotionally injured.

We need to remember that God is never to blame for our mistreatment. God loves every one of us, He is always faithful, He does everything right, and He deserves our trust.

We also need to understand that if God is truly causing unpleasant circumstances in our lives, then He is doing it for our own good to motivate us to redirect the course of our lives toward a better end. We can always pour out our hearts to God and trust Him to do what is right and fair.[67]

It is often only after we choose to trust God that our eyes are opened and we begin to recognize that He is indeed faithful and that He repeatedly demonstrates His trustworthiness within our own lives.

How about you? Were you hurt, disappointed, or misled a long time ago and now you are hesitant to trust anyone, including God? Do you keep your heart closed because you're afraid you'll be hurt or disappointed all over again? Are you at the place where you realize you are harassed and helpless and need help? Are you ready to let go of every possible misconception that you've believed about God and His Word?

---

[66] Psalm 10:14-18
[67] Psalm 62:8

I assure you, but more importantly, God promises you, that if you put your hope and trust in Him, then He will never let you down.[68] Why not trust your Creator and believe the One who knows all things? Why not place your trust in the author of the Bible and pour out your heart to Him today?

Trust is a Choice

I've heard it said that love is a choice, but trust has to be earned. I agree whether or not to love someone is a choice, but I believe to trust or not to trust is also a choice that we make. And this choice can be made regardless of past events or hurtful experiences.

Our perception of whether or not a person appears trust-worthy usually affects our decision to trust. When we perceive that a person or entity is trustworthy, we often choose to trust them, but when we have been injured or know of others who have been injured by a certain person, we often choose not to trust them unless we are convinced they have changed and are now trustworthy. We say in these cases that trust has to be earned.

Our propensity to trust is certainly influenced by our own perception, but it can also be affected by external sources. We have an enemy who uses tactics of fear and doubt and tries to distract, deceive, and convince us that others are against us and should not be trusted.

These tactics, combined with our own suffering and mis-understanding, convince many of us to choose not to trust people who are actually trustworthy. We also fall into the trap of not trusting God. This is obviously not good. All too often, we follow our own misguided understanding and our feelings instead of the truth.

---

[68] Romans 10:11

Most young children, however, follow their hearts, and they are trusting even when things may not physically make sense. Before they are warned or become hurt themselves, they have faith that others can be trusted and will not harm them. It doesn't matter if the people around them are the most untrustworthy people in the world; innocent little children will still trust them.

Have you ever met a little child who cried or appeared afraid when you reached out to him or her? If so, didn't you feel a little rejected? On the other hand, have you ever met a child who smiled or openly spoke kindly to you? I've experienced both, and it warms my heart whenever a young stranger demonstrates trust toward me in this way.

I also think it warms God's heart when we demonstrate our trust in Him as well. He probably feels rejected when we refuse to open our hearts toward Him.

Have you ever noticed how easy it is to convince little children to believe something even if it's not true? Most parents teach their children to be careful around strangers which is prudent, but some then fall into deception and take advantage of the trusting nature of their children by trying to convince them that they should believe lies about Santa Claus, the Easter bunny, or some other false concept.

People sometimes think it's fun to deceive little children. They mistakenly say to themselves that they are simply playing harmless games and having fun, but unfortunately, spreading lies is never harmless and always leads to trouble.

Eventually, the lies are exposed, little hearts are wounded, callouses form, and the trust and confidence that the children once had in their parents is diminished to some extent. If parents try to convince their children that they should believe and trust in God in addition to Santa Claus and the tooth fairy, then when the lies of the imposters are exposed, they often conclude that what they were taught about God is a lie as well. What a tragedy this is.

Unfortunately, deceiving children and causing them to believe lies in the name of fun and games or false religion is very common today. No wonder we have so much trouble in the world. We too often fail to seek the truth or walk in the light, so we don't even realize how destructive our actions are until it's too late and the darkness has spread beyond our control.

Sometimes, all it takes for a person to prove him or herself trustworthy is for someone to take a chance and demonstrate their trust of them. I know for myself that when another person willingly entrusts someone or something to my care, I feel honored and want to justify the trust that they have chosen to place in me. God is honored when we choose to be thankful and place our trust in Him as well.[69]

Sometimes, when we choose not to trust others, it's because we have judged them and concluded that they are not worthy of our trust. We should be very cautious about judging others. Visible attributes and past behavior patterns can sometimes be used to accurately predict future behavior, but not always.

When a person recognizes the wrong he or she has done, has a real change of heart, and turns from their wicked ways, then it is not right to hold their past actions against them. When we truly repent, God doesn't hold our past mistakes against us.[70]

Obviously, if the person is not truly sincere, and they repeatedly tell you what they think you want to hear in order to gain favor, then they are dishonest, and I would suggest minimizing your involvement with the person until such time as true repentance takes place. You may not always be able to justify placing your trust in others, but you can always trust God to direct you along a safe path.

---

[69] Psalm 50:14-15
[70] Ezekiel 18:21-32

We need to remember that God always welcomes us when we humbly come to Him for help regardless of whether we've exhausted all of our other options.[71] He wants us to place our trust in Him, depend on Him, and come to Him first – not last.

We do well when we remember and apply what King Solomon once wrote,

> "Trust in the Lord with all your heart, and lean not on your own understanding. In all your ways acknowledge Him, and He shall direct your paths."[72]

Therefore, let's open our hearts and place our trust in God as we seek the truth and take steps along the paths on which God directs us.

My Difficult First Step

I grew up believing that the Bible was only partially true and many Bible stories were exaggerated for effect. I could not believe that stories like God choosing Noah and his family to build a huge boat and gathering up all the animals to survive a worldwide flood, the parting of the Red Sea for the Israelites to cross over but not the Egyptians, Jonah being swallowed by a whale and delivered to a beach, Jesus turning water into wine and raising dead people to life, and other incredible stories. To me, they appeared exaggerated to teach life lessons.

I had never witnessed anything supernatural like these events, so by the time I was in my late teens, I decided that the Bible was simply man's creative attempt to justify how we got here and why we should be nice to each other.

---

[71] Isaiah 57:15

[72] Proverbs 3:5-6 (NKJV)

Since I decided that I couldn't trust the Bible, I didn't believe what the Bible said about God either. After all, if God were truly real, then why would He need to make up outlandish stories to convince us of His greatness?

The Bible made no sense to me, so I thought it was a waste of my time to read it. I also didn't want anything to do with someone else's opinion of how I should live.

I had been misled and hurt by people whom I originally thought I could trust. They disappointed me and let me down repeatedly, so I hardened my heart and decided that I couldn't trust anyone but myself. After all, I was smart and willing to work hard, so I chose to believe that the only person I could depend on was myself and I would surely never let myself down.

When I was twenty-seven years old, however, I found out that I was wrong. After finally graduating college, working as an engineer, and struggling financially and in my marriage, I became desperate. I had done it my way, and I failed. I was finally ready to give up on myself, but if I couldn't trust myself, who could I trust?

One spring day, while driving back to work after having lunch with my wife, who was also struggling through life, I finally gave up on myself and cried out to the God that I had been taught about in church.

"God, are you real? Are you listening? Can you please help me?"

Amazingly, right after I asked for help, I found myself debating with a voice in my head about the validity of the Bible. That was an odd business.

The concluding argument that I heard went something like this:

> Who are you to question the validity of the Bible? If what the Bible writers wrote was not true, and you don't believe it, then you've

lost nothing. If what they wrote was not true, and you believe it, then you may learn to be a better person, which is good, and you would not really have lost anything. If what they wrote was true, and you choose not to believe it, then you will have missed a great opportunity and end up in a terrible place. But if the Bible is really true, and you believe it, then you will have much to gain and will reap great rewards.

Was God speaking to me, or was I debating with myself? I decided it must be God since I had never had conversations in my head like that. So I pondered those arguments for a moment, and I decided believing the Bible appeared to offer the potential for the greatest gain with little risk or cost.

So I changed my mind and decided to wholeheartedly accept the Bible as God's true, accurate, and inspired message to everyone, including me, and I let go of my prejudices and beliefs about what I had heard about God and the Bible.

Right away, I felt like some cloud or weight had been lifted, and I had a new hope for life. I somehow knew I had made a good decision.

I started reading the Bible with an open heart, believing every word to be literal and true, and I somehow seemed to understand more of what I read. For the first time in my life, the Bible was truly interesting and made sense. I now began to see God's active involvement with people in a way that I had never seen before.

Two weeks later, I heard the Gospel in a way that made perfect sense to me. I finally understood that I needed help, and that God had already provided everything to help me through Jesus. That day, I thankfully chose to believe in Jesus and accepted Him as my personal Lord and Savior.

I had been blind and deaf, but I chose to open my heart and trust God and His words. Then I began to see, hear, understand, and experience the truth that God is all that the Bible claims He is. It was a great day!

Are You Ready to be Free?

If you've been lied to and hurt, and you've decided to harden your heart in order to prevent more damage, then you now have another choice to make: Either you continue down the familiar path of misery that you're on, or you turn to God, choose to trust Him, and ask Him for help.

Satan pretends to help us, but in reality he hates people and wishes all of God's creation to come to ruin, as he eventually will.[73] He will never willingly set you free, and you are powerless to free yourself. Yet, as Jesus declared,

> "If the Son sets you free, you will be free indeed."[74]

Only Jesus has the power to set you free. Do not believe the old saying, "God helps those who help themselves" because if you rely upon yourself to figure out how to free yourself, then you will remain captive and trapped in the painful self-destructive rut that you were born into.[75]

God knows you inside and out, and He understands that you have been mistreated and often feel hurt, rejected, and disappointed. God cares, and He wants to help you, but because you've been hurt, you may have allowed what you thought were self-preserving callouses to form around your heart.

---

[73] Romans 16:20, Revelation 20:10
[74] John 8:36
[75] John 3:36

Those calloused walls may help prevent you from being hurt by others, but you have also effectively blinded the eyes of your heart so that you cannot see God or anything beyond your own pain-stricken life.

Be encouraged! There is still hope. Believe what your Creator says about you. God loves you and wants to rescue you. You are highly valuable to Him, and He wants to bless you. However, you have to turn away from the old ways that have taken you down the path of emptiness and choose to put your hope in God.

The best part of my life started after I changed my mind about the Bible, opened my heart toward God, and decided to turn away from my own understanding. Then the ears and eyes of my heart were opened and God revealed to me His great love and plan for me and all people.

God knows your pain, and He wants to heal your heart. He will help you if you turn to Him with a thankful heart and depend on Him to help you tear down the walls that encircle your calloused heart. God has not rejected you, and when you call on Him, He will rescue you and set you free![76]

---

[76] Isaiah 41:9-10

5

STEP TWO: SEE WITH YOUR EYES

<hr/>

G od's written Word says Jesus was sent to "open eyes that are blind."[77] Have you ever acknowledged that you have blind spots and might need help seeing some things? It took me a long time, but I finally realized I had several blind spots and needed lots of help.

A good example of my own mental blindness happened to me on Mother's Day when I was thirty-seven years old. I had invited my mom and dad to join me and four of my children—ages five, seven, nine, and ten at the time—to take my boat out for a leisurely afternoon cruise on the lake.

My parents had not been boating with me for at least fifteen years, and my mom had been battling cancer for three years, so I wanted the experience to be pleasant for them. Everything went well until we stopped along a sandy beach to let the children swim around for a few minutes.

The children had been swimming around for about thirty minutes when my parents decided they were ready to move

---

[77] Isaiah 35:5, 42:7, Luke 4:18

on. So I called the children, and they all returned to the boat. After everyone was settled, I paddled us away from the shore and turned the key to start the motor.

Nothing happened. The motor would not start or make noise or anything.

I decided it must be some kind of electrical problem, and since I considered myself good at fixing things, I paddled us back over to the shore so I could work on it. I was quite confident I could fix the problem quickly.

The children were happy since they got to swim again, but by the time I had been troubleshooting for at least thirty minutes, I had become embarrassed and frustrated. My parents became unsettled as well.

I tried everything I could think of, but I could not figure out how to solve the problem. I spent more than ninety minutes disconnecting and reconnecting all of the wires going to the battery and to the motor. I switched batteries and checked all the wiring connections behind the dash and inside the motor. Finally, I gave up. I felt humiliated and defeated, and I finally admitted I needed help.

We decided to call a nearby marina for help, but our cell phones had no signal. So we started paddling out to where we might get the attention of someone passing by in another boat who might help us by towing us the few miles back to the boat launching area where our cars were located.

Then a surprising thing happened. Right as I began paddling, my cell phone rang. Amazingly, I now had a signal!

It was a good friend of mine calling to let me know he no longer needed my help with a project that afternoon. That was great news considering our current circumstances. Before we hung up, I told him about the predicament we were in on the lake, and I asked him to pray for us. He said he would. I thanked him, and we hung up.

Moments later, as Mom tried to get the attention of a man in a passing boat, it occurred to me that I needed to make sure the gearshift/throttle was in the neutral position to start the engine.

Of course! Why didn't I think of that? I said to myself.

I wiggled the gearshift around neutral while turning the key, and *vroom!* The motor started right up! Praise God! It seemed like a miracle! Mom immediately waved off the passing boat, and we were happily motoring down the lake again.

I had been piloting boats for over twenty-five years at that time; so of course, I knew the motor had to be in neutral for it to start. Why, at that point in time, for more than ninety minutes, had I been completely blind to that one critical detail? This question baffled me for days.

Several times prior to this trip, I had experienced the same starting issue with this boat, and within seconds, I had always remembered to solve it by wiggling the shifter around the neutral position while turning the key. And the motor would always start. Why was this time so different?

I finally concluded that for some reason I had been blinded and completely unable to see the solution of which I had previously been fully aware.

Perhaps I was being prideful about my ability to fix things, and God allowed this event to occur to teach me to humble myself and depend more upon Him. It was only moments after I humbled myself, decided to ask for help, and asked my friend to pray for me that my eyes were opened. Then I saw the answer as clear as a bell.

I learned some valuable lessons about blindness that day. First, when I pridefully lean on my own understanding, I blind myself to things that I would otherwise see if I was thankfully depending upon God. Also, I now have more compassion for people who cannot see what others see so clearly because I have experienced mental blindness for myself.

I'm convinced that my boat blindness was mainly caused by my own prideful and self-reliant attitude. Oftentimes, when we discover that we are blind in some area, or we find ourselves stumbling around in the dark, in order for us to see the right path from a true perspective, we must humble ourselves and ask for help like I finally did.

Spiritual Blindness

Have you ever noticed times in your life that you were blind to something? Have you ever been unaware of something one minute, and then it dawned on you and you could suddenly see that thing in a whole new light?

On a rainy day, years ago when my children were young, I was driving with two of my sons on a street through a shopping center parking lot when seemingly from out of nowhere another car crashed into me. The driver, a young college student, had driven through an intersection where she was supposed to stop.

We both got out of our cars, and after surveying the damage, I looked at her and she looked at me. She had a surprised and offended look on her face like she didn't know why I had just crashed into her. She appeared to have been completely blind to the fact that she was the one who had failed to stop at the intersection.

So I asked her, pointing to the letters spelling "STOP" painted on the road, "Didn't you see you were supposed to stop over there?"

She looked down, and suddenly it dawned on her what she had done. Shocked, embarrassed, and filled with remorse, she immediately started crying and apologizing for her mistake.

She said she had driven through that parking lot and stopped at that intersection many times, but with the rain and things on her mind she didn't realize where she was. She was extremely sorry and freely confessed to the police officer that it was her fault as she continued weeping. I felt sorry for her.

It was easy for me to see where the young lady went wrong, but at first it wasn't so easy for her. Later I reflected on what had happened, and it occurred to me that the young lady had a temporary mental blind spot, and it took another person seeing from a different perspective to help her see the truth.

I'm convinced that people naturally want to enjoy life and pursue happiness, so they usually don't purposefully choose a path that they know will lead to misery. When we choose to go down a dangerous path, it's usually because we have been deceived and our minds have been blinded to the truth.

To be physically or mentally blind is bad enough, but to be spiritually blind can be eternally deadly. Spiritual blindness is the inability to see spiritual things. A spiritually blind person has perhaps lost sight of the fact that he was created in God's image, and his purpose is to enjoy fellowship with God.

Spiritual blindness is often caused by one's own disobedience and refusal to believe God. [78] Our own choices cause us to be blind by creating barriers between ourselves and God.[79]

It is therefore important that we conduct ourselves in a way that does not hinder our own ability to see clearly. According to the Bible, when we purposefully do things that hurt each other, we walk blindly, as it is written,

> "Whoever hates his brother is in the darkness
> and walks in the darkness, and does not know

---

[78] John 9:39-41
[79] Isaiah 59:1-2

where he is going, because the darkness has blinded his eyes."[80]

So if we choose to retain the offenses that others commit against us and pass judgment so that we become bitter and resentful and do hateful things or think hateful thoughts, then we are walking in the dark where we are blind and can't help but frequently stumble.

If we turn to God and do things His way, however, He will give us the vision to see and ears to hear spiritual things while leading us along safe paths where we will seldom stumble. This path is safe, but it will not be familiar as He promised,

> "I will lead the blind by ways they have not known, along unfamiliar paths I will guide them; I will turn the darkness into light before them and make the rough places smooth. These are the things I will do; I will not forsake them."[81]

Jesus also addressed the unfamiliar nature of the places God would take us when He said,

> "The wind blows wherever it pleases. You hear its sound, but you cannot tell where it comes from or where it is going. So it is with everyone born of the Spirit."[82]

Therefore, even in the best of times, we will sometimes feel uncomfortable because the paths we are going down are new

---

[80] 1 John 2:11
[81] Isaiah 42:16
[82] John 3:8

and unfamiliar. We may not know where we will go from one day to the next, but that's not a bad thing because it's often part of God's plan for us to feel unsettled so we will depend upon Him more for our guidance and provision. We should remember that God's strength is perfected through us when we acknowledge our weaknesses and our need for Him.[83]

When we humbly acknowledge our weakness and depend on God, He will clear the path in front of us and make the rough places smooth. So when we feel unsettled with life, we must not give in to fear because God will guide us by illuminating one step at a time as we trust in Him.

Paul, the Blind Man

Events in the life of the Apostle Paul present a good demonstration of how someone can crossover from blindly stumbling along a familiar path to seeing clearly and safely walking with God along a new unfamiliar path.

As a young man, Paul wanted to devote himself to serving God, so he chose to submit himself to the teachings of the Pharisees who were considered to be the most devoted followers of God.

He diligently studied the Scriptures and learned to apply what he was taught. He thought the information he had been taught was accurate and truly honoring to God, so over time he became proud of his accomplishments.[84] Unfortunately for him, however, many of the Pharisees were misguided in their teachings about God.

Apparently, many of his teachers focused more on keeping up appearances than they did on loving others and serving God with a sincere heart.[85] They studied the

---

[83] 2 Corinthians 12:9-10
[84] Acts 22:3-5, Philippians 3:4-6
[85] Matthew 15:12-14

Scriptures, but most didn't properly apply them because they were blinded by pride, greed, and a selfish desire to receive admiration from the people.[86]

Paul became caught up in this blind web of deception, and so he, like the other blind Pharisees, was serving only himself while he blindly insisted that he was serving God. Paul was spiritually blind.

Spiritual blindness is like deadly poison, and if the antidote is not sought after and received, it results in death to the one who is blind. It is also dangerous and destructive to others as the blind lead the blind.

Jesus saw through the whitewashed appearances of the Pharisees into their deceitful hearts, and He often exposed the truth about their misguided ways and called them blind guides.[87] Therefore, they felt uncomfortable around Him and wanted Him to go away.[88]

Many of the Pharisees were so blinded that they thought they were right before God and could interpret and dictate God's instructions as they saw fit. They also believed they could justifiably imprison and kill anyone who opposed their views of what was right and wrong.[89]

Many of them were convinced that because Jesus didn't agree with them, and He ate and drank with sinners, He was the one who wrongfully taught lies about God and deserved to die.[90] It wasn't long before Paul and the rest of the Pharisees set out to kill Jesus and His followers because their teaching of the truth posed a real threat to their self-serving and prestigious ways of life.[91]

---

[86] Matthew 23:13-36

[87] Matthew 15:14, 23:16, 24

[88] Matthew 12:14, 15:12, 22:15

[89] John 16:2

[90] Matthew 26:3-4

[91] Matthew 12:14

It's interesting how twisted our perception becomes when we allow ourselves to be misguided by selfish ambition.

It's also interesting that after Jesus rose from the dead and appeared to Paul along the road to Damascus, He blinded him physically to match his spiritual blindness.[92] Then Paul was compelled to stop and reevaluate all that he had been taught and believed for so long. I'm sure there are times when we all need God's disciplinary action to cure our blindness.

Stop Pretending

Are your eyes closed to the truth in any areas of your life? Are you sure that everything you see and believe is the absolute truth? Do you even care if you're blind in some area? When we can't see clearly, it becomes easy to fall into the temptation to fear and doubt, and we find ourselves stumbling around.

Another good example of spiritual blindness was recorded concerning Elisha and his servant who were surrounded by the Aramean army with horses and chariots in the book of 2 Kings. The servant thought he could see well enough, but after going out early in the morning and seeing the Aramean army surrounding his master's home, he was afraid and ran back to the house in a panic to ask Elisha what they were going to do.

Then Elisha replied, "Don't be afraid. Those who are with us are more than those who are with them."[93]

Elisha prayed, "O Lord, open his eyes so he may see."

Then the Lord opened the eyes of the servant's heart, and he looked and saw the hills full of God's horses and chariots

---

[92] Acts 9:7-9
[93] 2 Kings 6:16

of fire all around Elisha's home.[94] Then his confidence in God's protection was restored and his fears subsided.

It's amazing that even today, like Elisha's servant, we can also be completely blinded to the truth one minute, and the next minute, after receiving help, we can see so clearly. Many times we are blind, and we don't even realize it.[95]

Therefore, one of the first major steps toward being able to see more is humbling ourselves and admitting that we have blind spots and need help to see things more clearly. We get ourselves into trouble when we pretend we can see just to fit in with others.

I spent the first twenty-six years of my life attending church fairly regularly and learning about God, but I never truly knew Him. I considered myself a Christian, but in my heart I knew something was missing. I was blind, but thought I could see, and since I was outwardly a quiet and nice person, no one appeared to see through my hypocrisy.

Yet, certainly, God knew the truth. When I was twenty-seven years old, I was miserable and I finally decided to give up and stop pretending I was something that I was not. Thankfully, God met me where I was and began revealing Himself and the truth that He loves me and wants to help me.

Instantly, I found peace and discovered that in order to maintain that peace, I had to be true to myself instead of pretending to be something that I was not. Pretending and posing through life, which are based upon lies and deception, cause us to walk in darkness.

When we purposefully do anything wrong, we walk in darkness. Many people realize they're walking in darkness, but they don't know how to move into the light. They may occasionally notice others walking in the light, and secretly

---

[94] 2 Kings 6:17
[95] Revelation 3:17

wish they could walk in the light, but for various reasons, they remain in darkness.

They often remain trapped until God sends someone along to help open their eyes so they can see and step out into the light, as Jesus once explained to Paul,

> "I am sending you to them to open their eyes and turn them from darkness to light, and from the power of Satan to God, so that they may receive forgiveness of sins and a place among those who are sanctified by faith in Me."[96]

Obviously, since God sends others to help us, it's clear that we all need help recognizing we're blind in some areas. Then it takes us letting go of lies, choosing to embrace the truth, and doing what is right in order to be set free from the bondage of darkness.

Taste and See

In order to start the journey toward complete freedom from the pain that has been slowly eating away at our hearts, we must first accept that we have blind spots in our lives and we need help.

Sometimes, our blindness is caused by our own choices, like when we knowingly choose to do wrong, which takes us along dark paths. When we get tired of stumbling around and are ready to see, we must turn away from our old selfish ways, commit ourselves to doing only what is right, and choose to open our hearts and turn to God for help.

Unfortunately, due to the high level of deception in the world today, people often find it difficult to truly believe God

---

[96] Acts 26:18

and trust that He cares about us enough to help us and give us the comfort and guidance we need.

When we feel down, instead of turning to God, we often reach for pacifiers like candy, soft drinks, alcohol, sexual pleasures, pornography, music, movies, tobacco products, drugs, religious activities, adulterous relationships, and the list goes on. People everywhere turn to pacifiers to try to fill empty hearts and provide comfort when life gets uncomfortable, but the reality is that there is no real nourishment in a pacifier.

Not all pacifiers are inherently bad, and we can obtain some level of legitimate comfort with some pacifiers. However, when we repeatedly depend upon pacifiers instead of God, we get ourselves in trouble. When the temporary excitement, pleasure, and comfort of a pacifier fades away, we realize that we're still hungry and hurting, the pain is still there, we're still empty, and we still need help. So what do we do?

If we have enough resources, many times we look for a new pacifier to try. This is one reason why it is so difficult for a rich person to enter the kingdom of God.[97] Sometimes the cycle continues until we run out of money or encounter another crisis in our lives. We keep reaching for things that don't really satisfy, and we begin to become disappointed and frustrated with ourselves and life until we are finally ready to give up.

When we are ready to give up, we must be careful not to give up on everything, as our enemy will try to convince us to do. Instead, we must give up on ourselves and our own ability to fix our problems. We must turn to our Creator for help.

Unfortunately, it's not always easy to choose to turn to God. Many who have been raised in broken homes with

---

[97] Matthew 19:16

moms and dads who were abusive or absent much of the time often have a difficult time turning to God because they can't see that He is good.

Many have had misguided parents or some other leader who misled them down a path that resulted in disappointment and pain, so they've closed their hearts and shut their eyes and decided not to put their trust in God or others anymore.

They don't want to take a chance and believe in the invisible God because they've been hurt, and they've hardened their hearts and shut their eyes so that the truth of God's goodness is not visible to them. Plus, our enemy tries to prevent us from turning to God. I used to be in this category.

Much of the time, many of us simply meander through life in our own little worlds, and we assume we're seeing everything as it truly is. Sometimes, it takes a major incident in our lives that causes us to step out of our routines where we can see things from a different perspective. Then we realize we were at least partially blind to some element of truth. At other times, we just seem to stumble across the truth in unexpected places.

Thankfully, there's no need to wander around and hope we stumble across the truth because most of us have access to the rich deposit of truth found in the Bible. Even better news is that the Author of the Bible is alive, and He still makes Himself available to anyone who earnestly seeks after Him.[98]

The words that are written in an accurate translation of the Bible can be trusted as the very words of God, but you must choose for yourself whether or not you will believe them. King David knew God and experienced His faithfulness repeatedly. In his excitement regarding God's goodness, David once wrote,

---

[98] Deuteronomy 4:29, Matthew 7:7

> "Oh, taste and see that the Lord is good.
> Blessed is the man who trusts in Him!"[99]

The words here are ordered in such a way as to imply a cause and effect relationship. First we taste, and then we see. In other words, to recognize God's faithfulness, we must first choose to turn away from our own ideas and choose to believe our Creator and trust Him.

To taste something is to try it or perceive or experience the flavor of it.[100] So to taste of the Lord is to try Him or experience His flavor. Also, in order to experience God and His goodness, we must first choose to believe God exists and that He rewards those who diligently seek Him.[101]

The passage might be just as true if it was written, "Try trusting God for yourself, and you will see that He is good." In God's economy, we have to choose to trust and believe Him as if we were little children before we will clearly see His goodness. Refusing to trust God certainly blinds many people to the truth that God is good.

Before we can see evidence of God's goodness, we first must choose to believe, as Jesus once told His friend Martha,

> "Did I not tell you that if you believe, you will
> see the glory of God?"[102]

He also told His followers,

> "Whoever has my commands and keeps them
> is the one who loves me. The one who loves

---

[99] Psalm 34:8 NKJV

[100] Google.com

[101] Hebrews 11:6

[102] John 11:40

me will be loved by my Father, and I too will love them and show myself to them."[103]

So not only must we choose to trust and believe God, we must also listen to Him and follow His directions in order to be able to see Him. God has taken the first step by creating us and promising to help us. Now we have to do our part to believe, trust, and follow Him in order to see His goodness.

Jesus also once explained to His disciple Thomas that those who choose to trust and believe God without having yet personally seen physical evidence of God's glory will be blessed by God.[104]

Therefore, before we can see that God is great and good, we must choose to believe. As long as we choose not to believe God exists or that He does not love us or desire to help us, we will be blind and deaf to His communications.[105]

God does not need to prove anything to any of us, but He is honored when we choose to believe Him, accept His words, and follow Him. When we choose to believe what God says, God changes things, and He blesses us in ways that reveal His goodness.

Where Did the Beauty Go?

Have you ever wondered why so many people get married and then divorce so quickly? Most newlyweds find each other very attractive and are full of hope that they will enjoy long lives together. Within a few years, however, some husbands and wives no longer even tolerate looking at each other. The same thing once happened to me.

---

[103] John 14:21
[104] John 20:29
[105] Hebrews 11:6

During the early stages of our relationship, Angel and I were very much in love, and she was beautiful to me. Then somewhere along the way, my feelings became hurt, I became disappointed, I built up walls around my heart, and I became bitter.

Consequently, I also became blind to her beauty, lost my attraction for her, and started neglecting her. Eventually, we separated for two years. I only began to see her beauty again after I started forgiving the hurts, disappointments, and judgments that I had held against her.

After I learned and began practicing forgiveness, I particularly noticed how lovely she was one afternoon while visiting with some old friends. In one of their photo albums, I saw a photo of my wife taken at a baby shower after we had been married about seven years.

In the photo, she was laughing, and she looked extremely beautiful to me. I could hardly believe how gorgeous she was. Why didn't I remember her looking that good? Where was I during that time?

Of course, I wasn't at the baby shower, but regretfully, I don't remember ever seeing her look that beautiful during that time in our lives. I recall others telling me how blessed I was to have such a beautiful wife, but I disagreed with their assessments because during that time I could not see any beauty in her.

I would actually go out of my way to "set the record straight" by telling them that they had obviously never seen her true colors. Then they would look at me in disbelief.

At the time, I was convinced they were blind, but it turns out that I was the one who was blind. I don't recall seeing her at that time as the incredibly beautiful woman that she was (and still is) because I constantly held things against her and battled my own feelings of rejection.

We didn't laugh together much, and I'm sure that for years in my presence, she found nothing to laugh about because I did little to make her feel loved and cherished.

Looking back, I realize that because I held so many grudges, hurts, and disappointments against my wife, my lens was terribly clouded by bitterness. The beauty that had once been so clearly visible to me before we were married was invisible to me because of my walls of bitterness.

I was so self-centered that I was not able to see how beautiful my own wife was. I regret being so hard-hearted for so many years. What a blind fool I was!

If I only knew then what I know now, I would have fought every day to take my focus off of myself and turn it toward God asking Him to show me where I was carrying offenses, judgments, or disappointments so I could release them and see more clearly. Then I would have been able to see the beauty in my wife much sooner and not wasted all those years.

God sees us through eyes that are not clouded with offenses because His only begotten Son has already provided for the forgiveness of our offenses that once created barriers between Him and us. When we receive Jesus, He sees us as the beautiful and unblemished people that He created us to be.

If you no longer see the value in your spouse, another person in your life, or even yourself, ask God to open your eyes to the truth and help clear out whatever is blinding you before another day passes. You won't be able to see clearly until you rid yourself of the logs that cloud your own vision.[106] You'll be glad you did!

---

[106] Matthew 7:5

The Log in Your Own Eye

Sometimes we cause our own vision to be blocked by holding on to false beliefs. At other times we hinder our vision by pridefully holding on to offenses and judgments. We simply can't see clearly when we are looking through eyes that are clouded with offenses or filled with pride or judgment.[107]

We tend to judge others in the same areas in which we struggle.[108] When we see others do the same things that we struggle not to do, we can easily get frustrated and fall into the trap of passing judgment against them. We might tell ourselves that we are frustrated because we don't like seeing others doing wrong, but the truth is that our frustration is often rooted in our own failures to do better in that area.

When we have areas in our own lives that we know we are not doing right, our vision is hindered and we often allow ourselves to pridefully pass judgment and hold on to offenses against people that we see doing those things with which we struggle. We give ourselves major blind spots in those areas of our lives, which greatly hinder our ability to help them.

Our goal should be to see clearly so we will be able to successfully help others, but when we hold on to judgments and offenses, they stack up and create barriers in front of our eyes so that we can't see clearly at all. We first have to remove those barriers that hinder our vision.

It's interesting that Jesus spoke in parables and word pictures so that His listeners would use their imaginations to envision scenes in their minds that would more effectively communicate His points. Imagining ourselves with logs in our eyes and others with specks certainly makes it clearer that

---

[107] Matthew 7:3-5
[108] Romans 2:1

we need to carefully examine our own hearts before we offer critical advice to others.

The Eyes of the Imagination

In addition to teaching us through parables and true accounts of people that were recorded in the Bible, God also communicates to us through our thoughts, dreams, and visions.[109] His truth is not always visible to us on the surface, which is why we must purposefully choose to turn to God and learn from Him ourselves.

God has given each of us the amazing ability to visualize and create things in our minds. For example, before we create anything physically, we almost always hear words or see images through what we call our imagination, which is directly tied to our hearts.

We might visualize something in our minds, and we write, draw, sculpt, or otherwise record the new ideas. Then we take clay, wood, stone, steel, paint or some other material to construct the new things that we first designed in our imaginations.

We also use our imaginations and our voices to create sounds through words and music that convey unique messages. Just as we can create words and music seemingly out of thin air, we can also use our imagination to create and build things in our minds out of nothing. We can also go places in our minds and even revisit events of our past. Our imaginations are quite remarkable, and they may be more useful and valuable than we have realized.

Have you ever read a book or listened to a story and imagined the scenes that were being described? If you answered, "yes," then your imagination works just fine. You should also read the Bible and visualize events using your imagination

---

[109] Numbers 12:6, Joel 2:28-30

while opening your heart to God, so you can also see and better understand what God wants to show you.

When we follow Jesus and are committed to doing only what is right, we can also visualize ourselves in His presence, ask Him questions and hear Him answer.[110]

We can look into His compassionate eyes and hear Him speak to us while He fills our hearts with love and acceptance. Then all pain and fear melt away.

We can consciously direct our own imaginations, and that's amazing, but that may not be the best part. Have you ever had a random dream while you slept or a vision while awake that seemingly came out of nowhere? Have you ever considered that God may be speaking to you or showing you things for some good reason through your imagination?

He often reveals things to us through dreams and visions,[111] and He gives us words to speak when we find ourselves in challenging situations.[112]

So we should not be surprised when we have random dreams and visions or we hear God speaking to our hearts because God may want to show or tell us something through the eyes and ears of what we call our imagination.

Imaginary or Real?

At least once a week, a misguided thought comes across my mind, and I am tempted to do something wrong or give in to doubt and fear. When I am not alert, I often passively give in to the temptation and do something wrong for which I feel disconnected from God and polluted.

When I'm alert, however, I remember that God would never direct me to do something wrong, and He hasn't given

[110] Hebrews 4:16
[111] Numbers 12:6, Joel 2:28-29, Acts 2:17-18
[112] Luke 12:11-12

me a spirit of fear,[113] so I quickly arrest and reject the troubling thought and say, "No," to the spirit from which it came. Then I pray for God to help me conduct myself in ways that honor Him.

This all takes place through what seems like my imagination, which doesn't always feel real since I can't immediately see or hear anything with my physical eyes and ears. It's only after a few moments pass that I realize the temptation has vanished, and what happened in my imagination or heart actually made a difference in my physical world. We need to remember that what we imagine in our hearts has real implications to our spiritual, emotional, and physical health.

Of course God can reveal things to us through our imaginations, but not every dream or vision is introduced to us by God's Spirit. Satan and his evil messengers can also introduce thoughts into our heads.[114] Therefore, we need to learn to take every though captive, test the spirits, and reject those that are not from God.[115]

Our enemy wants us to believe that what goes on in our imaginations is not important, but the truth is that we can see and do things using our imaginations in the spiritual realm that truly impact lives and often become visible in the physical world around us. What we envision in our hearts and the thoughts we entertain can change attitudes and events in the physical realm.

Jesus once explained that the selfish and evil thoughts we imagine in our hearts become spiritual realities that defile us when He said:

> "What comes out of a person is what defiles
> them. For it is from within, out of a person's

---

[113] 2 Timothy 1:7
[114] 1 John 4:1-3
[115] 2 Corinthians 10:5

heart, that evil thoughts come—sexual immorality, theft, murder, adultery, greed, malice, deceit, lewdness, envy, slander, arrogance and folly. All these evils come from inside and defile a person."[116]

Jesus also spoke about adultery and murder and the correlation between our thoughts and spiritual reality when He said:

"You have heard that it was said to the people long ago, 'You shall not murder, and anyone who murders will be subject to judgment.' But I tell you that anyone who is angry with a brother or sister will be subject to judgment."[117]

Also,

"You have heard that it was said, 'You shall not commit adultery.' But I tell you that anyone who looks at a woman lustfully has already committed adultery with her in his heart."[118]

Therefore, when a person is angry with someone and they entertain hateful thoughts about them and imagine getting revenge or seeing them killed or repaid with harm in some way, they are obviously conducting murderous acts in their hearts which affects their spiritual condition in a way that separates them from God like all sin does.[119]

---

[116] Mark 7:20-23
[117] Matthew 5:21-22
[118] Matthew 5:27-28
[119] Isaiah 59:1-2

Similarly, when a man desires to be with any woman that is not his wife, and he imagines seeing her naked or getting together with her sexually, he is effectively committing adultery with her in terms of spiritual reality. This is one reason that viewing pornography is so destructive to marriages.

Angry or lustful thoughts may seem harmless to us, but Jesus clearly taught what happens in our imagination plays out in our hearts as spiritual reality where there are real consequences.

Therefore, we should guard our thoughts and be careful where we allow our imaginations to wander. In my opinion, most mental disorders have spiritual origins and are caused when we allow demons to influence our perception at the heart level.

Have you ever felt close to a person at one time and then felt like something was between you the next time you see or talk to them? That's what happens when one of you has done something or thought about doing something dishonoring to the other. Our thoughts and actions are sometimes affected by messengers of Satan who routinely try to influence our thinking and perception of reality in order to cause trouble and division between us.

Take marriage for example: When a man and a woman come together physically, they also become connected emotionally and spiritually.[120] They mysteriously become "one" in God's eyes, and this is a good thing.

Unfortunately, however, much like our offenses to God cause a separating wall between us and God,[121] when we offend each other or imagine ourselves doing something offensive or dishonoring toward one another, a wall of separation is built, and we both feel disconnected. The "oneness" is restored only after repentance and forgiveness occurs.

---

[120] Matthew 19:5-6, Mark 10:8, Ephesians 5:31-32
[121] Isaiah 59:1-2

The act of forgiving from the heart is a perfect example of how amazing and real the events of our imagination can be. When we just say words that sound right, we don't always notice any improvements. But when we take the time and make the effort to purposely identify and release offenses and judgments within our hearts through our imaginations, we actually feel and experience the liberating effects of that invisible but true spiritual exercise.

Forgiveness and spiritual salvation both take place in the invisible areas of our imaginations and hearts, so we might be tempted to question their validity. In reality, however, they both are actual spiritual events that directly impact our lives and result in visible physical and emotional benefits and blessings.

According to the Bible, one of the physical signs that spiritual rebirth has occurred is that we are given a new foreign language that we can audibly speak.[122] Not all of us who believe and receive Jesus choose to exercise our gift of speaking in our new languages, but it's edifying and encouraging to us when we do because it is a reminder of the validity of our spiritual rebirth. It also reminds us that God keeps His promises to us.[123]

Therefore, our imaginations actually serve as spiritual conduits to our hearts through which we communicate with God, and He communicates His living words to us. His words nourish us like spiritual food.[124] We simply have to recognize that truth and open the eyes and ears of our hearts like trusting children in order to see and hear what God wants to reveal to our hearts in the spiritual dimension.

Let's remember that we must be careful not to use our imaginations to defile ourselves by wandering down

---

[122] Mark 16:17, Acts 2:4, 10:46, 19:6, 1 Corinthians 14:5, 14:21
[123] 1 Corinthians 14:4
[124] Deuteronomy 8:3, Matthew 4:4, Luke 4:4, John 6:63, 14:16-17

self-condemning, self-indulging, hateful, fearful, or other dishonoring paths in our minds. We must also be careful to avoid using our imaginations to wander into other areas of darkness. God hates when we endanger ourselves in this way.[125]

Instead, we should open the eyes and ears of our hearts and humbly seek after God's kingdom purposes and His good and great plans for every moment of our lives. As we do so, He will empower us to accomplish in the physical realm what we see and hear Him doing in the spiritual realm.[126]

Seeing Past the Next Corner

We are usually not given the ability to see beyond our current circumstances and experiences. Each minute is new and the circumstances we will encounter during the next minute in time are not always predictable.

Circumstances change, and no matter how well we think we know ourselves, we cannot always predict how we will respond to those changes. Sometimes we perceive circumstances as changing for the better, and sometimes we perceive them as changing for the worse. Either way, we must remember that we can always trust God to guide us down a good path.

God always gives us good things and allows all things in our lives to accomplish good purposes. When we choose to give thanks to God, especially when we are facing challenging circumstances and don't really feel thankful, God is honored and in return He honors us by showing us the path we should take.[127]

---

[125] Deuteronomy 18: 10-12
[126] John 5:19-20
[127] Psalm 50:14-15, 23

In the presence of the Lord, time is eternal and there is fullness of joy,[128] and in order to abide in God's presence we must maintain an attitude of thanksgiving.[129] Complaining about our circumstances separates us from God.

Therefore, whenever we find ourselves in challenging situations, we should find something for which we are honestly thankful and work to maintain a humble dependence on God so that we can remain in His presence. Together with God, we can fully embrace the blessings of the moment or safely endure the turmoil until we turn the next corner.

God always knows what's coming around our corners, and the sooner we stop lamenting over our challenging circumstances, turn to God for help, and thank Him for all the great things He has done for us, the sooner He will bring us around the next corner, beyond our challenging circumstances, to a place of victory and blessing.

Are You Ready to See?

Are you ready to stop leaning on your own understanding and start trusting God to reveal the truth from His perspective?

Our beliefs dictate how we respond to our circumstances and the events we face in life, so what we choose to believe is very important. If we're not careful, then we will waste much time and energy believing and acting upon lies. Eventually, when the truth is revealed, we will truly regret the fact that we embraced such foolish beliefs.

As you open your eyes to the truth, you might come to realize that much of what you have learned in the past was based on false information. Don't be discouraged, and don't condemn yourself. Since the time that Satan acquired

---

[128] Psalm 16:11 (NKJV)
[129] Psalm 100

dominion over the earth from Adam and Eve, he has filled the earth with lies, so we all face challenges as we try to identify what is true and what is false.

The only pure source of truth is God Himself.[130] And the number one physical resource that He has provided for us to gain understanding about the truth is the collection of Holy Spirit-inspired Scriptures that we call the Bible.

So if you are ready to see through the eyes of your heart, then let go of any misconceptions that others may have taught you, ask God to enable you to see with His eyes, and trust Him to reveal to you the truth about who He is, about the good plans He has for you, and about what's really going on behind the scenes in your life.

As long as we rely on ourselves and our own understanding, we will stumble through life like blind people, but as soon as we choose to depend on God, instead of following our own agenda, our vision is amazingly enhanced so we can see where we're going and recognize what we should do next.

It's amazing that when we believe the words of God, confess our sins and our need for a Savior, and imagine that we are opening the doors of our hearts and receiving the Spirit of Jesus as was promised,[131] then the chains of sin that once bound us are truly released in the spiritual dimension making us right with God and giving us unrestricted access to communicate directly with Him.[132]

Therefore, if you haven't already done so, why not turn away from your old ways and place your trust in Jesus? Receive Him into your heart so that your spirit will be made alive and you will be reborn with a new heart, new vision, and new life.[133]

---

[130] John 1:14-18, 14:6
[131] John 14:15-21, Acts 1:4-5
[132] Psalm 107:13-14
[133] Ezekiel 11:19, 36:26

If you are already a Christian, then why not make it your daily practice to deny the impulses of your flesh, along with your own limited ability to understand, and let God's Spirit be your guide? Begin each day by finding a quiet place and close your eyes and clear your mind. Open your Bible and open the eyes and ears of your heart and spirit. Seek God, and let Him fill your "imagination" with His spiritual words and visions of life for you for that day.

6

STEP THREE–HEAR WITH YOUR EARS

⁂

The first two steps toward healing involve softening our hearts to allow God into our lives and opening the eyes of our hearts to see and believe the truth that God is good, loving, merciful, and just.

Next, we must learn to listen to the voice of God who conveys the truth, encouragement, and guidance that is essential for our growth and development as His children.

According to Jesus, His sheep know His voice, listen to Him, and follow His instructions.[134] Our hearing and choosing to listen is not limited to just certain times. God directs us and shows us the choices we should make when we fear Him and trust in Him,[135] and we can choose to humble ourselves and listen to God's voice at any time on any day.

God spoke to people long ago and no God-fearing believer disputes this fact. God also speaks to us when we

---

[134] John 10:1-4
[135] Psalm 25:12, Proverbs 3:5-6

read the Bible with open hearts. We also know that God is the same today, yesterday, and forever.[136]

Therefore, if God spoke to men in the past, and He speaks to us today when we read His written words found in the Bible, then why would anyone question that He could speak to us today when we are driving a car, standing in line at the grocery store, meeting with friends or family, or sitting alone in the woods with open hearts?

According to Jesus, you must belong to God in order to hear what God says.[137] Once you've made the decision to wholeheartedly follow Jesus, He will dwell in your heart,[138] you cross over from death to life,[139] and you will have ears to hear God's voice.[140] Jesus explained,

> "Whoever belongs to God hears what God says. The reason you do not hear is that you do not belong to God."[141]

For Christians, hearing God's voice is not a difficult task involving some complicated process.[142] The ability to hear God's voice comes automatically when we are received into His family.[143] The important thing to remember is that it's up to us to believe this truth and resist giving in to distractions while we listen.

God speaks to our hearts in ways that we can understand. His communication is pure and undefiled by the physical

---

[136] Numbers 23:19, Psalm 55:19, Hebrews 13:8, James 1:17
[137] John 8:43-44, 47
[138] John 14:15-20
[139] John 5:24
[140] John 10:27
[141] John 8:47
[142] Deuteronomy 30:11-14
[143] Jeremiah 31:33, John 1:12-13, 8:47, James 4:8

aspects of this world. God's words bring life and hope, so we do well when we take the time to listen to His voice. He loves to reveal Himself to those who seek after Him and trust Him wholeheartedly.[144]

Some people try to persuade others that God doesn't speak to people today, and that even if He did, normal people don't hear Him. This is dangerous thinking. To claim that God no longer speaks to His people today is to say that He is no longer God or that He is mute or dead. Those who believe these lies have been captivated by the father of lies, and he will certainly not let go of his captives without a fight.

Other people claim that our ability to hear from God is restricted and that the only reliable source for God's instructions is the Bible. They sometimes claim that we cannot rely upon our own ability to hear from God unless we are reading His written words. I agree that it is often easier to stay focused and hear God's voice as we open our hearts and read the Bible, but God's speaking and our hearing is certainly not limited by how often we read the Bible.

God the Father sent His Son Jesus to accomplish the humanly impossible task of breaking down the barrier of sin that existed between Him and us because He desires to have an ongoing close relationship with each one of us. Why should our relationship with God be limited to only the time we spend reading His words?

If you discover that some people in your life have either unintentionally misled you or purposefully lied to you about certain things, then you should stop listening to those people. You would certainly be justified in closing your ears off to those people, but be careful not to close your ears altogether. If you have also closed off the ears of your heart to God, then you cannot hear the words of God, and you will

---

[144] 2 Chronicles 16:9

certainly struggle unnecessarily and miss out on many rich blessings in life.

It is therefore very important as followers of Jesus that we learn to listen to His voice and follow His directions. Just like the sheep need to listen for and obey the voice of their shepherd, we need to learn to recognize and follow the voice of our Good Shepherd as we navigate the many dangerous paths in this world.[145]

The Author Speaks

God inspired every word written in the Bible, so it's a different kind of book.[146] We can trust everything written in an accurate translation of the Bible to be true because the Author is always faithful and true.[147]

Therefore, when we open our Bible and simultaneously open our hearts to hear directly from God, we frequently learn something that perfectly applies to whatever situations we are facing at that time. This is because the Author of the Bible still lives, He speaks directly to our hearts, and He reveals relevant truth to us as we open our hearts to hear and receive it.

Throughout history, more effort has been put forth by non-believers to destroy the Bible than any other book in the world. Of course, no other book threatens the advancing of Satan's work more than the Bible, so it's understandable that the enemies of God would want to destroy it. Nevertheless, God has miraculously protected and preserved His written words for thousands of years so that the people of today can see and hear the truth about God for themselves.

---

[145] John 10:14-16
[146] 2 Timothy 3:16
[147] Psalm 33:4

We should all thank God that we have access to Bibles that have been translated into modern languages that we can read and understand. According to the psalmist, the Word of God is a lamp to our feet and a light to our paths.[148]

The Holy Scriptures are extremely useful for learning about God, understanding His plan of salvation for us, training in righteousness, and general spiritual growth. [149] We should, therefore, all make it a top priority to read or listen to the entire Bible for ourselves instead of simply relying upon others to teach us what they have discovered.

The Bible is obviously one of the primary tools through which God enlightens all people, but the Bible is not the only means through which God delivers truth to people. God also delivers truth directly to us through His Holy Spirit, teachers, pastors, missionaries, evangelists, friends, co-workers, neighbors, other people, and other created things like the heavenly bodies and things in nature.

When we rely upon the Bible as a doorway and step through it by opening the eyes and ears of our hearts to God while we read His words, His Spirit enlightens our minds to deeper understanding as He guide us into all truth.[150] We must be careful that we don't rely upon the written words of God more than upon God Himself who lives and still speaks today.[151]

Contrary to what some say, the Bible does not speak to us; it's the Spirit of the Author of the Bible who speaks. We should highly value and appreciate the Bible as well as the people who teach what is written in it, but we must be careful not to make idols out of them. The Bible and Bible teachers can show us the path of life obtained through Jesus,

---

[148] Psalm 119:105
[149] 2 Timothy 3:15-17
[150] John 16:12-15
[151] John 5:37-40

but it is God Himself who gives us this life – not His words written in the Bible.[152]

Jesus often spoke to the people and taught lessons using parables, which were meant to teach general concepts and principles of right living to people with sincere hearts who were eager to walk with Him in the light. His teachings were rarely understood by those who religiously followed rituals or traditions. Yet, even those who were sincerely trying to honor God, like the first disciples, had trouble understanding everything that Jesus taught until the Holy Spirit was released to them on the day of Pentecost. [153]

God has given us the Bible to use as a physical instrument through which He reveals His general plans and purposes to all people. As we open our hearts and earnestly seek God while reading the Bible, however, God speaks to us by His Spirit and reveals specific plans and purposes for our lives.

If we regularly open our Bibles and read God's words with open hearts, then we will regularly hear God's voice, and we will begin to also recognize His voice when He is speaking to us during our daily activities.

We know God inspired every word written in the original manuscripts of the Bible, but does He inspire words to be written in other books today? Of course He does. He also inspires art and music and other things. However, according to my understanding, the Bible is the only book in the world that is universally accepted by believers as having been completely inspired by God.

Over the course of history the many translators of the Bible may have inadvertently or, in some cases, purposefully altered the meaning of some passages. Satan works diligently

---

[152] Isaiah 42:5, John 5:21, 6:26-35
[153] Matthew 13:13, Mark 9:32, Luke 2:50, 8:10, 9:45, 18:34, 24:45, John 10:6, 12:16, 13:7

to pepper the truth of God's Word with a few strategically placed misrepresentations in order to mislead people.

The devil also wants people to adhere to archaic or foreign translations of the Bible so they will feel disconnected and struggle to relate to the ordinary people who lived and interacted with God during the time in which the Bible was originally written.

Thankfully, since the original Author still lives and guides the believer's understanding of His written words today, the truth revealed by the Holy Spirit as we read modern reputable translations of the Bible in our own common languages can always be trusted and embraced with confidence.

God can inspire any author to write His words of truth. Yet, as we read other books as well as translations of the Bible itself, we need to make sure we are careful to open our hearts and allow only God's Spirit to guide our thoughts and understanding. No matter what we read or to whom we listen, we should always ask God to teach us as we open our hearts to learn from Him.

God will also strengthen us to do all that He asks of us as we commit ourselves to following Him and doing right as it is written:

> "For the eyes of the Lord range throughout
> the earth to strengthen those whose hearts
> are fully committed to Him."[154]

Please notice that God strengthens those whose hearts are loyal and fully committed to Him—not just to His words, works, principles, or followers. Jesus spoke repeatedly about the need for people to listen to Him and follow Him. Are you fully committed to following God?

---

[154] 2 Chronicles 16:9

Many well-meaning Christians often seem to follow and depend more on church leaders, traditions, family members, friends, or even Biblical principles to guide their thoughts and actions rather than following the living God Himself. They follow the teachings and doctrines of men or they follow popular Christian movements or worship trends instead of the One who inspired all of those good things and continues to do so today.

We need to be careful whom we turn to for help. For example, if you loved and respected your grandfather, who was a successful fisherman, and he sincerely offered to teach you everything you needed to know about how to succeed in fishing, wouldn't you want to learn directly from him?

Likewise, if we want to learn how to walk closely with God and live the joy-filled and abundant life that God has promised to all who believe and follow Him, then why would we not turn to the One who wrote the Book, created us, loves us, and knows everything about us? God is the Author of the Bible, and He offers to teach us and help us anytime,[155] so why not ask Him for help and learn from Him directly?

In fact, wherever we go and whatever we do, we should always be mindful of the fact that God may want to teach us something. Jesus is the living Word who became flesh, and our spirits are nourished when we consume His words. He promised to give His followers His Spirit who would teach us all things and guide us into all truth.[156]

Therefore, let's choose to depend on Him and learn from Him.[157] Our efforts should not be directed toward obtaining man's wisdom and ideas of how to study the Bible or how to do anything else for that matter. Let us believe God, seek

---

[155] Isaiah 41:10, John 14:26
[156] John 14:26, 16:13
[157] Matthew 11:29-30, John 1:14

Him, depend on Him, and listen to and obey the voice of His Spirit.

Spending Time with God

In order to be able to hear and recognize God's voice as we journey throughout our busy days, we must purposefully set aside quiet time to spend with God apart from distractions where we can get accustomed to hearing His voice.

God once said,

"Be still and know that I am God."[158]

One reason that we often find it difficult to hear with our spiritual ears and hearts is that we are too distracted, and we don't stay still long enough to hear the gentle voice of God. Just like a child naturally learns to recognize the voice of his mom or dad because he or she has spent a great deal of time with them, we must also make time to spend with our Heavenly Father in order to learn how to recognize His voice.

I've found that the best way to learn to recognize God's voice is to spend time reading the Bible with an open heart and undistracted mind because God speaks to us and enlightens our minds as we open our hearts to Him and seek understanding.

God doesn't make it difficult to hear His voice.[159] He simply speaks to us in a normal tone that can be easily drowned out if we're not paying close attention. Too often we busy ourselves and allow unnecessary chatter and distractions to keep us from being still and from focusing our attention toward God and listening. That's another reason

---

[158] Psalm 46:10
[159] Deuteronomy 30:11-14

why it's good to make time daily to eliminate distractions, get still, and read God's written words with open hearts.

When you read the Bible, don't make the mistake of setting a goal to read a certain amount before moving on to something else. It doesn't matter how many words you read or how much time you set aside. What matters is that you read with an open heart.

For some people like me, it's also a good idea to listen to audio versions so we can listen for God's voice and obtain spiritual nourishment while driving or doing other things. I've found that I am more able to connect with God when I'm listening to someone else read the Bible because I can more easily visualize what I'm hearing, and I comprehend more easily.

In the past, this is the way most people used to hear God's written words because there were only a small number of copies of the Scriptures in a given area. For thousands of years teachers and other leaders would read a Bible aloud to large groups of people.

Later, after printing presses were developed, copies of the Bible were made more affordable so families could purchase their own copy of the Bible that was read routinely by parents to their children at home. Children would listen intently and imagine what life might have been like for the people of the past who experienced and personally witnessed God's supernatural interactions with the people on earth.

Reading the Bible should not feel like a chore because it's about spending quality time with God. The Biblical account of sisters Mary and Martha is a perfect example demonstrating the contrast between busying ourselves as we try to serve God and just resting in His presence.

The Apostle Luke wrote how one day Jesus came to Mary and Martha's house for a visit. Martha stayed busy making preparations for dinner or something while Mary simply enjoyed sitting at the feet of Jesus listening atten-tively to Him.[160]

Martha was upset because she had to do all the work, so she asked Jesus to tell Mary to help her. Surprisingly, Jesus rebuked Martha and told her that she was too busy and upset about things and that Mary was doing better by spending time with Him. He would not direct Mary to do anything else at that time.[161]

From this account, we learn that it's important that we do like Mary and take time to rest in the presence of God. We must be careful not to get so caught up in the busyness of life that we neglect the more important task of spending quality time with God, pouring out our hearts to Him, and listening to what He wants to tell us.

God wants to spend time with us, and once we know God, we will want to spend time with Him. It would be a tragedy if we go through life doing lots of things with the intent of serving God without ever spending time with Him. If we refuse to turn and rest in the presence of God and listen to His loving guidance, and instead, busy ourselves simply doing things that we hope will please God, then we will miss out on many blessings.[162]

When we consistently spend time with God, which requires that we walk in ways that honor Him, He calls us His friends. We see this intimate relationship between God and Abraham,[163] King David, and between Jesus and His early fol-lowers.[164] When we conduct our lives in such a way that we consistently walk in His presence, He also calls us His friends.

---

[160] Luke 10:38-40
[161] Luke 10:41-42
[162] Matthew 7:21-23
[163] James 2:23
[164] John 15:15

God is a friend who will never let you down, and He wants to spend time with you and get to know you. So why not pour out your heart to Him and listen to Him today?

Don't Believe Everything You Hear

It would be nice if God's voice was the only voice we heard during the day. Unfortunately, it's not.

It's not always easy to tell where our thoughts are coming from, but according to the Bible, they come from only three sources: our own mind, God, or the devil.[165] Therefore, we need to practice taking every thought captive, pause, and think twice to determine where each thought originated and whether or not we should act upon it.

We can usually tell when our own minds are generating thoughts because we control what we think about. God's words often come from out of the blue, through a calm and gentle, but authoritative voice, and what He tells us is always true, always agrees with His character, and is never contrary to Scripture.

That's one reason why the Bible tells us to:

> "Be still before the Lord, and wait patiently
> for Him"[166]

and

> "Be still and know that I am God."[167]

We often have to quiet our minds so that we can identify God's gentle, encouraging, and loving voice above all others. With practice backed by familiarity with God's written words, we can learn to discern His voice.

---

[165] Jeremiah 31:33, John 10:42-47, 2 Corinthians 10:5, 1 John 4:1
[166] Psalm 37:7
[167] Psalm 46:10

Thoughts introduced by messengers of Satan, however, are not always easy to discern because the words are manipulating and deceiving. His messengers are good at what they do. They study our habits and listen to our words so they can introduce ideas that we will find familiar and reasonable.

In order to motivate us to step into their traps, they tell us what they think we want to hear, and they usually mix in some truth to confuse us. Sometimes their voices are louder and more hostile sounding than the gentle voice of God, so we can sometimes detect a manipulating tone, but many times they are so crafty and skilled at deception that we fail to recognize them.

Messengers of darkness also speak to us in first person saying things like, "I'm stupid," "Nobody loves me," "I'll never get this right," "I'm fat," "I'm ugly," "Nobody cares about me," or some other false and self-condemning words to which we often carelessly agree.

Satan's messengers are skilled at motivating us to feel discouraged, confused, and fearful. They know they don't have any power over us, so they use deceptive, intimidating, and manipulating tactics to try to prevent us from walking in the power and authority that God has given us through Jesus.

Sometimes I have sought direction from the Lord, and I have heard a voice in reply that sounded a little harsh. As our ears become more sensitive to hearing the voice of the Holy Spirit, we will also be more aware of hearing other spirits.

So when you know you didn't come up with a particular thought on your own, how do you determine whether the voice you are hearing is from God's Spirit or some other spirit?

Fortunately, the Apostle John explained how to get through this dilemma as follows:

> Beloved, do not believe every spirit, but test
> the spirits, whether they are of God; because

many false prophets have gone out into the world. By this you know the Spirit of God: Every spirit that confesses that Jesus Christ has come in the flesh is of God, but every spirit that does not confess that Jesus Christ has come in the flesh is not of God.[168]

Therefore, whenever you hear a voice in your head that you know your own mind did not generate, and you're not sure if God gave it to you, ask the spirit whether or not he acknowledges that Jesus is the Son of God who became a man. Then listen because the spirit will answer.

Since you were able to hear the voice the first time, you will be able to hear it again. Every single time that I've questioned a spirit in this way, I've heard his answer. It all seems to take place in my imagination, but it's quite effective and real.

In my experience, if the spirit replies, "no," then I tell it to go away, and I disregard everything I heard. If the Spirit replies, "yes," however, then I wait and listen for further clarification because demons are notorious for lying. They might say yes to my question, but they will not confess that Jesus is the Messiah. A Spirit that is from God, however, will not hesitate to confess that Jesus is the Christ, the Son of God.

We must stay alert and remain aware of the devil's tactics to distract us and keep us busy doing non-productive activities. When you recognize the manipulating and pretentious voice of our enemy, then you should resist him as the Apostle James directed, and he will go away for a while.[169]

Respectfully say, "No" to any spirit who tells you to do something that you know is contrary to God's best for you. You don't have to get loud or excited. If you don't waiver, then the agent will go away without much of a fight.

[168] 1 John 4:1-3 NKJV
[169] James 4:7

If, however, you arrogantly tell him to go away and that you will never do what he says again, then you will cause trouble for yourself because that reveals a prideful weakness that he will certainly detect and use against you later.[170]

A good example of a small battle happened to me one Saturday afternoon as I was driving with my son William who had just turned seven years old. As usual, I was running late for a meeting, and this particular day I felt a little downcast because I was worried I wouldn't have enough work to make the money to pay the bills that month.

When we came upon a man holding a sign asking for help at a green light, I quickly drove past him and avoided eye contact because I didn't feel like giving away what little money I had.

Immediately, I felt convicted, so I decided to pull over to ask God whether I should go back and give the man some money. I asked William to pray and listen as well.

Immediately, as I began praying I heard in a rather agitated tone of voice, "Don't go back and give that man any money."

Hot dog! I thought to myself. Since I was short of cash and I was glad to have gotten such a quick reply to my question, I quickly agreed with the spirit. Then I asked William if God had told him anything.

He said, "I think God told me that He wants you to go back and give that man some money."

Okay . . . I had a feeling that William would be more willing to give money if God directed it since he wasn't depending on it like I was. Since I still felt convicted, and the voice I had heard didn't sound friendly, I decided we should pray again. So we prayed silently again, and speaking seemingly to a voice in my imagination, I asked the spirit, "Do you acknowledge Jesus as Lord who came in the flesh?"

---

[170] Matthew 12:43-45

I clearly heard in the same hostile voice, "No!"

So I said to the spirit in my imagination, "Get out of here then!"

Then I prayed, "Lord, I want to hear Your voice."

I heard in a firm but more friendly voice, "I am the Lord your God. Go back and give that man twenty dollars. Give and it will be given to you, pressed down, shaken together, running over and poured into your lap."

I knew I recognized these words as something God might say, and the voice was friendly. So I asked William if he thought twenty dollars would be good to give, and he agreed. I then took twenty dollars out of my wallet and turned around to drive back up the hill to where the man was standing.

Traffic was surprisingly clear, so I was able to make a U-turn right after passing the man. Then I pulled up to him and said, "God told me to give this to you."

He grinned, enthusiastically took the money, and quickly replied, "Thank you. God bless you."

I said, "God bless you too," and I drove away. Within a few minutes I noticed my depressed feeling had lifted, and I felt joyful. That was a welcome surprise. On Monday morning I was given a job that paid me more than two thousand dollars! What a blessing that was!

We can never know exactly how our choices to honor God and follow His guiding voice today might enable us to turn a corner where we will find a blessing tomorrow. We simply have to listen to Him and follow His instructions.

Draw Near to God

After we develop a daily routine of reading or listening to the written words of God and we learn to recognize God's voice, we must continually seek His guidance and exercise our spiritual ears and resist distractions as we go through each day so that our ears do not grow dull of hearing.

Some days God seems a million miles away, and I feel alone and downcast. Then, other days, it feels like God's presence is near, His voice is clear, and life is joyful.

Life on this earth is full of hostile forces and challenges that affect everyone differently. Sometimes we're up, and sometimes we're down. I think that's fairly common today because in our high-tech world, temptations to do wrong appear to be everywhere. We can be close to God one minute, and the next minute we can stumble into temptation, forget God, and drift away for a time.

Even when we are walking with God, however, with all the loud distractions of life, sometimes we can have difficulty recognizing God's voice. Also, when we are caught up with our own issues, pleasures, or greedy ambitions and not committed to walking with God, we will drift away from God where we will have more trouble hearing His voice.

Therefore, it should also be our goal to draw near to God so that He will draw near to us where we are able to hear His words of instruction and encouragement. When we trust God and follow His will for our lives on a daily basis, He will instruct us in the choices we should make, empower us to carry out those choices, and work things out for us. [171]

---

[171] Psalm 25:12-13, Proverbs 3:5-6

7

STEP FOUR–UNDERSTAND WITH YOUR HEARTS

Once we've opened our hearts, and we can see and hear the truth, we need to truly embrace and process that truth so we can grow in our understanding and learn how to apply it to our own lives. We certainly can't understand everything at once, but over time God gives us understanding in whatever area we need it as long as we continue to seek Him.

In this chapter I unpack what I've come to understand about offenses, disappointments, judgments, and forgiveness so that as you read, you will hopefully grow in your understanding of these topics and learn to apply whatever God wants you to teach you.

As much as it saddens God's heart that so many people have been hurt by family members, friends, and others, I'm sure it grieves Him even more to know there are so many people who are still carrying their pain after having been introduced to Jesus.

Jesus once expressed God's heart of compassion for His people who refused to turn to Him when He said to the people of Jerusalem,

"How often I have longed to gather your children together, as a hen gathers her chicks under her wings, but you were not willing."[172]

I'm sure His heart also laments over us today as we struggle through the challenges of living in this world while refusing to turn to Him for help. Even among regular churchgoers, I often see more sorrow and sighing than gladness and joy. Why is this? Why do people who receive Christ still walk around wounded and weighed down?

I'm convinced the answer to this question is rooted primarily in unbelief and a lack of understanding. I know that before I decided to turn to God and believe in Him, I used to carry loads of pain and heartache because I didn't fully understand all that He had lovingly done for me.

Jesus once explained how many people would come to Him boasting about the good things they did while on earth, but their words and actions did not overflow from a heart of understanding. Their deeds were apparently born out of selfish motives, religious exercises, and misunderstanding, so they will miss out on the blessings that come with a personal relationship with God.[173]

People can read and learn all about Jesus, but not everyone who learns and knows about Jesus understands and believes all that He has done for us and continues to do for us. If we truly understand how much He loves us and how much He has done for us, then we would humbly and thankfully spend more time pouring our hearts out to Him and listening to Him.

We should all spend time seeking out the truth and processing it to obtain a right understanding of our purposes and who we are in relation to our Creator. If we seek God,

---

172 Matthew 23:37
173 Matthew 7:21-23

listen, understand His words of truth, and apply His instructions with thanksgiving, then we will see clearly the path that leads to life.[174]

Until we commit ourselves to doing right and obtaining understanding, however, we will struggle to find the path that God has established for us. The same is true of forgiveness. Many of us will struggle to forgive until we have a clear understanding of what God has done for us. I'm certainly glad God is so patient with us.[175]

We are Slow to Understand

God created us and knows that we are often slow to understand and believe. He understands our skeptical tendencies, He is patient with us, and He doesn't give up on us or condemn us when we are slow to understand as long as we continue to humbly seek Him for the truth.[176]

In fact, God is never disappointed with you because He doesn't have any unmet or unrealistic expectations. He knows every choice that you will ever make before you make it. He rejoices with you over your good choices, and He laments with you over your bad choices. He cannot tolerate your sin, but He still loves you and has made provision to clothe you in His righteousness through the work of Jesus.

A good example of God's patience and forbearance with us was demonstrated in the account of the prodigal son who demanded his share of his inheritance early, squandered it all, realized he had acted foolishly and needed help, humbled himself, and returned home where his father welcomed him with open arms.[177] God knows we often give in to our

---

[174] Psalm 50:14-15, 23
[175] 2 Peter 3:9
[176] James 1:5
[177] Luke 15:11-32

selfishness, and our understanding is often lacking, so we sometimes go astray, but through Jesus, God offers forgiveness and always welcomes us back whenever we humble ourselves, repent, and turn back to Him.[178]

Much of what is recorded in the Scriptures and what Jesus taught is difficult to understand. In fact, many times it is recorded how the disciples asked Jesus to explain something to them, and He always did.[179] Even still, many disciples didn't grasp the full meaning of everything Jesus did until He returned to the Father, and the Holy Spirit was released into their hearts.[180]

It makes perfect sense that the teachings of Jesus would be difficult, if not impossible, for people without supernatural spiritual insight to understand, as He explained,

> "It is the Spirit who gives life; the flesh profits nothing. The words that I speak to you are spirit, and they are life."[181]

Even His closest disciples, who walked with Jesus every day for months, made comments like, "This is a hard teaching. Who can accept it?"[182] Still, they continued to search for understanding and ask Jesus for help. Jesus always helped them, and He wants to help us too.

It's not that God wants to make it difficult for us to understand His words. On the contrary, God wants us to wholeheartedly seek Him, trust Him, and open our hearts and minds so that He can reveal Himself to us. The words of

---

[178] 1 John 1:8-9
[179] Matthew 13:36, 15:15, Mark 4:34
[180] John 16:7-15
[181] John 6:63 (NKJV)
[182] John 6:60

God are spiritual, and it takes a spiritually minded person to understand them.[183]

A good example of God wanting to help us understand things was when two of Jesus' disciples were traveling to Emmaus and discussing and wondering about all that had happened to Jesus in Jerusalem.[184]

As you may recall, Jesus joined the two disciples without disclosing His identity, and He explained the Scriptures concerning Himself to them. The two men were filled with excitement, as they now understood how Jesus had fulfilled all the Scriptures written about the Messiah's first coming.[185]

After those two disciples spent time with Jesus and they returned from Emmaus, they found the other disciples and explained what had happened. Then Jesus appeared to all of them. They were confused and frightened, so Jesus "opened their minds so they could understand the Scriptures."[186]

Sometimes our ability to understand is so limited that God Himself has to "open" our minds like He did here with these disciples. Therefore, when we are having trouble understanding something, we should pray and ask God to open our minds, so that we too can understand more completely.

Many people, even scholars, think one can come to understand the Bible using one's own limited human intellect. According to Jesus, however, only those who have "ears to hear" can truly understand God's words.[187]

The Bible is a spiritual book. It is a collection of writings inspired by the Spirit of God, so we cannot understand it using our own reasoning.[188] The mysteries of the Bible

---

[183] 1 Corinthians 2:6-16
[184] Luke 24:13-27
[185] Luke 24:32
[186] Luke 24:45
[187] Matthew 11:15, 13:9, 13:43, Mark 4:9, 23, Luke 8:8, 14:35
[188] John 6:63, 1 Corinthians 2:6-16

remain hidden to those who do not fully depend on God for understanding.[189]

We need spiritual guidance, and we should be grateful that since the day of Pentecost, when the Holy Spirit was released to all believers, God's people have been taught directly by God, just as He promised.[190].

When we are born of the Spirit, we are given spiritual eyes to see God and ears to hear His voice.[191] God equips us, as His children, to see Him and hear His voice so that we are able to understand His words, follow Him, and live a fulfilling life today and forever. This journey begins with opening our hearts to God in humility and repentance.

Studying the Scriptures without allowing the Spirit of God to enlighten our minds and bring understanding to our hearts is like trying to drive a car without any fuel in the tank. The only way to move forward is to push and steer the vehicle ourselves. Every step forward is challenging and the farther we go, the more exhausted we get.

It's no wonder intelligent people get burned out and give up as they try to read God's Word without depending on God's Spirit for guidance. They can't get any nourishment. Eventually, people who are not humbly depending upon God avoid even trying to read the Bible because it seems impossible to understand and get anything out of it.

We cannot understand God's Word by simply relying upon the world's training techniques or our own efforts. I believe there are no systematic or scientific approaches that can provide the keys to unlocking the spiritual mysteries found throughout the Bible. We have to have ears to hear

---

[189] Daniel 2:28, 47, Matthew 11:25-27, 16:17, Luke 2:26, 10:21-22, Colossians 1:27
[190] Jeremiah 31:33
[191] John 10:27

and eyes to see what the living Author Himself chooses to reveal to us.

We must also carefully choose to whom we listen because Satan influences many teachers in this world today to mislead many people. We must not depend on man's earthly wisdom to shape our thinking about God or His words.[192]

We must learn to depend on the Author of the Bible to guide us in every way so that we can be able to recognize and reject any teaching or guidance that does not follow His perfect plan for our lives. We need to study the real article with help from the Author and not risk learning from a counterfeit.

If you want to gain understanding, then turn to God for the answers. When you humbly ask for help, God will find a way to open the eyes and ears of your heart and mind so that you can understand.

Do Good to Those Who Hurt You

Some time ago my wife and I saw a good movie titled, "The Vow" which was based on events in the lives of Kim and Krickitt Carpenter.

During the movie, Leo (representing Kim) and Paige (representing Krickitt) are involved in a car accident that results in Paige losing the memory of her life over the past couple of years. There's some heart-wrenching drama between Paige and Leo as she returns to the life she remembers prior to meeting him.

One day, at a local grocery store, Paige crosses paths with Diane who she recalls being her best friend. When she sees her, Paige is excited and greets her warmly, but Diane is embarrassed and apologetic and cannot embrace Paige. Diane knows their friendship ended roughly two years ago

---

[192] 1 John 2:18-27

over a major offense for which to her knowledge Paige had not yet forgiven her.

Paige, on the other hand, has no recollection of any issues or events that would have caused a breech in their relationship. She treats Diane with kindness and is bewildered by her response until she learns Diane and her dad had had an affair.

I found it intriguing that the loss of the memory of the affair left Paige with no emotional scars and enabled her to wholeheartedly embrace her old friend and dad with kindness without any reservations until she learned of the affair.

How great it would be if we were all able to just flip a switch in our hearts to completely forgive our offenders and their offenses so that we could always happily do good to those who hurt us.

As it turns out, many times we can choose to forgive in a way that's like flipping a switch. It's just not about forgetting the memories of certain painful or offensive events. It's more about making a deliberate choice to switch from holding on to judgments, offenses, and disappointments to releasing them while trusting God to work everything out.

Paige's accident was not her fault, but her own choices and actions had led her down the path that brought her to that challenging time in her life. In the same way, our choices take us along certain paths, and like Paige, some of those choices lead us in directions that cause us to have trials and tribulation.

The Bible says if you want to experience abundant blessings and great reward, you must

> "bless those who curse you, pray for those who mistreat you,"[193] "not repay evil with evil or insult with insult," "repay evil with blessing,"[194]

---

[193] Luke 6:28
[194] 1 Peter 3:9

"do good to those who hate you,"[195] and "not
be overcome with evil, but overcome evil
with good."[196]

If you're like I once was, then you might ask, "Are you kid-
ding me? How in the world can this be possible? Why does
God want me to be nice to the mean people who hurt me?
Doesn't God care about justice for me? How can my being
nice to someone who has hurt me bring about justice? How
can that be fair?"

It may not seem fair at the time, but God can indeed be
trusted to execute justice at the right time. Unless and until
you and I forgive the offenses from others and release the judgments made against those who have hurt us, we will never be
free, and we will be unable to truly bless those who have hurt us.

One might ask, "Why can't I just keep on thinking bad
thoughts toward the people who have hurt me? Don't they
deserve to be punished for hurting me? Does God love them
more than me? Why does He want me to be nice to them?
Does God even care about me?"

Of course God cares about you, and He loves you and
everyone equally.[197] If you want to carry all or some of the
offenses that are delivered to you, then you are free to do
so. God won't force you to let them go, but you will have to
suffer the consequences of holding on to them.

When you die, of course, you will automatically let them
go, but you can choose to hold on to offenses and grudges
and stay weighed down by them as long as you live on the
earth. You simply don't have to, and your life will be miserable and likely cut short for doing so.[198]

---

[195] Luke 6:27
[196] Romans 12:21
[197] John 3:16
[198] John 20:23

We don't need to worry about whether others get punished for hurting us. It's the Holy Spirit's responsibility to "convict the world of sin."[199] We simply have to release the evidence of the offensive actions others have committed against us so we can be free, and God can bring about that conviction which, when received, will bring about a burning sense of regret in the heart of the offender and hopefully, a desire to make things right.

Remember how Jesus addressed Judas after he had led the band of soldiers to arrest Him? Jesus still called him "friend" demonstrating that He did not hold the betrayal against him.[200] Since Jesus did not hold the sin against Judas and even blessed him by calling him "friend," it was as if Jesus was heaping burning coals of conviction upon his head. [201]

Of course Jesus would not have poured burning coals on anyone's head, but that's the effect that forgiveness and subsequent acts of kindness have on a person's offenders because the offenses are unbound and released so that God can judge the evidence and apply conviction where it belongs. Since Jesus did not hold on to any offenses, Judas felt the overwhelming weight and regret of his actions.[202]

God gives us authority to bind and to loosen, [203] and when we loosen offenses they fall on Jesus.[204] As long as we are still holding their offenses against them and passing judgment, however, we cannot truly bless them, and the evidence of their offenses remains bound up in our hearts. In order to acquire the ability to be nice to mean people, we must first understand binding, loosening, and forgiveness.

---

[199] John 16:8
[200] Matthew 26:50
[201] Proverbs 25:21-22, Romans 12:20
[202] Matthew 27:3-5
[203] Matthew 16:19, 18:18
[204] Psalm 69:9, Isaiah 53:6

Binding and Loosening

In Matthew's account of the life of Jesus, he recorded Jesus' teaching about forgiveness and how our binding and loosening on earth changes things in the heavenly realm. Jesus explained,

> "I will give you the keys of the kingdom of heaven; whatever you bind on earth will be bound in heaven, and whatever you loose on earth will be loosed in heaven."[205]

Jesus also said,

> "If you forgive the sins of any, they are forgiven them; if you retain the sins of any, they are retained."[206]

One of the keys to the door of a healthy and fulfilling life is forgiveness. When someone offends us and we choose to retain their offenses, we are binding those offenses to ourselves in the heavenly realm, which weighs us down and prevents God from considering those offenses as evidence, judging the matter, bringing convicting reproof to the offender, and executing justice.

If we loosen the ties that bind offenses, judgments, and disappointments to our hearts, however, then they are free to fall onto Jesus in the heavenly realm so that He can weigh the evidence, judge the situation, and execute justice when and where it's needed. Meanwhile, we are freed from the weight of those burdens.[207]

---

[205] Matthew 16:19, 18:18
[206] John 20:23 NKJV
[207] Psalm 69:9, Matthew 11:28-30

A person saying, "I forgive you," is basically saying, "I no longer hold the evidence of your offenses against you, and I release you to answer to God to face His judgment."

When we hold offenses against others, however, we are effectively demonstrating that we don't truly trust God. Each of us must decide for ourselves whether or not we choose to believe God and trust Him enough to loosen the ties that bind to us the offenses that others have made against us as well as the disappointments that we carry against ourselves and others.

If we choose to hold on to them, then our offenders may never fully understand how they have hurt us because the evidence is bound to us and the convicting influence of God is prevented from penetrating their hearts. They will not realize how offensive their actions are, so they will likely hurt us in the same way again.

Therefore, not only does our binding and retaining offenses often cause us to be hurt repeatedly in the same way by the same people, but we also cut ourselves off from God because our sin of holding on to offenses creates a barrier between ourselves and God.[208]

Furthermore, as if cutting ourselves off from God and others wasn't bad enough, when we refuse to forgive, we also open doors of opportunity for Satan to sneak in and pollute our lives with more darkness, and we give him a foothold. Retaining offenses is a losing proposition no matter how we look at it.

Our enemy works hard to convince us to hold on to offenses whenever someone sins against us. He even tries to influence us to judge others and condemn them when no real offense has occurred.

We must stay alert to his schemes and resist every evil spirit who tries to fill our minds with condemning thoughts

---

[208] Isaiah 59:2, Matthew 6:15, Mark 11:25

toward others. Think twice before acting. There is no riding the fence on this issue. We must learn how to release offenses quickly so that we leave no room for our enemy to sneak in and try to wreck our lives.

I've witnessed the tragic results of binding offenses and the life-giving results of loosening offenses over and over through the years. It's simply amazing how this spiritual law impacts our lives, but if we've not yet developed the habit of loosening and releasing offenses, then it's time to learn.

Learning a Foreign Language

Some people grow up around others who are forgiving, so they learn good habits early and find that forgiving the offenses of others is no big deal. Just like learning a first language, learning to forgive can be picked up naturally from family members.

Other people, however, grow up with family members who easily take offense and hold grudges against each other. For these people, learning to forgive can be much more challenging, like learning a foreign language. Unfortunately, I've encountered more people who struggle with forgiveness.

The concept of forgiveness is not complicated. However, in the same way that learning a foreign language requires learning new skills, such as proper pronunciation, grammar rules, and word meanings, the act of completely forgiving offenses and offenders also takes learning new skills, understanding how and when to apply those skills, and practice.

The sooner we learn the new techniques and develop the good habit of effectively forgiving others and their offenses, the easier it is to consistently walk it out, and the more freedom we will enjoy.

Learning a new language is easier if you are constantly around others who speak the new language. For those of us who grew up in homes where forgiveness was not taught and demonstrated, we have to find teachers who are skilled in the practical elements of forgiveness and willing to teach us. Many teachers have emphasized the necessity of forgiving others, but they don't always teach forgiveness from a perspective that includes identifying each of the components of the specific offenses and judgments held against others as well as themselves. If not taught properly, most people will struggle to truly forgive from their hearts, and so their lives remain marked by misery, regrets, bitterness, and sickness.

I've heard teachers explain that sometimes it can take years for deeply wounded people to truly forgive their offenders. I believe it's true that some people have piled up so many offenses against others that it may take a long time to identify and release all of them, but we don't have to forgive the same offenses over and over to be free of them. Once is all it takes.

Not everyone, who teaches about a particular subject is 100% accurate, so instead of relying upon teachers that might be misinformed in some areas, why not learn from the best? God Himself wants to be our teacher and counselor.[209] Whenever we listen to or read anyone's teachings, we should open our hearts to God and ask Him to develop our understanding of the subject from His point of view.

At first, the forgiveness process can be quite challenging, but thankfully, with proper training and practice, it gets easier. We have to remember, however, that we will likely always face opposition from our old selfish nature or agents of darkness as we work to do what's right.

We must also choose to remain humbly dependent on God. As soon as we think we've mastered the ability to forgive, and we boast about it, someone will hurt us, and we will fall back into the old patterns of holding a grudge and feeling resentful again. Then, if we act too hastily, we may retaliate

---

[209] John 14:15-18, 16:13-15

against our offender or hurt someone else, after which we will have to do the extra work of making things right.

If we find ourselves stumbling and falling back into old patterns of wrong behavior, we need to be careful not to condemn ourselves. Even adults who mastered the ability to walk decades ago still stump their toes and trip occasionally.

Each time we find ourselves feeling angry or resentful toward ourselves or someone who has hurt or disappointed us, we must quickly identify the root cause and take steps to release the offenses and emotional pain. While holding offenses, if we retaliated against anyone, we also need to make things right in that area. This process should be repeated every time offenses are recognized.

At first, the forgiving process may seem rather tedious as we work to identify offenses and let them go while allowing God to reshape our thoughts and renew our minds. But over time, with constant practice, the act of releasing offenses and judgments becomes easier and easier. And believe me, the blessings that we receive will be well worth the cost.

Just don't be surprised or discouraged if you find yourself being tempted to hold on to another offense soon afterward.

Our enemy hates it when we start moving in a positive direction toward the light, so he tries more diligently to trip us up. Expect opposition. In this world we will continue to have troubles that often come through other people, so we will get plenty of practice as we are learning to forgive from our hearts.

Forgive and Forget

When my son Eric was eleven years old, while riding through the country, we spotted a church marquee with the following message upon it: "True Forgiveness is Forgetting." I started to ponder that statement, wondering if it were true. I asked Eric what he thought, and he quickly said, "No."

"Why not?" I asked.

"Because," he replied, saying something like, "you can watch a movie and forget about your hurts for a while, but that doesn't mean you've released those hurts or the people who hurt you. When the movie's over, you'll remember your hurts again."

I liked his answer. Some people say we should try to forget about our hurts, and over time, forgiveness will take place. This way of thinking is harmful because forgiveness is not a byproduct of forgetting. Forgetting, however, is often a byproduct of forgiveness.

If we try to forget something by choosing not to remember it, that does nothing to remove the source of the pain. If someone shoots you with a bullet, does taking pain relievers and forgetting about the bullet enable it to go away? Of course not.

Let's look at some Scriptures. One passage that comes to mind says,

> "For as high as the heavens are above the earth,
> so great is His love for those who fear Him; as
> far as the east is from the west, so far has He
> removed our transgressions from us."[210]

Thus, in forgiving our sins, God purposefully removes our sins from us and casts them far away. That's great news, but is that the same as forgetting about them?

Also, consider the following passages:

> "I will forgive their wickedness and will
> remember their sins no more."[211]

---

[210] Psalm 103:11-12
[211] Hebrews 8:12, Jeremiah 31:34

Also,

> "I, even I, am He who blots out your trans-
> gressions, for my own sake, and remem-
> bers your sins no more...I have swept away
> your offenses like a cloud, your sins like the
> morning mist...."[212]

So in saying, "I will remember your sins no more," is God saying He will forget our sins? Is "remember no more" the same as forgetting? You may be thinking, "Aren't they saying pretty much the same thing? What's the difference?"

One big difference is that "forgetting" is the unintentional result of not remembering something, and to "remember no more" is to intentionally choose not to remember or bring up something. Forgetting is passive and accidental. Choosing not to remember is actively done on purpose.

If we choose not to remember or recollect the memories about some specific information or event, then we are doing that on purpose, and with the passing of time, since our minds are not perfect, we eventually forget things.

Technically, we can choose to remember or not to remember something, but we cannot purposefully forget something.

Isaiah recorded that God once said,

> "Forget the former things; do not dwell on
> the past."[213] Those two statements go hand
> in hand, for in order to forget the past, we
> must choose to not dwell on, rehearse, or
> remember past events.

---

[212] Isaiah 43:25, 44:22
[213] Isaiah 43:18

Then, over time, because our minds are limited, new events and ideas consume our attention, and we unintentionally forget some things. The more often we remember past events, the easier they are to recollect.

In reality, however, because of our busy lifestyles, we forget more things than we remember. We even forget many things that we want to remember, like names, birthdays, and anniversaries or where we put our car keys.

We've already shown that "not remembering" is not the same as "forgetting." I cannot find in Scripture where God claims to have forgotten our sins, or anything else for that matter. Since God is all-knowing and perfect,[214] I believe God doesn't accidentally forget or lose anything.

Since God truly forgives our sins, and it is not possible for God to forget like we do, it follows that true forgiveness is not about forgetting. Forgiveness is not a passive act of forgetting offenses, but the willful act of choosing to release them.

When God forgives us, He purposefully separates our sins from us. They don't simply disappear. It's like they are swept away when they are placed upon Jesus, who willingly took our punishment and accepted separation from the Father, physical torture, and death.[215]

By saying "I will remember your sins no more," God is promising He will not bring them up against us ever again because Jesus has now taken our punishment once and for all. The job of redemption is finished.

This is much better than passively forgetting our sins because rather than being unable to remember our sins, which, if one day remembered, He might choose to hold against us again, God chooses to intentionally *not* remember our sins after removing them and placing them upon Jesus.

---

[214] Matthew 5:48

[215] Isaiah 53

Forgiveness, therefore, is not about forgetting the offenses of others. God forgives and promises not to hold our sins against us ever again, and He never breaks a promise. I think this is great news!

An Eye for an Eye

How often have you been hurt by someone and immediately felt like you wanted to hurt them back? I've not met many people who are so self-disciplined and humble that they don't at least complain after being assaulted. Many people consider it quite proper to return insult for insult or to avenge themselves, but is this the best course for us?

I have heard or read many times that when you forgive someone you "give up your right to punish the person who has hurt you." This description of forgiveness seems legitimate to our natural minds, but for a long time something about it bothered me.

Finally, it occurred to me that it's misleading because we have never been given the "right" to avenge ourselves and get back at those who have hurt us. Therefore, we certainly cannot give up a "right" that we've never had. God commands us to love, not hate; to heal, not hurt, to build up, not tear down.

God also said that He will judge with righteousness, execute justice, and avenge the wrongs that others do to us.[216] He specifically told His people not to avenge themselves.[217] He often employs other people to execute justice, but

---

[216] Deuteronomy 32:35, Psalm 9:8, 50:4, 96:10-13, 98:9, Isaiah 66:16, Ezekiel 18:30-32, Mic 4:3, John 16:8, Romans 12:19, Hebrews 10:30, Jude 1:14-15

[217] Romans 12:17-19, 1 Peter 3:9

those people would be acting under authority given by the Supreme Judge, not acting according to their own authority.

People who want to justify their vengeful actions and claim they have been given the right to "get even" often refer to the passage in the Bible where Moses said,

> "If there is serious injury, you are to take life for life, eye for eye, tooth for tooth, hand for hand, foot for foot, burn for burn, wound for wound, bruise for bruise."[218]

Many argue that through these instructions an injured person has been given the right to get even. Unfortunately, however, these statements are too often quoted out of context and misapplied. We have never been given the right to act as our own judges and avenge ourselves upon our own offenders.

God Himself, acting as Supreme Judge, prescribed the sentences for each of the crimes listed. In this passage Moses, who was God's spokesman and chosen judge over His people, was directed by God to execute His predetermined penalties upon those who had been formally tried before a judge and convicted for the specific offenses based upon the testimony of at least two witnesses.[219]

Too many people blindly accept the teaching of people who themselves have been misled, and it is disturbing to me that so many people don't open their hearts and take the time to read and understand God's words for themselves. In order to experience the blessings of walking with God on the earth, we must discover for ourselves the truth about God and His great plans for us.

---

[218] Exodus 21:22-25, Leviticus 24:17-23, Deuteronomy 19:16-21
[219] Deuteronomy 19:15-21

Learning to Forgive

Forgiveness always involves releasing something. In many cultures a visual demonstration of forgiveness occurs when a father releases his daughter into the hands of her new husband during the wedding ceremony. It's called "giving away the bride," and the minister asks, "Who gives this woman?" Usually the father gives her willingly and completely into the hands of her new husband with no intention of taking her back. That's a good picture of forgiveness.

One primary key to unlocking the door to joy and fulfillment and better health in this life and eternal life in the next is the practice of forgiving offenses and offenders. Some people are able to forgive relatively easily, but that's never been easy for me.

During the first thirty-four years of my life, I did not understand what forgiveness was all about, and I didn't think I needed to learn. I don't like following rules or learning to do something unless I think it is necessary or beneficial for me, so I never developed the habit of forgiving offenses or offenders.

I thought forgiving was the same as forgetting, so I tried to forget about the times that I had been hurt, but that didn't help me because the pain was still there. I also wanted to see justice served, so I did not want to let others off the hook when they mistreated me.

I thought forgiving someone let them off the hook so they didn't get punished, which gave them approval to hurt me again. I was wrong. Was I wrong to want justice? No. In fact, God loves justice, and He loves those who are just,[220] so wanting to see justice served is not a bad thing. However, I was certainly wrong to pursue my idea of justice through my own means and on my own timetable.

---

[220] Psalm 11:7, 33:5, 37:28, 99:4

When we let our offenders off of our hooks, they are automatically released to fall onto God's hook. Only when we choose to release the evidence is God able to take it up and judge the matter. It doesn't matter what you believe about God, when you release an offense it automatically falls onto the account of Jesus where He can deal with it.[221]

Because of my independent attitude and calloused heart, I was unwilling to learn and unable to understand that my holding on to disappointments and petty offenses and my judging others were destroying my heart and my relationships.

God once said,

> "My people are destroyed from lack of knowl-
> edge ... a people without understanding will
> come to ruin."[222]

I have personally experienced the truth of these statements because after many years of applying my ignorant habits, my lack of knowledge and misunderstanding about forgiveness was indeed causing my life and family to come to ruin. Just before my wife left me, we were emotionally distant, and we constantly argued. Our relationship was a mess. After she left, I was devastated and began crying out to God for help.

I was finally ready to learn what God wanted to teach me about forgiveness and other important things. Thankfully, He was there to comfort me and teach me how to forgive the offenses and disappointments, and He also convinced me to trust Him to be the judge over others and myself.

Once I learned how to forgive from my heart, my outlook became radically more hopeful, and my countenance

---

[221] Psalm 69:9, Isaiah 53:6, 1 John 2:2
[222] Hosea 4:6, 14

became marked by joy. I began to see the hand of God at work in my life and in the lives of those whose offenses I had released. I was also able to see each offender as more valuable and worthy of my respect.

God was healing my broken heart, setting me free, and gluing the pieces of my life and family back together. My family, friends, and co-workers noticed these changes in me. If you are feeling like your life is in ruins, then know that God wants to help you too.

I learned we should all practice releasing offenses and judgments quickly – even from those who hurt us repeatedly[223] because forgiveness is a primary key through which the chains that keep us in bondage are eliminated so that healing can begin.

Retained offenses always damage hearts and relationships. They prevent intimacy between husbands and wives, mothers and daughters, brothers and sisters, friends, co-workers, and so on. Retained offenses also create barriers between God and us. [224]

When we pridefully hold on to the offenses of others, God doesn't hear our prayers.[225] That's another big reason why forgiveness is so important.

Oftentimes, our natural response to being hurt by another person is to hold on to the offense, pass judgment against the offender, and try to avenge ourselves by hurting the offender back. This is a dangerous thing to do because if we were wounded by some painful event in the past, and we refuse to trust God and let it go, then we will continue to be damaged by it, and it will negatively affect all of our relationships.

---

[223] Matthew 6:12-15, 18:21-22, Luke 17:4
[224] Isaiah 59:1-2
[225] Isaiah 59:1-2

People who are quick to forgive offenses, however, enjoy healthier relationships and appear to be much happier than others who hold grudges and frequently find fault with others. Furthermore, clinical trials conducted by Duke University Medical School and Cancer Centers of America have shown that people who are quick to forgive are also healthier and less likely to develop chronic diseases like cancer.[226]

At the onset, a victim may be innocent of any wrong-doing. If he or she cries out to God, refuses to pass judgment, and releases the insults, then God Himself will step in to comfort and heal the victim, weigh the evidence, judge the situation, and set into motion the execution of justice against the offender.[227]

If, however, the victim holds on to the offense, passes judgment, and tries to avenge themselves, then he or she sins against God which separates him or her from God[228] and causes their own pain and suffering to increase.

We can know for sure that as we act in obedience to God, He will orchestrate events in ourselves and others so that in the end we are blessed.[229] Regardless of what another person has done to you and how badly they have hurt you, if you choose to believe God and act according to His will, then He will bless you.

Invisible Pain, Invisible Cure

Have you ever noticed that when someone insults you, the words that were directed at you are heard by you and others around you, but the offense and emotional pain that you may have received into your heart are invisible?

---

[226] www.Medscape.com
[227] Psalm 10: 14, 17-18
[228] Isaiah 59 1:2
[229] Romans 8:28

Your visible countenance may have reflected your emotional pain, but the actual offense you took was invisible. It had nothing tangible that could be detected by sensory perception, but as long as the offense or sin is kept stored away in your heart, its effects will be felt directly by you and indirectly by those who are close to you.

Furthermore, if you don't forgive the offenses that others direct toward you, then not only will you have to endure the painful effects of carrying the offenses, you will also suffer because you offend God by not releasing them.[230]

The spiritual effects of carrying sin may be invisible to us, but they are no less real than anything visible that we can see with our eyes. Sin always causes separation and pain which are always invisible side effects of doing wrong. [231]

We were not designed to carry offenses, and it was never God's plan that we would have to carry them or the sorrow and pain that accompanies them. Therefore, just as we search for and apply visible remedies for physical ailments that are visible, we must also find and apply invisible remedies for our emotional and spiritual ailments that are invisible.

Thankfully, our invisible God provides the cure, and it's available to everyone, as it is written,

> "Surely He took up our infirmities and carried
> our sorrows ... The Lord has placed on Him
> the iniquity of us all."[232]

Since all sin causes sorrow and suffering, when God placed all sin upon Jesus, which was spoken of in past tense even before Jesus was born, the corresponding pain and

---

[230] Matthew 6:15
[231] Isaiah 59:1-2
[232] Isaiah 53:4-6

punishment for all sin passed to Him as well. In the spiritual realm, there is no time dimension, so any person from any time period who believes in Him can accept God's provision and be healed.[233] It's as simple as that from our perspective, but that doesn't mean it was easy.

The wages of sin is separation from God, punishment, and death,[234] so when the sins of the world were placed onto the account of Jesus, He experienced physical torture, emotional abandonment, spiritual separation from the Father, and death.[235] These experiences were in no way easy to endure.[236]

Jesus poured out His blood for us, so our sins would be atoned for and forgiven. This was necessary in order for us to be reconciled to God, as it is written,

> "without the shedding of blood, there is no forgiveness."[237]

God did the difficult part, which is an incredible gift for us.[238] We should remind ourselves of this truth and give thanks repeatedly for the great sacrifice that Jesus made to bring healing and salvation to us.

Jesus has already carried upon Himself the pain and affliction caused by our offenders' sins against us. So we should remember that once we receive Christ as Lord and Savior of our lives, we no longer have to carry the burden and pain of the sins that others commit against us.

---

[233] Isaiah 53:4-5

[234] Romans 6:23

[235] Psalm 22:1, Matthew 27:46, Mark 15:34

[236] Matthew 26:36-45, Luke 22:39-45

[237] Hebrews 9:22

[238] Romans 5

We have, in Jesus, provision for carrying our sorrows and grief. Every sin that someone else commits against us has already been placed upon the account of Jesus and paid for. Therefore, when we look upon Jesus as our Redeemer, who provides for our eternal peace and saves us from eternal punishment, we should also see Him as our burden-bearer who carries our sorrows and heals our hearts.

Indeed, part of the joy of our salvation is knowing that the pain of every offense that has ever been done or ever will be done to us was already received by Jesus where He willingly carried it upon Himself so that we could be free. [239]

Just because we didn't know Him or have a relationship with Him long ago doesn't change the fact that He has already carried our emotional hurts. Jesus carried our past hurts, our present hurts, and our future hurts.

We therefore have no right or reason to try to carry any of the pain and sorrow that has already been carried by Him. Our responsibility is to trust God, believe what He has done for us, and release all of the offenses that we carry along with the pain and suffering so that it can be included in His finished work.

Since there is no time dimension in the spiritual realm, all sin for all time and the pain and sorrow that goes with it has been applied to Jesus on the cross. The work is finished.[240]

You may ask, if Jesus already carried my sorrow and emotional pain, then why do I still feel it? Good question. This is the supernatural, awesome part about faith. We have to choose to believe God and respond to His instructions before we will be able to see and experience His goodness.[241]

One time, when Jesus encountered a man who had been unable to walk for thirty-eight years, He asked what I

---

[239] 1 Peter 5:6
[240] John 4:34,5:36,17:4,19:28-30
[241] John 11:40

consider to be a strange question. Jesus asked, "Do you want to get well?"[242]

The man answered that he did, but he said he needed help. Jesus then told him to get up, pick up his mat, and walk. As soon as the man decided to believe Jesus, he was instantly cured, and he was empowered to do what he was told to do. The path to his healing had already been established, but he had to choose to believe it and take action before his healing was activated.

In the same way, we choose what we believe and how we act upon those beliefs. When Jesus told Peter to come to Him on the water, Peter had to choose to believe he could walk on the surface of the water because Jesus told him to, before he could actually do it.[243]

The same holds true for us. We have to choose to believe what God says and act accordingly before we can experience the results that He promises. I can attest from my own experience that the joy and freedom that comes into my heart after I have believed God and followed His instructions, like forgiving offenses and judgments, is real and supernatural.

Usually, the bigger the offense is, the harder it is to let go and the more Satan tries to convince us to hold onto it. But when we finally decide to trust God and give it over to Jesus, we experience an abundance of joy, peace, and freedom.

If, after hearing the truth about offenses, we choose not to release them, then we are either refusing to accept God's provision or choosing not to believe His words are true. In either case, the result is that we are rejecting God, so we will continue to experience the pain and suffering of carrying the insults and injuries ourselves.

Whether you are deeply hurting because of past abuse that was sexual, verbal, physical, emotional, or some other

---

[242] John 5:1-9
[243] Matthew 13:25-31

kind of mistreatment, Jesus suffered with you and carried your pain and sorrow to the cross where it has been forever cast away. If you accept this truth by faith and release all of the evidence of your victimization to God, then you will experience the incredible rest and freedom that He has already purchased for you.

There is no time dimension within the spiritual realm, so no matter how terribly you've been hurt or how long ago you were mistreated, you can be set free. God's invisible cure is still available to all of us.

Therefore, every time someone hurts us in some way, let's believe God and claim by faith that Jesus already dealt with the pain and the insults that caused the pain. Let's not add to His pain by refusing to accept what He did for us.

Sticks and Stones

Do you remember the old saying, "Sticks and stones may break my bones, but words will never hurt me"? When I was a child and someone said hateful words to me, I repeated this sentence, and I wanted to believe it, but harsh words and insults still hurt me.

I tried to be tough and forget about the painful insults that others hurled against me. I even successfully covered up the feelings of hurt and rejection for a while, but later the pain would come to the surface and negatively affect my attitude and behavior. Thankfully, I eventually learned the truth about insulting words and offenses.

According to what King David wrote in the Bible, unkind people "sharpen their tongues like swords and aim cruel words like deadly arrows."[244] The Apostle Paul compared the insults and temptations of the enemy to flaming arrows.[245]

---

[244] Psalm 64:3
[245] Ephesians 6:16

Years ago, flaming arrows were often used as weapons launched through the air to effectively penetrate an enemy's defense system, inflict some immediate injury with the sharp points, and then eventually completely destroy the targets by fire.

Like deadly, flaming arrows, the lies and hateful words that come through the air from other people can be very destructive and inflict much pain upon us if we don't shield ourselves.

One of Satan's tactics is to try to convince us that if we ignore offenses when they come our way, then they won't hurt us. This is dangerous thinking. If someone throws a rock at you, will it just go away if you ignore it? Or if someone shoots a bullet toward you, will it disappear simply by hoping that it goes away? Of course not.

In the same way that physical pain is felt when you are hit with a rock or a stick, emotional pain is felt when you are insulted with words or mistreated in some other way. In fact, the emotional pain from being hurt by a few hateful words spoken or texted over the telephone can be much more lasting and damaging than the pain from being physically hurt by something like a bullet or a punch in the nose.

Think about how destructive words can be. Assaulting words like, "You will never amount to anything," "You're ugly," "You're a loser," "You're a bum," "You're stupid," "You're good for nothing," "You're fat," or some other hateful or discouraging words often remain in people's hearts and cause them trouble for many years.

Thankfully, it doesn't require going to a hospital or a doctor and spending money to treat an emotional assault. When someone launches a verbal offense against us, we can identify it and let it go quickly so the flames of the offense are extinguished and don't cause us much trouble.

It's not our fault when someone else's offensive actions or words invade our lives, but we must be diligent to shield ourselves from the resulting emotional and spiritual consequences for our own health and safety.

We also need to understand that we were born into a world that is currently under the influence of Satan, and he opposes everything good and everything that God loves, including us. As children of light,[246] we face battles frequently, and it is dangerous for us to pretend like our enemy of darkness doesn't exist.

We must recognize this truth in order to effectively shield ourselves against his attacks. The agents of Satan constantly target prideful, vulnerable, and unsuspecting people, who have wandered away from the Truth, to manipulate them so they will deliver flaming arrows of insults and offenses to stir up trouble.

We need to stay alert because attacks come when we least expect them. I can't even count how many times my wife and I have been enjoying time together when out of nowhere we began arguing over some petty issue. Before we knew it, we both felt angry and divided. This still happens today.

When we finally cool down, we usually realize that an unkind comment or some misunderstanding initially triggered the conflict, which was then fueled by prideful and defensive thoughts and comments. Sometimes, it seems like agents of darkness are laughing at how easily we take their bait and go off track.

Satan and his agents delight in causing us trouble, so they look for our weaknesses and focus their efforts on tempting us when we are most vulnerable. Therefore, it is essential that we, as Christians, stay alert and take up the shield of faith, as Paul called it, to prevent insulting words and offensive actions from penetrating our hearts, coming out of our mouths, and poisoning our lives.

---

[246] Ephesians 5:8, 1Thessalonians 5:5

Currently, Satan is called the prince of this world and the ruler of the air, and he is quite effective in twisting our words to cause trouble.[247] Since words are usually transmitted through the air or some medium like the internet, we must remember that any word that we say, hear, or see can be discovered by Satan's messengers. They often then add their own deceptive thoughts and words to the receiver in order to twist the intended meanings as they work to disrupt relationships and destroy lives.

Therefore, we should be careful not to allow ourselves to jump to conclusions or make assumptions about what we hear or read. If something is not clear, then we should ask the other person to clarify their communication.

Furthermore, we should not say or do anything out of selfish ambition, pride, or retaliation because when we do, we expose our weaknesses to our enemy who will certainly take note and use what we say and do against us. The Apostle James did well when he instructed his fellow believers to be

> "quick to listen, slow to speak, and slow to become angry."[248]

We have to be careful about what we say. You've probably heard on TV a police officer dictating to a person who has just been arrested the Miranda Rights: "You have the right to remain silent. Anything you say can and will be used against you." Believe it or not, this statement holds true everyday whether you've been arrested or not.

The devil, who is called the prince of demons and the prince of this world,[249] and his agents listen to what we say. Every word we say can and will be used against us by enemy

---

[247] John 12:31, 14:30, 16:11, Ephesians 2:2

[248] James 1:19

[249] Luke 11:15, John 12:31, 14:30, 16:11

agents who listen to find out where we are most vulnerable so they can sneak in and gain a foothold in our lives.

Remember when Jesus said Satan had no hold over Him?[250] That's because Jesus believes only the truth, speaks only the truth, and has never said or done anything wrong, so there are no holding points of access.

If you often find yourself battling temptations and feeling harassed by what you think are your own thoughts, then it may be that you have given Satan a hold or open door to access your life by believing lies, speaking lies, or doing something else wrong.

The devil's agents, who are very crafty and resourceful, often introduce misguided thoughts and tempt us to judge and condemn those who may be completely innocent of any wrongdoing. They also distract us to prevent us from facing the real source of our own pain, they tempt us to blame others for our disappointments and heartaches, and they even try to convince us to blame God for our troubles.

Therefore, we need to stay alert, analyze every thought that comes into our minds, and think twice before we say anything or respond in any way. Also, we should always try to think the best of others, and let go of perceived insults quickly, before we say or do something we will regret.

The longer we hold on to insults, the more damage they do to our hearts. Every insult for which we needlessly choose to take and hold eventually takes root in our hearts and will cause a destructive fire of resentment, bitterness, anger, and hatred to burn within us that will affect the innocent people around us, lead to spiritual separation from God, and eventually lead to physical sickness and death if left unchecked.

So if we think by ignoring the words of others that they cannot be used against us, then we are badly mistaken. We need to remember to stay alert and be careful what we

---

[250] John 14:30

write or let come out of our mouths and what we choose to believe about what others are saying about us.

When harsh words are delivered to us, instead of letting our understanding of their meaning affect us in a negative way, let's choose to identify and let go of them so they will fall on Jesus.[251] Let's purposefully shield our hearts from taking offense by remembering what Jesus has done for us and releasing to Him any perceived insults.

As we walk in humility, practice forgiveness, and bless those who mistreat us, God's supernatural power is released through us to build His kingdom and change the world around us. So when sticks and stones or harsh words and insults come our way, let's not ignore them. Let's focus on the truth and take up our supernatural shields of faith.

Take up Your Shield

Paul directed the believers at Ephesus to "take up the shield of faith" to "extinguish all the flaming arrows of the evil one."[252] This shield is supernatural, so exactly what is a "shield of faith"?

The "shield of faith" is a real and effective shield that protects our hearts from being pierced by the deceptive tactics of our enemy, and it's necessary to deflect or "extinguish" the harmful effects of all of the lies, insults, and abusive or discouraging words that come our way.

This supernatural "shield" is composed of our wholeheartedly believing and trusting God while embracing and applying His truth to our lives daily.[253]

When we study the truth, choose to believe God, actively trust that He will do what He says He will do, and act

---

[251] Psalm 69:9
[252] Ephesians 6:16
[253] Psalm 28:7, 115:11

according to His directions, then our faith becomes a shield. Consequently, the lies and manipulating tactics of the enemy are easier to identify and can be quickly rejected so that they have no effect on us.

We must ground ourselves in the knowledge of God, turn away from our own self-reliant tendencies, and learn to rest and apply the shield of believing the truth and trusting that God will defend us every time someone insults, offends, mistreats, or tries to discourage us.

In this way our faith in God becomes a shield that we carry in our hearts as a defensive weapon against the offensive actions of others and the temptations of Satan. For God Himself is our shield and strength,[254] and He will protect, defend, and strengthen us as we trust and rest in Him.[255]

Since God is our provider, doesn't it make sense that He would make provision for the protection of our hearts so that we would not have to remain hurt or polluted by the insults of others? God does indeed protect us, for as the Psalmist once wrote:

"He is a shield to those whose walk is blameless, for He guards the course of the just and protects the way of His faithful ones."[256]

Of course, as the old saying goes, "An ounce of prevention is worth a pound of cure." The key to maximizing the shield's effectiveness is deciding to believe God and commit to walking in ways that honor Him before we come under attack. We also do well to remain in fellowship with other

---

[254] Genesis 15:1, Deuteronomy 33:12, 29, 2 Samuel 22:3, 31, Psalm 3:3, 7:10, 18:2, 30, 28:7
[255] Isaiah 30:15
[256] Proverbs 2:8

believers so that we can encourage one another and help each other identify possible areas of vulnerability.

We can also prepare ourselves by spending time with God and consuming His words because our knowledge of the truth enables us to identify and reject all of the lies that the father of lies shoots in our direction. Our faithfulness activates God's shield.

If we are not faithful, however, and we take on offenses, then our sins of holding on to those offenses create walls that cut us off from the loving and protective presence of God.[257] If we are not paying attention, then we can be easily lured away from the light with lies and begin to walk in darkness where Satan traffics and tries to gain additional footholds into our lives.

Of course, Satan who is called the father of lies[258] takes every opportunity he can to discourage and distract us while filling our minds with thoughts of fear, doubt, and discontent to try to lure us into the dark and keep us there. We must therefore be careful to faithfully ground ourselves in the truth and stay alert so we know when we are coming under attack.

As we go through life, let's expect that insults will come our way, and let's prepare ourselves by faithfully believing and trusting God and casting off any offensive words or actions that may be tossed in our direction. That way the fiery darts that come from our enemy are deflected, and we are able to avoid unnecessary emotional and spiritual challenges.

God speaks. We believe. And God changes things for our benefit. Let's take up our shields!

---

[257] Isaiah 59:1-2
[258] John 8:44

Sin and Forgiveness

To fully understand the forgiveness of sin, first we must understand sin. Sin is the spiritual dimension of any thought, word, or deed that is contrary to what is right and pleasing to God. Sin always causes pain or offense to someone, including God or yourself.

The pain, sorrow, and suffering that occur are tied directly to the sin. The two are inseparable. Where there is sin, there is pain, sorrow, or suffering.

At one time Christ spoke through King David saying,

> "The insults of those who insult you fall on me."[259]

So when we release offenses, they don't fall by the wayside; they fall onto the Way.[260] Jesus carried all sin for all time.[261]

One might ask, "If God has already credited the sins of the world to the account of Jesus, then why does it matter what we do?" Good question. It matters because God gives us freedom to make our own choices and believe what we want to believe.

In the spiritual realm, there is no time dimension, so the spiritual truths that applied in the past are still applicable today. We must choose to believe God, accept His provision, and act accordingly before we can experience the benefits of that provision.

Regarding our individual lives, God doesn't force His will upon us but gives us the freedom and authority to make our own choices. With that freedom and authority, however,

---

[259] Psalm 69:9
[260] Isaiah 35:8, John 14:6, Acts 22:4
[261] Isaiah 53:6-12

comes the responsibility to accept the consequences for those choices.

Every action begins with a choice, and we are ultimately responsible for every word that we speak and every act that we commit.[262] When we choose to hold on to things, such as sins and burdens, that are not ours to carry, we weigh ourselves down unnecessarily and reap painful consequences.

We don't have to follow God's plan for our lives, but when we choose to do so, God blesses us.[263] When we choose not to follow God's good plan for our lives, we encounter misery.[264] Thankfully, God offers a way of escape for that misery when we humble ourselves and turn to Him for help.[265]

When we repent and turn to God for help, He separates our sins from us, and He also separates the pain, sorrow, and suffering that accompanies our sins from us as well.[266] By faith in Jesus, our sins are forgiven, and God heals us as we understand and apply this truth.[267]

Forgiveness of sins is the intentional, willful act of releasing the specific offenses along with the pain, sorrow, and suffering that accompany them. Forgiveness of offenders is the intentional, willful act of releasing the specific judgments that we've made against them.

Every sin builds a barrier between the sinner and the one who is offended as well as God, but the barrier with God exists only between God and the one who commits the sin. Your relationship with God is not directly hindered by someone else's actions.[268]

---

[262] Matthew 12:36, Ecclesiastes 12:14

[263] Deuteronomy 28:1-14

[264] Deuteronomy 28: 15-24, John 5:14

[265] Deuteronomy 30:1-10

[266] Isaiah 53:4-5

[267] Matthew 9:2-7

[268] Ezekiel 18:1-20

If someone sins against you, however, and you hold on to that sin and entertain condemning thoughts toward the offender, then you have sinned against God in two ways. Your sins of retaining offenses and passing judgment separate you from God and His comforting and healing influence.[269]

After a sinful thought is conceived, delivered, and received by another person, then pain is inflicted and now the victim has an offense with which to deal. In a similar way, someone may throw a dart or pull a trigger to launch a bullet, but it's the bullet or dart that actually causes the pain and needs to be the focus of attention – not the shooter.

Generally, when a person has been shot with a gun, he or she is rushed to the hospital so that hopefully, a skilled physician can carefully and quickly remove the bullet. Removing the bullet is top priority because only after the bullet is removed can complete healing begin to take place.

The doctor does not care who shot the bullet because it makes no difference to him. His job is to remove the bullet as quickly as possible.

Of course, the shooter should be arrested, tried, and convicted before a qualified judge, and sentenced appropriately.[270] But if the person who has been shot focuses only upon obtaining justice for his assailant and ignores the bullet, then his troubles from the wound will only grow worse. If not properly treated, the wound may become infected and cause even more trouble or even death for the victim.

The same holds true after being emotionally assaulted by offenses. If an offended person focuses only on his or her offenders and ignores the actual offenses, then they will remain in his or her heart where they will fester, cause bitterness, and possibly lead to physical illnesses like cancer, which could lead to death for the victim.

---

[269] Isaiah 59:1-2
[270] Matthew 18:7

So don't be misled into thinking that the person should be the only focus of forgiveness. If we lose sight of the actual offenses, then we may spend years struggling to break free by repeatedly releasing judgments made against our offenders without ever forgiving the actual offenses that are triggering the judgments.

Therefore, one of the main reasons we still feel the pain when we recall and revisit hurtful events is that they have never been released. I think this is why some people mistakenly claim that true forgiveness should take years to accomplish.

When we focus on releasing our offenders and not also their offenses we can spend many years feeling the weight of those offenses because we haven't yet let them go. During this time the wounds remain unhealed and bitterness festers which continues to breed condemning thoughts of hatred and vengeance toward our offenders.

By the time it reaches this stage, we feel like we have irreconcilable differences, and forgiveness seems like an impossible task. It doesn't have to be that way.

When someone offends us, it's the actual offenses we take on that cause the emotional pain—not the people who launched the offenses against us. So in order for healing to begin, not only must we release judgments, but we also must focus our attention and efforts on identifying and releasing the specific sins, hurts, and offenses.

As long as offenses are retained, pain remains, and the painful effects spread like fire within our own hearts and eventually to the people close to us. As soon as the offenses are released, however, healing begins and the pain fades away in time. When we can remember being hurt but no longer feel the pain, then we know all of the pain-inducing evidence of the offense has been truly forgiven.

Please remember that it is the offense itself that causes emotional pain, not the person through whom the sin is delivered. The identity of an offender can be useful to help correctly identify past offenses, but their identity is only necessary when judgments have been made against them that also need to be identified and released.

Sometimes our greatest obstacle to quickly releasing offenses and refusing to pass judgment is our prideful tendency to think we don't deserve to feel hurt or disappointed. Our pride can make forgiving challenging enough, but we often struggle even more because we are not grounded in the truth. Our believing lies gives Satan and his agents holding points of access into our lives to cause us more trouble.

The devil's messengers are constantly looking for ways to trip us up. They frequently come along at times when we are physically tired or emotionally compromised or otherwise vulnerable and try to talk us into holding on to grudges and seeking vengeance for ourselves. We must therefore take every thought captive and think twice before we act in order to reduce the number of times we trip and give in to the manipulating tactics of our enemy.[271]

We should also remember that sometimes other people fall into one of the enemy's traps and say or do something hurtful to us with no planned intention of being hateful. So it's important that we not be surprised when they carelessly fall into one of the devil's traps because we too fall into traps and carelessly hurt others at times.[272]

We don't see everything with unbiased vision, and we don't usually see much beyond the surface of the words and actions of others. Yet, God sees past the surface with perfect vision, and He knows the past experiences of every person as well as the thoughts and motives of their hearts. God alone is able to judge everything perfectly.

---

[271] 2 Corinthians 10:5
[272] Romans 2:1

Therefore, we must learn to let go and trust God. Otherwise, we will naturally harden our hearts in a futile effort to protect ourselves from the painful aspects of this world. Then we will lose sight of God's mercy and compassion, and we will find it nearly impossible to pardon our offenders and release their offenses.

Satan will use anyone who is willing to cooperate with him to hinder you and motivate you to hold on to hurts so you become calloused, bitter, self-reliant, and self-destructive. Make sure you don't fall into this trap of believing lies and holding offenses against another person.

It takes practice to develop the habit of quickly forgiving offenses because our natural inclination is to take and hold offenses and to avenge ourselves. When we train ourselves to forgive offenses, however, the freedom we experience is truly supernatural.

Forgive the Offense or Offender?

Have you ever honestly tried to forgive someone or let go of the wrongs they did, but then you still struggled with feeling hurt or wanting to see justice served? I certainly have. That's often because we haven't yet specifically identified and released both the offenses and the judgments.

As we read through the Scriptures, we find that the exercise of forgiveness is applied to both offenses and offenders. In many passages Jesus directed His disciples to forgive the sins, debts or trespasses, and in other passages He directed them to forgive their offenders. So what's the difference?

When we speak of forgiving a person, it is implied that we are releasing judgments against that person. When we forgive sins or trespasses, we are releasing the actual offenses along with their accompanying pain.

As odd as it sounds, sometimes we forgive our offenders by releasing the judgments we've made against them while still holding on to the offenses. Sometimes we release offenses while we continue to pass judgment against the people who hurt us and look forward to seeing justice served.

In some instances it's easier for us to forgive offenses first. At other times we move forward more quickly when we first release judgments made against our offenders. Regardless of which task we accomplish first, in order to be completely free and healed, we must forgive both the offenses and the offenders.

After we identify and forgive offenses, we are able to see our offenders with unobstructed vision without feeling pain because the offenses are no longer present. Then it is much easier to release any judgments that we may have formed against them. It's also usually easier to release judgments when we find out that the offender has been caught and punished for their crime.

Have you ever noticed that some people are more willing to forgive some offenders and offenses after they find out that their offender has died or is facing some major tragedy in their lives? That's because it's often easier to forgive when we believe the offenders have already received their just punishment.

Sometimes, when we are injured, we fall into the trap of quickly passing judgment and condemning our offenders. Then we're faced with the double task of having to release both judgments and offenses. We should try to avoid falling into these traps, but when we fail, we should act to release offenses and judgments as quickly as possible because the longer we wait, the more likely we are to cover up the pain and become bitter, and the more likely we are to give in to the temptation to avenge ourselves.

Sometimes we do not understand why we cannot get over the pain in our hearts and move on with life, so we conclude that we have to keep on forgiving people over and over again. That's because not all of the components of the offenses, including the actual insulting words, emotional pain, and judgments have been released. If not purposefully released, they remain in our hearts where they continue to fester, cause bitterness, and create holding points for enemy agents to influence our perception and cause more trouble.

When we fail to release offenses, anytime someone does something to hurt us in a way that is similar to the retained offenses, the enemy stirs up trouble by reminding us of them and feeding us lies that change our perception of the new offense in order to amplify the hurtful effects. When this happens, a small offense often triggers a noticeably inappropriate, exaggerated, and angry response.

Then we often blow up and ask things like, "Why do you *always* do that?!"

When we judge others in this way, then people will judge us in the same way because we will be found making the same or even greater mistakes than what we criticize others for making. This is one of the important topics that Jesus addressed when He instructed His followers:

> "Do not judge, or you too will be judged. For in the same way you judge others, you will be judged, and with the measure you use, it will be measured to you. Why do you look at the speck of sawdust in your brother's eye and pay no attention to the plank in your own eye? How can you say to your brother, 'Let me take the speck out of your eye,' when all the time there is a plank in your own eye? You hypocrite, first take the plank out of your own eye, and then you will see clearly to remove the speck from your brother's eye." [273]

---

[273] Matthew 7:1-5

Therefore, it is important that we release all offenses and condemning thoughts against ourselves and others because as long as they exist in our hearts and minds, they will distort our perception of reality and prevent us from being able to see accurately.

Just because someone does or says something to insult us, that doesn't mean that we have to take offense and carry the burden of the insults. We don't have to let another person's offensive attitude or behavior mess up our lives. We can choose to purposefully let go and actively trust God.

It doesn't matter how long we've held onto offenses, we can still take the appropriate steps needed to move toward healing, wholeness, and restoration. Obviously, the more scar tissue there is, the more concentrated effort it takes to uncover and release the root causes. If we persevere, however, we will more greatly appreciate the joy and freedom that we experience once those actual burdens are released.

After the insults, injuries, and disappointments are released, they no longer stand between us. We become free from those weights, judgments are more easily released, dividing walls are removed, and relationships can be restored.

It's imperative for us to remember that when we are hurting due to another person's actions, or we are frustrated with ourselves for making mistakes, we must focus on identifying and releasing the actual offenses, judgments, disappointments, or mistakes so that God can weigh all the evidence, pass judgment, and execute justice.

The Great Promise

During a traditional marriage ceremony a man and a woman usually make sincere promises to each other to care for, respect, and love each other until physical death separates them. As a result, both hearts experience feelings of acceptance, happiness, and security, and an intimate mutual bond is created. It's a beautiful thing.

In a similar way, our Creator, who loves each of us and wants to have an intimate relationship with us, has taken the steps to remove the barriers from between us, and He has made promises to us for which He is always faithful to keep.

When we choose to believe God, accept His promises, and promise to faithfully love and honor Him all the days of our life, then we too enjoy a bond of intimacy with our Creator that is beautiful.

A great example of God's loving faithfulness to us is demonstrated in what I call "The Great Promise." A long time ago a man named Abram chose to trust and obey God as he left his homeland and traveled to a foreign land as God had directed him.

Because of Abram's obedient heart, God blessed him, changed his name to Abraham, and promised to make him the patriarch of a great family. He also promised Abraham and his descendants,

> "Whoever blesses you I will bless, and who-
> ever curses you I will curse."[274]

Now, that is a great promise, and God has been faithful to keep it. He said He would weigh the evidence for every situation, pass judgment, and execute justice so that Abraham would not ever have to concern himself with acting as his own judge.

Throughout Scripture we read over and over again how God was faithful to this promise and repaid blessing for blessing and cursing for cursing to all those who interacted with Abraham's family and his descendants. This is

---

[274] Genesis 12:3, 17:5

reassuring when we consider how serious God is about keeping His promises.

Another reason this promise is so reassuring is that Jesus is a direct descendant of Abraham.[275] So if we have received Jesus into our hearts, then through Him we have been adopted into Abraham's family and God's family, and we are covered under this great promise.[276]

The implications of this promise are huge. God is faithful, and He always keeps His promises. As we serve God, receive Jesus, and walk with Him, He will bless those who bless us and pay back trouble to those who harm us.[277]

Therefore, we can forgive the offenses that others throw against us and the judgments that we make against them, knowing that God will indeed execute justice when the time is right.

Sometimes the most challenging aspect of freeing ourselves from burdens and the things that weigh us down is actually letting go. The struggle becomes especially apparent when we are trying to forgive and let go of repeated offenses and personal injuries.

When we consider, however, that God is faithful to bless those who bless us and punish those who hurt us, it becomes easier to let go. Our God is the One and only true God who actively works to maintain and defend the lives and honor of those who faithfully serve Him. The people of other religions fight to defend the honor of their gods, but our God actually fights for us.

The blessings promised by God are almost always dependent upon our fulfilling our part of the deal, which consistently involves believing God and following His instructions. That's why Jesus said our healing was directly dependent on

---

[275] Matthew 1:1-16, Luke 3:23-38
[276] Romans 8:14-17, 8:23,& 9:4, Galatians 4:5, Ephesians 1:5
[277] 2 Peter 2:13

our faith in Him.[278] When we choose to trust and believe God and submit to His authority, then we position ourselves to reap His promised blessings.

It is our faith in God, our knowledge of Him, and our trust that He will do everything He has promised that compels us to follow Him, walk with Him, and experience what He has promised.

Whenever we are tempted to take and hold on to offenses, we should stop and remind ourselves that our loving Creator will deal directly with anyone who causes us trouble that we don't deserve as long as we release the evidence of the offenses to God. We can always trust Him to keep His promises and administer justice when the time is right.[279]

Letting Go of the Evidence

Since we are all made in the image of God who loves justice,[280] it's natural that we want to see justice served in the world around us. When we don't see justice executed against the offensive people in the world, we are often tempted to take matters into our own hands.

When God created Adam and Eve, He gave them dominion over the earth and all the birds and fish and animals on earth.[281] God, however, did not give them dominion over each other.

Throughout history when people have gotten out of control and hurt each other, God has always served as judge and orchestrated the execution of justice.

---

[278] Matthew 9:29
[279] 1 Peter 2:20-23
[280] Psalm 11:7, 33:5
[281] Genesis 1:28, Psalm 115:16

When Cain killed Abel, it was God who stepped in, judged the situation, and executed justice.[282] When Joseph was done wrong by his brothers, God executed justice.[283] When the Egyptians oppressed the Israelites in the time of Moses, God stepped in and executed justice.[284]

When Miriam, the sister or Moses, grumbled and complained against her brother, God stepped in and taught her to be more respectful toward Moses.[285] Time after time, Moses humbly fell on his face before God to release all of the complaints and insults that had been directed at him by the people, and God always stepped in and took care of things.[286] God is always honored when we humbly submit to His authority and turn to Him for help.

The phrase, "Let go and let God," sounds like good advice when it comes to forgiveness because we need to learn to let go of offenses and other burdens that weigh us down while humbly trusting God to judge the situations and execute justice.

The phrase, "God helps those who help themselves," on the other hand, is misleading because God helps those who humbly depend on Him for help—not those who are self-reliant and pridefully think they can take care of things themselves.

When we hold on to offenses and pass judgment ourselves, we are pridefully withholding the evidence of our victimization and effectively communicating that we don't trust God to keep His word. Our refusing to forgive also communicates that we think we can do the job better than God, which is quite insulting or even rebellious.

---

[282] Genesis 4:1-16
[283] Genesis 30-50
[284] Exodus
[285] Numbers 12
[286] Numbers 12, 16, 21:4-9

No wonder we feel disconnected from God when we're holding on to offenses and judgments against others.

In order to accomplish the execution of justice all over the world, God establishes rulers, judges, parents, and other leaders in authority over the people to act as physical judges over the affairs between people.[287]

When we misbehaved as children, God often executed justice through our parents or teachers. As believing adults, God directs us through His Holy Spirit who works in us and through us to guide us, teach us, counsel us, remind us of what He has said, and to bring conviction when needed.[288] He also works through those in authority over us to maintain order and execute justice among us.

God often employs the systems that He has put in place to execute justice, but not all rulers and judges are faithful to execute God's commands. We all experience some injustice in the world, but God can always be trusted to ultimately weigh all evidence and execute justice in our lives and in the lives of every person on the earth, as it is written,

> "God will bring into judgment both the righteous and the wicked, for there will be a time for every activity, a time to judge every deed."[289]

Therefore, when we are victims of mistreatment, we should turn over the evidence and trust God to execute judgment through His systems of justice. We must be careful not to withhold evidence from God and try to act as our own judges. When we feel like judging or getting even with the people who offend us, we should remind ourselves that God said,

---

[287] Romans 13:1-2, Exodus 6:26-7:7, 1 Samuel 12, 16:1
[288] John 14:14-26, 16:13-15, Acts 5:32
[289] Ecclesiastes 3:17

"I will bless those who bless you, and whoever curses you I will curse."[290]

And

"It is mine to avenge I will repay."[291]

And

"Do not seek revenge or bear a grudge against one of your people."[292]

And

"I will contend with those who contend with you."[293]

God hates injustice.[294] Therefore, since God is sovereign, those who misjudge and mistreat others will certainly not go unpunished.[295] We can always trust God to keep His word.

God's ways are always right, but this world is currently under the dominating influence of Satan and his agents of darkness, so many of our world systems are often corrupt and unfair. Soon enough, however, Jesus will return, eliminate all evil influences, and restore righteousness, peace, and justice on the earth.

Beyond our physical lives on earth, God's righteousness and justice always prevails. When we understand this fact,

---

[290] Genesis 12:3
[291] Deuteronomy 32:35, Romans 12:19, Hebrews 10:30
[292] Leviticus 19:18
[293] Isaiah 49:25
[294] 2 Chronicles 19:7
[295] Proverbs 11:21, Romans 2:1-11

we can more willingly release the evidence of our mistreatment knowing that we can trust God to judge between us and bring about justice in the spiritual realm in His perfect timing.

Let's remember that as Christians we are qualified to judge between others when they have a dispute because we can listen and trust God's Spirit to guide our decisions to make a righteous judgment.[296] We may also be technically qualified to judge between ourselves and our own offenders, but that's never a good idea.

Besides being specifically instructed not to pass judgment against those who offend us, a few reasons that we should step aside as judge when we are personally involved with a case are as follows:

1. Our emotions often hinder us from seeing all the facts and weighing the evidence without partiality.
2. We cannot possibly see all of the motivating factors behind the offender's actions.
3. We cannot remain impartial, so we may hand down sentences that are not commensurate with the crime.

We should therefore always recuse ourselves from acting as judge when we are a party to the dispute.

When we are personally involved in a case with another person that requires judgment, we need to release the evidence of our mistreatment to God and trust Him to judge between us and our offenders, and we need to show kindness toward our offenders. Only God is capable of weighing all the evidence and making a perfect judgment without showing partiality, and He takes that responsibility seriously.[297]

---

[296] Luke 12:57, 1 Corinthians 5:12-13
[297] Deuteronomy 32:35, Romans 12:19, 1 Corinthians 4:3-5, Hebrews 10:30

We should also trust God for the timing. When we pridefully act as our own judge and withhold evidence of the offenses, we are effectively saying we know better than God, which is certainly not possible. When we fall into the trap of judging our offenders, we act contrary to God's plan for us, and we always get ourselves in trouble.

God is the Chief Justice who ultimately can be fully trusted to administer justice. This is comforting if you are on the side of right because God sees everything, He knows the hearts of everyone, He loves everyone equally, He is perfectly fair, and no situation is beyond His ability to handle.

Anytime God appears to act slowly, it's always for good reasons that we may not fully understand. Sometimes God quietly brings conviction and patiently waits so that those who have done wrong will have an opportunity to change their minds and repent.[298]

We need to remind ourselves that it is the responsibility of the Spirit of God to "convict the world of sin."[299] It's not our job, and that's good news because properly judging and convicting can be a very challenging, if not humanly impossible, task.

God is perfect at lovingly and accurately bringing our attention to the areas in our lives that we need to change in order to bring about blessing in our lives. However, even God's convicting influence does not always motivate people like Cain, who have severely calloused hearts, to turn from their offensive ways. So why do we sometimes think we should take on the task of convicting others?

Furthermore, we shouldn't worry about whether or not our offenders ever apologize for hurting us. They may never choose to accept responsibility for their actions while living

---

[298] Ezekiel 18:30-32, Romans 2:4, 2 Peter 3:9
[299] John 16:18

on this earth, but they will certainly face God's judgment at some point in time. [300]

We don't have to dwell on the past and let the misdeeds of others or some challenging events in our lives weigh us down and dictate what we think about ourselves or what paths we take in life. The trials that we face in this world don't last forever. Some last longer than others, but we can remain hopeful that the troubles will fade away soon enough as long as we continue to put our hope in God.

Therefore, if you feel like you've been unjustly treated, just release the evidence of your mistreatment to God, and remember that no wrong act will go unpunished.[301] God cares about you, and you can always trust Him to execute justice at the right time.[302]

Unrecoverable Debts

Throughout the Bible, sin is referred to by several more descriptive terms such as trespass, transgression, offense, insult, iniquity, fault and debt. It's interesting that each of these words for sin carries a slightly different meaning.

For example, a trespass is generally considered to be an intrusion or violation of a boundary. A transgression is an act that violates a rule or law. An offense is an injury or violation of another's rights. An insult is a verbal offense. Iniquity is a habitual tendency to engage in unrighteous acts of wickedness or injustice. A fault is a defect or shortcoming. And a debt implies that something is owed to someone else. The concept of sin encompasses all of these meanings.

Have you ever made an unkind remark or done something that resulted in reducing someone's hope or happiness

---

[300] Romans 2:6
[301] Job 10:14, Proverbs 11:21, 16:5
[302] Acts 17:31

for a time? Afterward, did you see how your insult, trespass, or other offense impacted the other person and wished you could take it back, but it was too late?

All you could do is say, "I'm sorry," ask for forgiveness, and try to make things right.

It was like you had taken something intangible from them and now owed a debt that you could never repay. I've known that feeling far too many times.

When someone insults us, violates our trust, or otherwise hurts us in some way, a piece of our happiness is taken from us. Once happiness is gone for that time, it can never be repaid. It is like an unrecoverable debt.

I find it interesting that Jesus compared the forgiveness of sin to the forgiveness of debts.[303] As I explored this parallel, I realized that whenever we offend another person, it is like we are taking something, such as joy, hope, or happiness, from them that we should repay but cannot. We owe them a debt. Likewise, when someone offends or trespasses against us, it is like they are stealing part of our lives from us for which they can never truly repay or reimburse us.

In a just and fair world, whatever is stolen would have to be returned or repaid, plus interest, just like a financial debt. Unfortunately, many things that people take from us cannot be repaid. Intangible things like innocence, virginity, time, hope, and happiness cannot be repaid by others. Lost lives cannot be repaid. The list goes on. Can you think of any intangible things that have been taken from you for which you have never been repaid?

I certainly have. But before we get caught up in feeling sorry for ourselves, let's remember that God can repay and restore anything, as He once promised,

---

[303] Matthew 18:23-35

"It is mine to avenge; I will repay."[304]

God said He will repay what? In this passage God specifically spoke of avenging Himself against His adversaries who mistreat Him and His people, and He went on to mention paying ransom and making atonement for His people.[305]

God repays negative consequences or curses to those who act wrongly, and He also repays positive consequences or blessings to those who act rightly.[306] If we give up something, someone, or everything to follow God, then He will always pay back more than what was given up.[307]

We therefore don't have to worry about keeping a record of wrongs and hiring a debt collector to collect the intangible and seemingly unrecoverable debts that others owe us. You can always depend on God to repay your offender with what he or she deserves, and you can depend on Him to repay, restore, or replace any intangible things that have been taken from you.

God also rewards those who do right and repays to them the seemingly unrecoverable debts that others owe for lives and things that have been stolen or damaged by others. Furthermore, like the good Father that He is, through Jesus, He provides debt relief for His repentant children who have carelessly taken intangible things from others.

We cannot always depend on other people to repay what they owe to us, but we can always depend on God to repay and restore because He always keeps His promises. Our God fights for the honor of His people and saves lives. Throughout the Bible, God has repeatedly demonstrated His faithfulness to us in this way.

---

[304] Deuteronomy 32:35, Romans 12:19, Hebrews 10:30

[305] Deuteronomy 32:43

[306] Deuteronomy 28

[307] Matthew 19:29

We should never take matters into our own hands and try to force repayment from others.[308] God instructs us to trust Him and turn over our unrecoverable debts and IOU's to Him so He can repay what is owed and take care of restoring us to a place of freedom, peace, and rest.

So remember that whenever someone injures you and takes something of yours, either tangible or intangible, turn over the debt to Jesus. Don't demand retribution. God will repay and reward you.[309] Just write down all of the IOU's that you think others owe you, and humbly present them to God.

Debts and Forgiveness

We can trust God to repay us when others are indebted to us for things that they cannot repay, and we can also trust God to help us repay others when we are the ones in debt to them.

One of the biggest weights that we often carry is the burden of being in debt to someone else. I hate being in debt because instead of working for the hope of having something positive and satisfying that I have earned; I feel like I'm working just to pay for something whose satisfaction expired long ago. That's an especially familiar experience for most of us with financial debt.

In our culture, it takes a great deal of self-control to be patient, save money, and resist the temptation to borrow money for the things we want. Many people spend their entire adult lives repeatedly borrowing money and working to pay off their debts. In my opinion, this is not a rewarding way to live. I understand, however, how easy it is to fall into this trap because I've lived that way most of my adult life.

---

[308] Luke 6:29-30
[309] Luke 6:32-36

Jesus once compared the debt that we owe God to a great financial debt that we could never repay. He told the story of a certain servant who owed a debt to his master that was too large to ever repay. The servant begged his master for mercy, and the master showed compassion toward him and forgave the debt.[310]

Then the forgiven servant tried to force his fellow servant to repay to him a much smaller debt owed to him. When the master found out, he became angry. Jesus concluded:

> "Then the master called the servant in. 'You wicked servant,' he said, 'I canceled all that debt of yours because you begged me to. Shouldn't you have had mercy on your fellow servant just as I had on you?' In anger his master handed him over to the jailers to be tortured, until he should pay back all he owed. This is how my heavenly Father will treat each of you unless you forgive your brother or sister from your heart."[311]

Initially, facing torture for not forgiving the sin debts of others sounded very harsh to me until I remembered that God's warnings are always for our own good. The consequences of our carrying offenses are devastating to us and harmful to others, so God's warning to us is understandably stern.

We all have sinned against God and owe Him a debt that we can never repay. God the Father, however, has a plan to help us. He sent His beloved Son Jesus to the earth, who lived a perfect life without ever doing anything wrong, to pay our debts for us.

---

[310] Matthew 18:21-35
[311] Matthew 18:32-35

According to the plan, all of the debts that we owed to God were placed upon the blameless account of Jesus who accepted them and paid the price and penalty for those debts, which included physical torture, separation from God the Father, and death.[312] After Jesus had fully paid our debts, His life was restored, and He was raised from the dead.

When we accept that our debts and old sinful nature were crucified with Christ, and we invite Him into our hearts, our spirits are reborn and made alive through Christ. God now sees us as debt-free creations clothed in the righteousness of Jesus.

We can now be reconciled to God because the barrier of insurmountable debt, which our sin created between us and God is eliminated when we choose to believe God and receive His provision by faith.

Therefore, we truly have no right to hold offenses against other people when we ourselves have committed similar, if not identical, offenses against others and countless offenses against God. If God forgives the many major offenses that we have committed against Him, then who are we to choose to hold anything against anyone else?

When we needlessly and defiantly continue to carry and hold the sins of our offenders against them while seeking retribution or repayment, we effectively communicate to God that we consider the debts that others owe to us superior to our debts once owed to Him.

Therefore, we nullify the priceless value of God's amazing gift to us, and we are left to try and repay our own debts to God on our own—a task that we can never possibly accomplish.

We must remember that we have no right to hold onto offenses or judge and condemn others, no matter how many times someone hurts us, and it's our duty as dearly loved

---

[312] Isaiah 53, Matthew 27:46, Mark 15:34

children of the merciful King of the Universe to show mercy and love those around us. As James put it:

> "Judgment without mercy will be shown to anyone who has not been merciful. Mercy triumphs over judgment."[313]

The consequence of our holding offenses and judgments against others is separation from God and punishment. It's no wonder that when we hold grudges, our lives are so empty of any real peace or joy. When we choose to extend mercy to others who have wounded us, however, we remain in His presence where there is fullness of joy.[314]

Certainly, we have the freedom to choose to hold on to offenses and pass judgment against others if we want to, but we will face the painful consequences for those actions because Jesus already carried all offenses for all time and for all people, and He told us to show mercy toward others and release the debts.

God empowers us to do what He instructs us to do, and He is always ready and willing to help us accomplish His instructions. Sometimes, our main obstacle to releasing the debts of others is our stubbornness and pride. We also face opposition to do right from our enemy, but God always equips us to stand and overcome those temptations when we humbly depend on Him.

God has made provision to pay our debt owed to Him through the life of His Son Jesus, and when we choose to believe God and accept this gift, we see and experience the goodness of God for ourselves. Therefore, let's humble ourselves before God and freely pardon the debts that others owe to us.

---

[313] James 2:13
[314] Psalm 16:11 (NKJV)

Pardons for the Guilty

Do you remember what Jesus said when He asked the Father to forgive those who had demanded that He be executed? Even as He was in physical agony and dying, He remained compassionate and merciful and said,

> "Father, forgive them, for they do not know what they are doing."[315]

He asked the Father not to judge and condemn His accusers for their wicked actions because they did not understand what they were doing. We too should follow His example and remember that many times people carelessly hurt us and others for various reasons without fully realizing what they are doing.

Do you understand all the motives behind the actions of those who have hurt you? Do you always understand the motives of your own heart? How about the experiences of those who have hurt you? Are you familiar with all of them? I would think it's not likely.

You understand only what you know, and that usually isn't all that much when it comes to other people's lives. Even if you've lived with someone for fifty years, you may still not be familiar with everything the other person has experienced.

You cannot possibly know everything that goes on inside the heart and mind of another individual. You can learn many things by hearing what others tell you and by studying their actions and attitudes, but you can't know everything.

God, however, knows everything. He knows the events of your past. He knows your future. He knows what you and your offenders have been through. He also knows what

---

[315] Luke 23:34

motivates you to do what you do. He knows your heart inside and out because He created you, and He wants to help you and everyone if we turn from our misguided ways and turn to Him.

God understands our motives, He loves us, and He wants us to turn to Him for help to free us from the consequences of sin, as it is written,

> "Let the wicked forsake their ways and the unrighteous their thoughts. Let them turn to the Lord, and he will have mercy on them, and to our God, for he will freely pardon."[316]

It's important to understand that our pardoning an offender and releasing judgments in no way implies that an offender is justified in their actions or that they should go unpunished. When we pardon our offenders, we simply release them to face God's judgment.

God, who knows the motives of our hearts and sees beneath the surface, may or may not choose to pardon someone, but He can always be trusted to do what is right and execute justice at the proper time.

Let's remember that people commit sins, and sins are always bad, but people are not always bad. God created us and loves us all, but the sins that we commit that inflict pain are what have to be released in order for the healing process to begin. For our battle is not against people, but against the powers of darkness in the world and spiritual forces of evil in the heavenly realms who influence and entice people to act in wrong and hurtful ways.[317]

People are naturally selfish and sinful, so if left alone, we will often make choices that result in hurting others. Add to

---

[316] Isaiah 55:7
[317] Ephesians 6:12

these tendencies the fact that Satan and his forces of darkness manipulate and entice us to sin even more, and it's no wonder that there is so much hatred and so many hurting people in the world.

We must always remember that our true battle is against Satan and his agents, not the people he deceives and manipulates to hurt us.

Even though we suffer through various trials and unpleasant or painful circumstances in this life, we can trust God to balance everything in the end. Jesus said that we would have trouble in this life, and as Christians we would face even more hostile opposition from the agents of darkness, but as long as we persevere and pardon those who offend us, He will pay back trouble to those who trouble us, and give relief to us when we are troubled.[318]

Repeat Offenders

The pain associated with having been hurt by a natural disaster is different than the pain associated with having been hurt by another person. And the pain inflicted by a stranger is different than the pain inflicted by a close friend or family member.

Any pain can be suppressed and covered up, but the wounds received repeatedly from the offensive actions of a close friend, wife, husband, mom, dad, or other relative can feel impossible to forgive because they are usually accompanied by strong feelings of betrayal or rejection.

If someone hurts you once and they say they're sorry, you can assume it was an accident and that maybe they were having a bad day. So you can probably forgive their offense fairly easily and resist judging them. That's commendable.

---

[318] 2 Thessalonians 1:4-10

You might even readily forgive someone who hurts you twice. But if someone with whom you are in regular contact keeps hurting you over and over, it becomes easy to conclude that they don't care about you, and they are hurting you on purpose.

When someone hurts you repeatedly, do you ever feel like saying, "I'm sorry" just isn't good enough? If they were truly sorry, then wouldn't they stop doing things that hurt you?

Plus you might wonder if God is paying attention and truly cares, then why doesn't He do something to punish or change the offensive person so they will stop hurting you?

Sometimes we truly forgive the offenses of others, but they continue to offend us repeatedly, and it becomes more and more difficult to resist judging them. When we don't see them being punished for what they did to us, we also sometimes fall into the trap of doubting God and His faithfulness.

When the same people hurt us repeatedly, then we may hear a voice slyly ask, "Did God say He will pay back harm to those who hurt you? If so, then why isn't He doing it?"

We must be careful not to fall into this trap and resist the temptation to doubt God. If God said it in the past or says it today, then we can trust that He will keep His word.

If God's promise to bless those who bless us and curse those who curse us is true, then why don't we see repeat offenders getting punished and learning their lesson? Why do they continue to be so mean to us? This same question has been asked for ages.

The psalmists asked these questions,[319] and even Jesus' first disciples faced the same dilemma. Have you ever noticed the only time it is recorded that the apostles asked Jesus to increase their faith was after Jesus instructed them to forgive repeat offenders? Jesus explained,

---

[319] Psalm 10:1-6, 42:9, 43:2, 73:11, 74:1

"It is impossible that no offenses should come, but woe to him through whom they do come! It would be better for him if a millstone were hung around his neck, and he were thrown into the sea, than that he should offend one of these little ones. Take heed to yourselves. If your brother sins against you, rebuke him; and if he repents, forgive him. And if he sins against you seven times in a day, and seven times in a day returns to you, saying, 'I repent,' you shall forgive him." And the apostles said to the Lord, "Increase our faith."[320]

This may be the only time recorded in the Bible that the disciples asked Jesus for more faith. Even they admitted it would be challenging for them to repeatedly release chronic offenders to face God's judgment when it didn't appear like God was doing anything to help.

Certainly, this passage confirms that it's not uncommon for people to be hurt repeatedly by others, and repeatedly forgiving them to face God's judgment, when nothing appears to be improving, requires a deeper level of trust in God. In these cases we have to be careful not to fall into the temptation of doubting God's faithfulness.

Notice Jesus started this teaching by saying that people who go around offending others would be severely punished. So our forgiving an offense and refusing to pass judgment doesn't let anyone off the hook. We simply need to believe God and release the evidence and burden to judge over to Him so He can deal with them.

It's also interesting that in these instructions, Jesus didn't mention forgiving the sins or offenses. Elsewhere, He instructs us to forgive offenses, but here, when discussing

---

[320] Luke 17:1-5

repeat offenders, He said our focus should be on forgiving our offenders because that's the bigger challenge.

Choosing not to pass judgment against someone who insults or hurts us repeatedly over a short period of time is extremely difficult to do because we would naturally be inclined to judge their behavior and conclude that the person must be hatefully hurting us over and over on purpose.

Yet, Jesus instructed His followers to refuse to pass judgment and to release the offender and the offenses no matter how many times they hurt us.[321] It's no wonder we need a lot of faith.

It's important to note that we do not have to let someone abuse us just because we are forgiving them and their offenses. Jesus instructed us to rebuke our offenders and to inform them of what it is that they are doing that offends us.[322]

He also said that in dealing with the people of this world, we should be on guard, be as shrewd as serpents and innocent as doves, and avoid abusive or unwelcoming people.[323] When we come in contact with hateful or abusive people we should not retaliate or fight against them, but we don't have to spend time with them either.

Sometimes people are simply careless and don't realize they are offending us. If they are strangers, then we can easily forgive and move on. However, if we live with offensive people, then we must exercise more self-control, forgive them every time they offend us, and constructively communicate how hurtful their actions are to us while trusting God to improve the situation. It's certainly more work, but maintaining good relations with God and others is well worth the effort.

---

[321] Matthew 18:21-22
[322] Luke 17:3
[323] Matthew 10:11-17

We also need to remember that we are in no position to judge God or question His motives. He has good reasons for everything that He allows to happen, and we have to guard ourselves against doubting God. If we find ourselves complaining about something, then we should take steps to give thanks instead of complaining, and remember that God is faithful to work things out for the best.

God always knows the circumstances and motivating factors surrounding everyone's actions, and we can always trust Him to judge correctly and to execute justice at the proper time.

It's often easy to judge repeat offenders and conclude they are never going to change. It's also easy to doubt that God is working things out for you. This is why forgiving repeat offenders and desiring to bless them can be so challenging and requires such a deep level of trust.

We can always release the offenses and release the offenders to face God's judgment so He can bring conviction and execute justice, but that doesn't guarantee that the offender will change for the better. Even if God has already judged and convicted our offenders, they still have free will to make their own decisions and choose how they will respond.

Many people act in hurtful ways out of habit, and most habits are hard to break. So even after we've let go and think God has had enough time to convict them, we don't always notice a change in their attitude or actions. That's where trust and faith comes in.

God is always trustworthy and faithful. He always keeps His promises, so as long as we release the offenses every time others sin against us, and we refuse to judge our offenders, then sooner or later, they will indeed have to face real consequences for mistreating us.[324] We may never see those

---

[324] Matthew 12:36

consequences with our natural eyes, but we can always trust that God will do what He promises.

We need to be careful not to doubt God, and as we rest in the knowledge that God will execute justice, we have to be careful not to wish bad things to happen to our offenders. If we do, then we are again judging and condemning them, and we have not truly released them to face God's judgment.

We cannot know all of the pain and motivating influences within another person's heart, but God does. Let us therefore release all offenses and remember not to repay evil for evil, but with blessing, for in the measure we give to others, it will be given back to us and multiplied.[325]

Signs to Forgive

When my children were growing up, I could easily tell when one of them had been hurt. All children differ in many areas, but in one area I've found them to be similar. When children feel hurt, they usually clearly demonstrate the pain in their heart through their attitudes, words, and actions because they have not yet hardened their hearts.

One moment we see smiles and tears of laughter, and the next moment we see frowns and tears of pain. Even if the pain is not made visible right away, sooner or later, the hidden tears of pain are made visible through outbursts of anger. We must not give in to the temptation to ignore the signs.

I've always hated to see discord between people, so for most of the years that my children were growing up, I took the job of investigating the causes of their downtrodden looks and angry outbursts seriously. What I discovered was that there were always legitimate reasons for their expressions and behavior.

---

[325] Luke 6:37-38

Their downtrodden look on the outside and hostility toward others invariably reflected their feeling hurt, rejected, or disappointed on the inside.

Since four of our children were still young when I discovered the importance of forgiveness, I made it my goal to train and encourage them to learn to identify and release offenses and judgments as quickly as possible so they wouldn't waste time feeling bitter and struggling with fractured relationships. Now that they are all adults, I must say I am quite pleased with how well they get along with each other and others.

There are several signs that can be good indicators of when a person is carrying offenses that he or she would do well to forgive. I highly recommend learning to identify the specific signs so that you can correct your own course and reach out to help others before relationships suffer. Several of these warning signs are as follows:

1. The most obvious of these indicators are hateful thoughts or behavior. If you secretly or openly wish harm would come to someone, then you have most likely passed judgment and condemned them for something.

2. The second indicator is anger. Anger is not always an indicator that we are holding on to offenses or disappointments, but anger, frustration, and irritability are usually present when a person is holding on to hurts after being repeatedly hurt or disappointed.

3. Another indicator that a person is holding on to offenses is avoidance. Of course, it's not necessarily wrong for us to avoid people who repeatedly hurt us, but if we have unpleasant or uncomfortable feelings whenever we think about a certain person who hurt us in the past, we cringe when we see their number show up on our phone, or if we try to avoid the person when we see them in the grocery store or

somewhere, then it could be that we are either still holding an offense against that person or we are still judging them over something.

4. A fourth indicator is depression or self-hatred. If you often battle depression or you have self-loathing, self-condemning, or other unkind thoughts about yourself, then that's a sign that you are believing lies and probably holding your own mistakes against yourself. Carrying offenses against ourselves weighs us down as much as carrying offenses against others. As long as we hold our mistakes against ourselves, we leave doors open for Satan's messengers to harass us and try to convince us that we should punish ourselves. Often, this results in acts of carelessness and more frequent occurrences of "accidental" injuries and sickness. Like any other offense, we must turn over the evidence of our own mistakes to God and ask Him to show mercy toward us like He instructs us to show toward others.[326]

5. Next, we feel disconnected from God. Of course, feeling disconnected from the peace and joy of God occurs anytime we sin, so feeling disconnected from God doesn't necessarily indicate we're judging or holding on to the sins of others. Yet, for many people, holding on to offenses and passing judgment is often the culprit.

6. Finally, when we see an old photo or remember certain events in our lives that still trigger feelings of being hurt, upset, irritated, bitter, or resentful, then we are probably still holding on to at least some of the evidence related to that event.

---

[326] Luke 6:35-36

When we see these signs in our own lives, we should examine our hearts and ask God to help us identify the offenses, judgments, or anxieties we are carrying so we can unbind them from our hearts and release them while trusting God to heal our hearts and work things out.

God may also employ friends or family close to us to help us see these signs, so we should be careful not to act deceitfully or try to cover up our true feelings. If we can't answer a question truthfully, then we should not say anything. Our willingness to act deceitfully only invites the father of lies to influence our lives and keep us stumbling around in the dark. Therefore, we should always be honest with others and ourselves.

If you often feel depressed or irritable, then it may be a result of holding onto disappointments, offenses, or grudges, and you will never be free until you specifically identify and release each one. Don't let yourself become complacent and accept feelings of self-condemnation or defeat. And don't try to ignore your feelings or try to cover them up by diverting your attention to something else.

Ask God to search your heart and to help you identify the hurts or disappointments that you have not yet released. When they come to mind, acknowledge them, confess them, release them, and trust God to pick them up and cleanse your heart. He wants you to let them go so He can deal with them and you can be reconciled and free starting right now.

My Reconciliation

As I mentioned earlier, the most difficult time of my life came when my wife and I separated in the summer when I was thirty-four years old. During this devastating time, I grew so dependent on God for comfort and support that I couldn't tolerate feeling separated from Him.

His loving presence was so real to me that every time I offended Him by doing something wrong, I felt separated from Him.

Whenever I did something that dishonored God, the feeling of isolation and abandonment was so pronounced in my heart that I was desperately driven to humble myself and ask the Lord to show me where I had done wrong so I could confess, repent, and return to His loving presence.

Nearly every time I felt forsaken by God, He showed me that I had either held on to an offense that I received from an insult, I had wrongfully judged someone who may or may not have tried to hurt me, I had retaliated against an offender, or some combination of these things.

After I realized what I had done to offend God, I had to confess, repent, and make things right in order to be reconciled with God. If I didn't let go of the pain and forgive the offenses and judgments and/or make things right with God and the people against whom I had retaliated, then I would feel terribly weighed down and alone.

As soon as I released the offenses and judgments and made things right, however, I felt the return of the comforting presence of the greatest friend I've ever had.

Jesus had given me the comfort and acceptance that no one and nothing else had ever been able to give me. He was always there when I needed Him, and He has never let me down. So I learned that every time I felt hurt and weighed down and alone, the sooner I turned and made things right, the quicker His joy and presence would return to my heart.

I was and still am quite stubborn, so it can take a while for me to let go of my old ideas to embrace the new ones. Thankfully, God is patient, and He is a perfect teacher. When I need correcting He often reminds me of several applicable truths written in the Scriptures.

I used to think that I reminded myself of these truths, but since I'm not that smart, I'm convinced that the Holy Spirit teaches me and reminds me of the truth just as Jesus said would happen.[327]

Therefore, pay attention to the signs of your heart and to the leading of the Holy Spirit. Depend on God to help you and don't hesitate to humble yourself and make things right anytime you feel the need for reconciliation.

Don't Wait

I've heard several teachers claim that we must be ready and willing to forgive as soon as our offenders repent. This sounds logical, but this teaching is misleading because our forgiving someone else or their offenses has absolutely nothing to do with whether they ever choose to show any remorse or repentance for their offenses. We should never wait to forgive.

Jesus said that a person would know we are His followers by the love we show one for another.[328] And according to Paul, one aspect of demonstrating love is keeping "no record of wrongs."[329]

If we keep a record of wrongs and wait for our offenders to apologize and make things right with us, then we are causing ourselves to needlessly suffer and delaying our freedom. If we do not keep a record of wrongs and refuse to retain insults or other offenses, then God will bless us. Peter described how Jesus demonstrated this love when he wrote:

> "When they hurled their insults at Him, He did
> not retaliate; when He suffered, He made no

---

[327] John 14:26
[328] John 13:35
[329] 1 Corinthians 13:5

threats. Instead, He entrusted himself to Him who judges justly."[330]

We too should follow Christ's example and immediately release all insults and offenses along with any judgments and entrust ourselves to God who will judge everything properly at the right time.

Retaining offenses and grudges always damages relationships. That's one reason why forgiveness is so important and why we shouldn't wait.

Remember that God sent Jesus to carry our sins to extend forgiveness to us before we were even born. So He provided for the forgiveness of our sins before we repented and before we even did anything wrong.[331] In the same way we should prepare ourselves to forgive long before we are actually offended.

Certainly, it's easier to let go of the pain and release the offense and judgment if the offender demonstrates he or she is sorry for hurting us, but their repentance should never be a prerequisite for forgiveness. If they apologize, then we should readily forgive. If they don't apologize, then we should readily forgive.

Sometimes the ones who have offended us may have already passed away. Or sometimes our offenders will not even consider repentance until we have already released our judgments against them, forgiven their offenses, and shown kindness to them.

Jesus never instructed us to hold on to offenses and judgments until the offender repents. Instead, He instructed His followers to forgive the sins of others so that our sins against God may be forgiven. [332] Also, Jesus directs us to confess our

---

[330] 1 Peter 2:20-23
[331] Romans 5:8
[332] Matthew 6:14-15

offenses and repent to those whom we offend before we attempt to come into the presence of God.[333]

Jesus instructed His followers to always take the first steps toward reconciliation, which includes repenting for hurting others, notifying others when they hurt us, releasing condemning judgments, and forgiving the offenses of others no matter how many times they hurt us.[334] In taking these actions, we supernaturally work to tear down dividing barriers between others and us and between God and us.

We must act quickly to release both the offenses and the offenders. We must not wait for the offender to act.

When we hold on to past offenses and then take offense over some new violation, the resulting pain felt in our hearts is compounded, and we are likely to overreact. That's why before I had released of all of the little disappointments against my wife, if she did something seemingly disrespectful toward me, I felt maliciously betrayed and abused.

She could not understand why I would blow up over such seemingly trivial things like her turning up the thermostat or buying something that I considered unaffordable. Obviously, I was not good at respectfully communicating my feelings to her.

The reality for me was that I had already held on to so many other little real or imagined offenses and disappointments that any additional infraction, no matter how small, triggered major feelings of disrespect and rejection to come to the surface. I would then overreact and respond harshly.

I was a blind and bitter mess, and it took my wife leaving me and months of soul searching and releasing offenses and judgments for me to finally find healing. I learned the hard way that if we hold on to offenses we blind ourselves to the

---

[333] Matthew 5:23-24
[334] Luke 17:3-4

reality of our true condition and greatly reduce our capacity to care for others.

Rarely does a person overreact to a situation without a reason. To an onlooker, many people's actions may seem irrational, impulsive, or over-reactive, but since one can bury and hide many painful experiences in his or her heart, explosive responses indicate the need for help with addressing deeper heart issues.

Therefore, instead of trying to forget our troubles, we should choose to remember and specifically identify each offense and judgment that we've carried and release them all to God so that He can work everything out according to His good plan before we explode onto the people around us.

If someone who hurt you communicates to you that they're sorry for hurting you, then it is important and extremely restorative to the relationship for you to release any offenses and judgments and to communicate that forgiveness to them.

After we release offenses about which we know the offender was aware, we should communicate to them that we have forgiven those offenses in order to help mend the relationship. Similarly, when we have judged those who offended us, and they are aware of their offense, then after we have released those judgments, we should also communicate that forgiveness to the offenders.

If an offender is not aware of any offense, however, then we should not stir up trouble by telling them that we have forgiven them for something about which they were not aware.

Telling a repentant offender that you have forgiven him or her communicates love and respect instead of condemnation, which helps to accelerate the mending of a bruised or broken relationship.

We should remind ourselves that our choosing to forgive offenses and offenders and moving toward healing are simply never dependent on the actions of another person. So let's not wait. We are always free to forgive to begin our healing process and help restore relationships regardless of what our offenders do.

Irreconcilable Differences?

When we first meet nice-looking people, it's typically easy to think the best of them. In fact, some people come across so friendly and attractive that we decide that it might be nice to become friends. It's easy to maintain high expectations and think highly of other people when we see only their best side.

Unfortunately, all people have a selfish side that is not usually on display at first. If people spend much time together, then sooner or later their best sides fade revealing a side that is selfish and unattractive or even hateful.

Eventually, when careless words or selfish actions offend us, those initial high hopes and expectations can easily turn into hurt feelings and disappointments. If the offenses are not quickly identified and released, then they often lead to passing judgments and can eventually cause broken hearts and broken relationships.

You may have unintentionally fallen into the trap of calling your differences "irreconcilable," but you must understand that for people who have at one time been emotionally close, few differences are truly irreconcilable. It takes intentional effort on both sides that is focused in the right direction to get out of the trap, but believe me: the rewards of working out differences are usually well worth the effort!

The Bible says that for the joy set before Him, Jesus endured the cross carrying our "irreconcilable differences" of sin so that we could be reconciled to God.[335] The sacrifices

---

[335] Ephesians 2:13-19, Hebrews 12:2

that God made for us clearly demonstrate that the rewards of reconciliation are indeed worth the price, even though the price usually involves dying in some way.

Do you ever feel like you and your spouse, family member, or friend are separated by so many differences that it seems impossible to find a way to reconcile? If so, then you might be tempted to say that the once compatible and loving relationship is ending or has ended because of irreconcilable differences.

Are all so-called "irreconcilable differences" really irreconcilable?

I think much too often, we give up on relationships when we've been hurt and reconciliation seems unobtainable. We give up when the going gets tough, but God can help restore any broken relationship no matter how many seemingly irreconcilable differences are identified and no matter how much hatred and animosity develop between two people. What seems impossible for people to accomplish is still possible with God.[336]

Anytime we have seemingly irreconcilable differences with someone close to us, we have three primary choices:

1) We can focus on our differences, complain about our disappointments, and continue to be miserable;
2) We can change our minds and expectations to accept what we cannot change about our circumstances or the other person, make efforts to compromise where we can change, and decide to focus on areas of agreement while we lower our expectations in areas of disagreement; or
3) We can give up on the relationship and walk away.

---

[336] Matthew 19:26

In most cases, option two is the best choice – especially in marriages and families. Option three would be the best option in cases of physical or emotional abuse. Unfortunately, option one is probably the most commonly chosen option.

Changing our minds to deny ourselves and accept compromise can be challenging — especially if we are stubborn and have strong beliefs about the subjects of difference. It can seem impossible, but as long as we are moving in the direction of love and truth, God will help us.

Even though some differences seem irreconcilable, with God's help, two people who sincerely want reconciliation and are willing to compromise can always be reconciled.

Sometimes, compromise involves a change in perspective and behavior without necessarily changing beliefs. For example, if you know that you and a friend disagree on politics, then you can choose to purposefully avoid discussing politics and look for something on which you agree to discuss. Open and effective communication is one key to reconciliation. Forgiveness is another key.

Sometimes, the only things that prevent change and reconciliation are dividing walls of hurt and disappointment, which are aggravated by couriers of darkness who constantly wage war against families and friendships. We should always be aware of how our enemy tries to sneak in to cause us trouble.

When we sincerely turn to God for help, He empowers us to overcome our enemy, stand up for the truth, and do the right things like forgiving others and their offenses. Afterward, we often discover new hope for reconciliation.

It makes little, if any, difference whether the person with whom you have had conflict has already passed away or still remains on the earth. Of course, it's always better to make things right sooner rather than later, but God will help you achieve reconciliation and make peace with others whenever you earnestly seek it.

The intimate connections and relationships with others that were once an exciting and fulfilling part of life can be restored once offenses and judgments are released and the walls of self-preservation are eliminated.

Therefore, regardless of how far you've drifted, if there was a time when you and another person were close, and both of you are willing to try to work things out, then there's always hope for reconciliation.

With proper use of the right supernatural weapons, the darkness can be driven out, hearts can be softened, and those dividing walls can be torn down and cleared away so that full reconciliation can be achieved. The battle belongs to God,[337] so continue to trust Him to help you, heal your heart, and mend the fractures in your relationships.

Anger and the Setting Sun

In order to remain emotionally stable and avoid angry outbursts, we must choose to rid ourselves of the root causes of our pain, and we should act before sundown each day, for as Paul explained,

> "In your anger do not sin. Do not let the sun go down while you are still angry, and do not give the devil a foothold...Get rid of all bitterness, rage and anger, brawling and slander, along with every form of malice. Be kind and compassionate to one another, forgiving each other, just as in Christ God forgave you."[338]

Therefore, since we are directed to control our behavior when we're angry, we obviously have been given the ability

---

[337] 1 Samuel 17:47
[338] Ephesians 4:26-27, 31-32

to restrain ourselves when we are experiencing anger, and we should exercise self-control to do so.

God put everything in order to establish times and seasons here on Earth. He created the sun and the earth and started the earth spinning so that the sun shines on the various surfaces of the earth as it spins. When He did this, He established that each day ends and begins for people at sunset.

That's why it was written that there was evening and morning on each day of creation[339]. Evening comes first, and sunset marks the end of one day and the beginning of the next. It was no accident that each day begins and ends with a time of rest.

I find it interesting that throughout the book of Leviticus, when God gave instructions about what to do when a person did something that made them physically unclean like touching a dead animal or something, He explained that the person would be unclean until evening when that day ended and a new day began.[340]

Apparently, God resets our days at sundown, and we are released from the effects of whatever polluted us physically that day. We can then begin the new day with physical and emotional rest. In the same way, before sunset we should confess and repent of any wrongdoings that would have polluted us spiritually that day so that we can enter each new day at rest spiritually.

Another good reason to do our part to resolve conflict prior to sundown is that after sundown, people are generally more likely to fall into temptation and do things they will regret in the morning. When we are tired, weak, or hungry, we usually find ourselves more vulnerable and less likely to control our emotions and actions.

---

[339] Genesis 1
[340] Leviticus 11:24-40, 14:46, 15:5-27

It's not surprising that according to the National Resource Center on Domestic Violence, most crimes involving friends or family members occur after sundown.[341] So resolving even minor relational conflicts prior to sundown could easily prevent much greater levels of conflict and injury that could be aggravated by nighttime fatigue. Satan wants to entice us when we're tired and vulnerable.

That may also be why at the end of the day, he and his messengers also entice us to drink excessive amounts of alcoholic beverages and pollute our minds by watching unwholesome TV shows or movies or by playing unwholesome computer games. He wants us to begin our days thinking about and doing things that lead us into trouble and set an unclean course for the rest of the day.

Our lives would be so much more light-hearted and joyful if we would simply refuse to carry any burdens over from one day to the next. So let us observe sundown each day as a time to reflect on the day's accomplishments and disappointments, and let us give over to God our sorrows, worries, and other burdens before sundown and give Him thanks and praise for the good things that happened that day and for His great provision for us.

Be Prepared to Say "No"

When we feel like we are being bombarded with too many challenges in life or too many temptations to do wrong, we need to consider that we may be under enemy attack.

We must remember that it is Satan's goal to steal our peace, to kill our joy, and to destroy our lives, and he often employs the people around us to entice us to steer the ships of our lives into the rocks. We must stay alert and learn to

---

[341] http://www.nrcdv.org

recognize his tactics so that we will be able to stand during times of temptation.

Satan's messengers are effective at hitting us when we're feeling irritable, hungry, tired, or discouraged. And they are looking to gain access into our lives by convincing us to believe lies so we will move away from the light of God and truth into the darkness.

Let's not be deceived; Satan's team is crafty, and if we crack open the door just a little by entertaining the idea to do something wrong, then one of his dark agents will likely take notice and quickly stick out a foot to hold the door open and try to entice us to follow through by actually doing wrong. They are sneaky and often use manipulating tactics like fear, intimidation, confusion, and doubt to influence our decisions.

We must stay alert and refuse to open the door to them, and we must refuse to even consider doing what we know is wrong. This includes believing lies. When we are tempted to do wrong, our best recourse is to humbly stand firm and say, "No" to the tempting voices we hear.

Demons serve the "father of lies," so they are very effective at convincing us to believe lies. They try to lure us into their traps by using just enough truth to catch us off-guard, so we need to refuse to even entertain them at all.

The demons, or agents of our enemy, are fallen angels,[342] and as such, there are a limited number of them. They are good at following the orders of their master, and they often use their influence to target Christians, but we shouldn't think that every wrong thought or act has been influenced by a demon. We also struggle against our own carnal nature. We simply need to remain alert to the possibility of their influence.

We don't have to open the doors of our hearts and entertain agents of darkness, and they know it. We simply need

---

[342] Matthew 25:41, Jude 1:6

to resist them. We also don't have to raise our voices or get all excited. Jesus didn't. He spoke rationally and respectfully whenever Satan tempted Him or He addressed his agents.[343] Even angels treat their fallen counterparts with dignity and respect.[344]

Therefore, like Jesus and the angels, we simply need to respectfully say, "No" to Satan and his messengers and mean it. When we are facing temptation and reminded of some truth that counters the deceptive enticements of the tempting spirit, we should speak out loud like Jesus did with Satan. It's powerful and effective for us to speak the truth out loud because words of truth carry authority on the earth and through space, and Satan's messengers recognize it.

Even if we've given in to the tempting spirits repeatedly in the past, we can start refusing to entertain them anytime and continue one step at a time. We have to learn to take a stand and tell them, "No," and then turn our focus to something productive and wholesome.

If the enticing spirit is familiar to us and we've entertained his suggestions repeatedly in the past, then I suggest telling the messenger, "No; not today" or "No; not now" instead of something like "I'm never going to do what you say again!"

If we take one moment at a time and refuse to give in, then the messenger will usually go away without putting up much of a fight and eventually will come knocking on our doors much less frequently.

We must remember to depend on God for guidance when dealing with our enemy because he is crafty. If we arrogantly tell him that we will never give in to his tempting messengers again, then he will certainly detect our prideful and vulnerable position and take on the challenge to send

---

[343] Matthew 4:1-10, Luke 4:1-12
[344] Jude 1:9

more high-ranking agents to hit us from many sides when we least expect it.

When we get arrogant, we undoubtedly find it more difficult to resist giving in to the bombardment of tempting suggestions, and we will likely fall. Believe me; I speak from experience. When I know that I will likely be facing tempting spirits, I try to remember to ask God for help. I also listen to the audio Bible that I have on my phone to help keep my thoughts on things that are good and right.

Therefore, let's stay alert so that we will be able to recognize and resist temptations when they come. At any time we feel overwhelmed, we should humbly drop to our knees and cry out to God for help.

Our True Battle

We must always remember that our fundamental battle is *not* against the people in our lives.[345] It's against the forces of darkness that are waging war against everyone who is on the side of truth. The people in the middle who we see, hear, and touch are often unknowingly used as instruments through which Satan tries to distract us and tear us down.

Certainly some people knowingly and willingly allow themselves to be used by Satan to inflict pain and trouble upon others, but other people unintentionally hurt them because they do not fully realize the destructive impact that their sinful words and actions have on them as well as on themselves.

Most usually don't realize that they are being influenced or even manipulated by Satan's messengers. They simply don't know what they are doing, as Jesus pointed out while He hung on the cross.[346]

---

[345] Ephesians 6:10-12
[346] Luke 23:34

It's time for us to wake up and stay alert so we will be able to recognize when the forces of darkness are at work around us. It's time for us to choose to stand up against the devil's forces instead of blaming and attacking each other. It's time for us to stop stepping on others while competing for attention, position, and fortune.

Satan is too crafty and too resourceful for us to stand against him while we are simultaneously at war with ourselves.

Thankfully, the power and authority to defeat Satan comes from God. He has given us His Son, Jesus, who has given us His authority to overcome all the powers of Satan.[347] As we allow His Spirit to work in and through us, we will be empowered to overcome the devil's temptations in our own lives as well as to help those around us. Yet, we must learn to work together so that we can all stand against his destructive efforts and experience victory together.

Paul wrote about forgiveness and how we need to guard ourselves against falling into the devil's schemes when he explained:

> "If you forgive anyone, I also forgive him. And what I have forgiven—if there was anything to forgive—I have forgiven in the sight of Christ for your sake in order that Satan might not outwit us. For we are not unaware of his schemes."[348]

Here Paul said that he had learned to release the offenses and condemning thoughts toward others so readily that he didn't even have to identify the exact sin or offense in order to release them. He simply refused to retain any sin or judgment against anyone.

---

[347] Luke 10:19
[348] 2 Corinthians 2:10-11

Paul understood how counterproductive and self-destructive it is to retain sins and judge others, and he knew how Satan tries to deceive us into believing that we should hold on to offenses, judge and condemn others, and avenge ourselves so that our idea of justice is served. Paul understood that when we respond in this way, we position ourselves away from God where the devil can easily "outwit" us and gain a foothold in our lives.

Far too often, we blindly sleep through life while Satan and his messengers cause trouble all around us. Our problems aren't always caused by outside forces, but often they are.

Therefore, we must open our eyes and remember that we have been given the power and authority to overcome our enemy, and we don't have to give in to the intimidating and paralyzing effects of fear.

In the Bible, the Apostle Luke recorded that after Jesus spoke of forgiving those who sin against us even seven times in the same day, He followed by telling His followers to maintain the attitude of unworthy servants who are only doing their "duty."[349]

We must be careful and stay alert because we have an enemy who is sneaky and is determined to destroy as many lives as he can. He wants us to get stuck in his traps of following the things of this world, but the reality is that none of the people and traditions or things that we follow will lead us to life and fulfillment. We must learn to let go of them and hold on to God.

So whether or not we understand the full life-giving impact of releasing every offense to Him, we should choose to routinely trust God's Way, release the insults of others, and refuse to pass judgment, even when we don't feel like it and we're acting only out of a sense of duty.

---

[349] Luke 17:10

When we understand the truth about mercy and forgiveness and actively apply what we know, God will bless us and empower us to fight against our true enemy so we can remain standing.

8

STEP FIVE – TRUST AND TURN

After we've softened our hearts and opened our eyes and ears to see and hear the truth, and after we understand what God would have us do, we have a critical decision to make. Do we decide to turn toward the path that He says is best, or do we continue down our own paths that we think are best?

Turning to choose God's path for each area of our lives is often the most difficult of all five steps because truly turning toward God requires a genuine change of heart that leads to action. We must change our habits and refuse to continue in our old selfish and hurtful ways in order to make room for better habits and patterns.

Whether it is due to pride, stubbornness, fear, or something else, most of us resist change, so we hesitate to turn, and we continue to stumble and face struggles that could have been avoided.

If we choose to stay on our own paths and follow our own ways and the ways of the world, then we will remain bound up in our sin and continue to be headed for trouble.

If, however, we choose to turn and follow God's instructions, then a new and much better life marked by blessings, joy, and freedom will emerge.

In every situation we face, as long as we are conscious, we always have choices. Even when we cannot change our circumstances, we can always choose to change how we respond to those circumstances.

We can choose to complain about things that we cannot control and make ourselves miserable, or we can change our minds, accept circumstances that we cannot change, find contentment with what we have, and trust God to work things out for us.

I especially don't like to change my mind and turn in a different direction when I don't know the reason or purpose behind the change. That's why it took me so long to learn how to truly forgive. I had to be convinced that there was a good purpose behind each step of instruction before I changed my mind and made any real effort to turn.

Turning toward an invisible path that we have been told leads to life can initially be challenging for several reasons. First, we may have been let down so many times by teachers who were themselves misguided that we find it difficult to trust other teachers, including God.

Secondly, choosing to take a new path might be intimidating because it is unfamiliar. Since it feels foreign to us, we usually feel apprehensive as we consider choosing that new path.

Finally, Satan doesn't want us to turn toward the Way that leads to life, so he will bring many distracting or alluring thoughts into our minds in order to keep us moving down the wide and familiar path that promises good things on the surface but eventually leads to isolation and destruction.

Therefore, in this life we must overcome many obstacles and courageously take chances as God directs us in order to reap great rewards. [350] As we choose to turn toward God, we must remember to persevere in order to remain standing through the difficult times. We must not give up.

Changing our Minds and Hearts

Some people teach that if we simply change our minds to think positive thoughts, then our hearts will change, our actions will improve, and doors of blessing will be opened. They claim that if we simply speak positive words of forgiveness and blessing, then a change of heart will eventually follow, and that over time our hurts and desires for revenge will diminish.

This routine may work for some people, but it didn't work for me with forgiveness until I learned and understood more about what forgiveness is all about. I changed my mind and asked God to change my heart.

I don't know which came first, but I do know I had to disregard what I thought I knew, actively turn to God to discover the truth, and pursue a better understanding of what forgiveness meant before I was able to trust God enough to forgive issues at the heart level.

Some people claim that changing our minds is a cheap substitute for actually making heart changes. For people who frequently change their minds over trivial issues, this may be true. Oftentimes, however, changing our minds is the first step toward allowing God to change our hearts, which leads to real change in our actions and our lives.

Sometimes all we have to do is change our minds to align our expectations with the truth in order to begin moving along the path to joy and peace.

Obviously, changing our minds and trying new ideas and new things doesn't always lead to good results. If we

---

[350] Matthew 16:24, 19:21-24, Mark 8:34, 10:21-24, Luke 9:23, 18:18-25

choose to change our minds to move in a direction that dishonors God, then we will sooner or later realize that we have stepped away from His protecting hand, and we will regret that choice. If, however, we have a true change of heart and change our minds to move in a direction that honors God, then He will honor us by clearing the path before us as He guides and protects us.[351]

Before some of us can have a genuine change of heart, we must be willing to stop doubting and change our minds to accept what we may not yet be able to see. We need to align our thoughts and expectations with the truth from God's perspective, and this requires faith — faith to let go of what is natural and familiar, and faith to embrace what is supernatural and new.

It does not take faith to change your mind to believe something previously doubted after you personally see evidence and are convinced of the validity of the new idea. This is what the apostle Thomas did when he changed his mind to believe that Jesus had indeed been raised from the dead only after personally seeing Him alive with nail and spear wounds.[352]

That's also like seeing rain falling outside and deciding to put on a raincoat instead of the sweater previously chosen before you go outside. It doesn't take any faith to make that choice.

It takes a little faith to change your mind to adopt a new idea when a person you trust makes convincing arguments in support of the change. That's like hearing a weather forecaster predict that your area will have rain on a certain cloudy day, so you decide to put on a raincoat.

Depending upon how reliable a person has shown themselves to be, it takes varying levels of faith to change your

---

[351] 1 Samuel 2:30, Proverbs 3:5-6
[352] John 20:24-29

mind to accept that you need to change directions when that person tells you that you should change.

It takes much more faith, and it's quite a bit more challenging to change your mind to believe something when the only evidence available is a stranger's testimony. That's what we have in the Bible – a collection of testimonies from people whom we've never personally met. When we believe that everything written in the Bible is true and that the people were ordinary people like us who were blessed as they honored God and cursed as they dishonored Him, it is easier to accept their testimony and learn from their triumphs and their mistakes.

Of course, when we open our hearts to Jesus, we are able to personally get to know Him, so that over time our level of trust in Him becomes established through personal experience rather than just faith.

God understands our hesitation to embrace change, which is probably one reason He rewards us when we completely change our minds to accept the truth and believe Him along with those who testify about Him, without first having personally seen evidence.[353]

When we choose to believe God before we personally see convincing proof, and we turn to follow Him, God is honored, and He will bless us and open the eyes of our hearts so that we then personally see and experience the proof of His goodness.[354]

In order to truly honor God so that He blesses us, we must begin by humbling ourselves, choosing to believe that what He says is always true, and developing an understanding of the truth and how to apply it. Then out of the overflow of our hearts we will turn, and our words and actions will

---

[353] John 20:29
[354] Psalm 34:8

demonstrate our alignment with the truth, and God's blessings will flow into our lives.[355]

Pleasing God is not just about saying the right words; we must have a sincere change of heart and choose to turn, because words are meaningless without a genuine change of heart, just as the Lord explained about the Pharisees and teachers of the Law: "These people come near to me with their mouth and honor me with their lips, but their hearts are far from me. Their worship of me is based on merely human rules they have been taught...Leave them; they are blind guides. If the blind lead the blind, both will fall into a pit."[356]

Just going through the motions to do what appears to be right in front of others and saying good things is of little or no value. We must honor God by seeking the truth and sincerely aligning our thoughts as well as our actions with that truth in order for His blessings to flow into our lives.[357]

God hates lying lips,[358] and those who practice deception and falsehood will bring trouble upon themselves.[359]

We must therefore be careful not to act as hypocrites or posers who say certain things around certain people just to make outwardly good impressions all the while knowing that we're not being fully honest. True repentance begins with a sincere change of heart.

True Repentance

Have you ever stopped to think about how valuable and lasting the words that Jesus left behind are? Many, but not nearly all of His words, were recorded by His followers for

---

[355] Matthew 12:33-37
[356] Isaiah 29:13, Matthew 15:8-14, Mark 7:6
[357] Matthew 7:21-27, Luke 11:28
[358] Proverbs 12:22
[359] 2 Peter 2:1, Revelation 22:14-15

us and others to read many years later.[360] One encouraging lesson that Jesus taught about repentance goes like this:

> "What do you think? There was a man who had two sons. He went to the first and said, 'Son, go and work today in the vineyard.'
> 'I will not,' he answered, but later he changed his mind and went.
> Then the father went to the other son and said the same thing. He answered, 'I will, sir,' but he did not go.
> 'Which of the two did what his father wanted?'
> 'The first,' they answered.
> Jesus said to them, 'I tell you the truth, the tax collectors and the prostitutes are entering the kingdom of God ahead of you. For John came to you to show you the way of righteousness, and you did not believe him, but the tax collectors and the prostitutes did. And even after you saw this, you did not repent and believe him.'"[361]

Here Jesus pointed out that the first son changed his mind and turned from whatever else he had planned to do to what his father wanted. That was true repentance because the change of mind resulted in a change of action.

Why did the first son change his mind? Who knows? Maybe he remembered that God wants us to honor our dads, so he decided to help him. Maybe his mom asked him to reconsider. Maybe he wanted to ask his dad for a favor later on. Does it matter why he changed his mind? Apparently not because Jesus didn't mention it.

---

[360] John 21:24-25
[361] Matthew 21:28-32

The second son said he would help him, but for some reason he didn't. Maybe he changed his mind or maybe he lied and never intended to help his dad. Apparently, it didn't matter since Jesus didn't mention a reason.

I find it interesting that it didn't matter that the first son had initially refused to help his dad before he changed his mind and did what his dad wanted. He was not condemned. The same holds true for us when we repent and turn from our own plans and choose to do what God wants us to do.

Jesus did not say that the son who changed his mind and chose not to honor his dad was condemned, but I'm sure he at least missed out on a blessing.

This story is encouraging and impactful for me because for many years of my life, I rejected God, and during that time I usually felt empty and alone. Thankfully, however, I changed my mind about God and the Bible, experienced a real change of heart, and decided to put my trust in Him during my late twenties. He has poured out many blessings to my family and me since that time.

I'm also encouraged because as I go through life, I'm often going in one direction, and God prompts me to change my mind and take a quick detour to accomplish some task like helping someone. I often hesitate because I don't like detours, but after a couple of clear promptings, I usually change my mind and do what God asks of me. Then He blesses me in some way.

This reminds me of how God blessed me after I changed my mind to give twenty dollars to the man that I mentioned earlier. Even though I did not initially want to give him any money, God didn't condemn me for hesitating. I'm sure He already knows that I can be stubborn in that way.

Sometimes we change our minds and repent after hearing some convincing argument, and sometimes we do so because we've had a sincere change of heart. Whether repentance begins with a change of heart or a change of mind is not as important as what we actually do because we will be judged for our actions, not our intentions.[362]

Remember that it's not how you start that matters – it's how you finish.

My Cheeseburger

When we find ourselves disappointed because our expectations aren't being met, and we change our minds to align our expectations with or even give thanks for our circumstances, we usually find that everything works out.

Several years ago, during the time that my wife and I were separated, God taught me a valuable lesson about how beneficial changing my mind can be through an experience with a fast food restaurant. Here's what happened:

Angel and I had arranged that I would pick up our four youngest children from school each weekday, spend time with them, eat dinner together, and take them back to stay with her at around seven p.m.

This one particular day, it was rainy, and I was running late as usual, so I decided to pick up dinner at our favorite drive-thru restaurant and eat in the car with the kids.

During that time in my life, money was especially tight, so I usually didn't look beyond the one-dollar value menus at fast-food restaurants. We were content with that, but that day I had worked efficiently and made some extra money, so I decided to give myself a treat. I ordered a deluxe chicken sandwich, and I was very much looking forward to it.

After I paid for and picked up the food, I happily drove off and found a place to park so we could distribute the food and start eating. I could hardly wait to bite into my deluxe chicken sandwich. The food was distributed by whoever's

---

[362] Revelation 22:12

turn it was to sit in the front passenger seat. The last sandwich was mine.

I reached into the bag, pulled out the sandwich, unwrapped it, glanced at it as I started to bite, and—

"What?!" I asked rather loudly in my angry voice. "This is not chicken! This is a burger! Where's my chicken?! Did somebody take my chicken sandwich?!"

"Not me," was everyone's response.

"Are you sure?!"

"Yeah."

"I ordered chicken! I paid for chicken! I didn't order a cheeseburger! What's the matter with those people?!"

Since I expected chicken and didn't want a burger, I was extremely disappointed, so I wrapped it back up and tossed it back into the bag. "Everyone else got the food they asked for! Why couldn't they get my order right?!" I whined in protest. I was having quite a pity party and creating a stressful atmosphere in the car.

I obviously overreacted because I had put too much hope into that chicken sandwich to bring me satisfaction. I could have gone back to exchange it, but I decided not to because I would have to leave the kids in the car and walk through the rain, and I was already late to get the kids back home.

After realizing I was setting a bad example, I decided I needed to calm down and let go of my disappointment and release the judgments that I had made. After all, they probably didn't purposely try to ruin my whole night. So I let them go.

Right away, something interesting happened. A thought popped in my head that said, "Why don't you change your mind and decide you want a burger instead of chicken?"

"Where did that random thought come from? How can I do that?" I replied in my head. "I don't want a cheeseburger. I want a chicken sandwich." But since I had nothing else to eat and I was hungry, I decided to try changing my mind about the burger.

I thought about how hungry I was and pictured a delicious-looking cheeseburger. Then I decided that a burger might be good after all. I reached into the bag, grabbed the cheeseburger, and took a bite. Surprisingly, it tasted great, and I was happy and very satisfied!

Two minutes earlier, I was ready to throw it out the window, and now I was happy to have it! I think I was more satisfied and thankful to have had that once-rejected cheeseburger than I would have been if I had eaten the chicken sandwich that I had originally wanted. I simply needed to change my mind to align my expectations with the reality of my circumstances. It seemed like a miracle!

I enjoyed every bite of that cheeseburger, and I apologized to the kids for having a bad attitude.

Who knows? Maybe a chicken sandwich would have made me sick, and God arranged for me to be given the burger. Maybe He wanted to teach me a lesson about changing my mind and learning to be content. Maybe it was all just a random coincidence. I don't know, and it doesn't matter what the reason was. I was simply glad that I had changed my mind and everything worked out. It was a good lesson.

Learning to Be Content

Since learning the cheeseburger lesson, I have successfully applied this same process to other discontented areas of my life. Apparently, feeling discontent but changing my mind to accept and be content or even thankful for what I already have or for circumstances that I can't control honors God because I always feel better, and I'm able to identify the direction in which I should go after doing so. [363]

---

[363] Psalm 50:14-15

It's not usually the first thing that comes to my mind when I'm facing difficulties, but this course of action works well when I'm facing car problems, tax bills, annoying people, work issues, bad weather, physical aches and pains, and other aggravating circumstances about which I have little or no control.

With every set of circumstances that we encounter, we always have options available in dealing with them. If nothing else, we can choose to change our attitude toward the circumstances and find something for which to be thankful. When we find ourselves disappointed with our circumstances but change our minds to align our expectations with what we have and be thankful, we demonstrate our trust in God, and He works everything out for us.[364]

I'm certainly not advocating that we should passively sit by and refuse to take action to improve our lives or to make positive changes in the world around us when it's in our power to do so. I'm simply saying that if we find ourselves complaining and feeling miserable about something that we cannot change, then we should adjust our expectations, find something for which to be thankful, and trust God to change hearts and circumstances as He sees fit.

God doesn't change His mind,[365] and He is always right. So when we find ourselves disappointed because our expectations aren't being met, we may need to change our minds to align our expectations with the reality of whatever we're facing at that time.

God does not make mistakes, and He does not allow circumstances to develop in our lives that He in unable or unwilling to bring us through. So the next time we find ourselves feeling frustrated or disappointed with something or someone or some circumstance that we can't change,

---

[364] Romans 8:28, Hebrews 13:5
[365] Numbers 23:19

instead of complaining and getting upset, let's try changing our own minds to align our expectations with what we already have so we can find contentment. The sooner we do this, the sooner God will bless us and restore our peace and joy. It's quite amazing!

Turn Toward the Light

We have only two options regarding how we conduct ourselves at any given point in time: Either we do what is right and walk in the light, or we do not do what is right and walk in darkness. If we don't purposefully choose to receive and follow Jesus to align ourselves with God's kingdom of light, then by default we are aligning ourselves with the world and darkness.[366]

Walking in darkness involves acting without regard for doing what is right. People who walk in darkness typically try to hide their deeds and motives from others so that they give a false impression to those around them with the hope that their misdeeds will not be exposed. [367] Furthermore, those who walk in darkness cannot see where they are going, so they stumble frequently as they go down a dangerous path.

God created each of us for this time and place with specific purposes to advance His kingdom on the earth. [368] He has also equipped each of us to engage in battles against the evil forces of this world. We simply have to decide whose side we are on, and we have to choose whether or not to fight.[369]

If we choose to honor God by doing right and fight against the darkness, injustice, and evil that's all around us, then we soon discover that we are inadequate to face

---

[366] Acts 26:15-18
[367] John 3:19-21
[368] Ephesians 2:10
[369] Luke 10:19, Ephesians 6:10-17, Acts 1:8

these battles alone. When we feel inadequate, we should acknowledge our weaknesses and turn to God for help. He is always honored when we humbly ask for His help, and He will empower us to stand and effectively advance His kingdom on this earth.[370]

It is only when we walk in the light that we can have fellowship with God because God is light, and in Him there is no darkness at all.[371] In the light there is nothing hidden, no secrets, and no deception. Everything is revealed and exposed as it truly is.

One of the turning points in our path toward healing is the moment when we allow a change of mind and heart and decide to turn and walk in the light. People change for any number of reasons, and those reasons ultimately don't matter because the end results are what are important. When we walk with God in the light, we can see where we are going and are much less likely to stumble and get hurt again. Also, we can be open and honest so that the true motives of our hearts are exposed, and we can effectively help each other.[372]

When we embrace lies, we walk in the dark where we acquire sinful patterns of thinking and behaving that can be so deeply rooted and familiar within our own lives that we forget they are there. Since we have blind spots that make it difficult for us to see how misguided we are in some areas, we should spend time with others, humbly expose our struggles, and allow them to speak truth into our lives.

A good example of a person who chose to turn and walk in the light was Simon the Sorcerer described in the book of Acts.[373] When Simon heard the good news about Jesus

---

[370] 2 Corinthians 12:9, Romans 5:3-5, 8:18-21
[371] 1 John 1:5-7
[372] James 5:16
[373] Acts 8:9-13

from Philip, he quickly repented, turned to God, and was baptized. Later when Peter came to visit, Simon spoke freely which brought his sinful way of thinking into the light. At this point Peter was able to identify Simon's root problem and suggested that he change his ways.[374]

Simon fell under conviction, and he quickly changed his mind and humbly asked for prayer to help him turn away from that sinful pattern in his life.[375]

We should learn from this example, choose to walk in the light, and willingly accept rebuke and correction like Simon did. We should also welcome the opportunity to get together with fellow believers regularly in a casual setting where we feel safe to be honest, open our hearts, share our struggles with each other, and testify about what God is doing in our lives.

Only when we share with others our true feelings and struggles with life can we have real fellowship with one another. As we trust God and open up about our struggles, the Holy Spirit will often reveal the root cause of our troubles. Then we can allow Him to change our hearts so we can more easily change our minds and turn from our selfish or misguided ways at which time God will bring healing and restoration.

God wants us to trust Him and walk in the light, so we must be careful not to give in to the temptation to fear what others will think about us because fear of man will hinder our walk with God and cause us to keep our lives hidden in darkness.

Regardless of whether or not we can see our own sinful issues clearly, we should be willing to accept that as long as we inhabit earthly bodies, there will be dark areas in our lives to which we are often blinded that God wants us to bring into the light.

---

[374] Acts 8:20
[375] Acts 8:20-24

If we are having trouble hearing from God or not feeling the joy that comes from being in His presence, or we feel unclean or polluted by something, then we have likely done something wrong that has taken us onto a dark path. We have to take deliberate action to turn and move back into the light.

Like Simon, we should humble ourselves, ask God to show us what we did to carry us into darkness, listen for the answer, confess the wrongdoing, repent, and commit to doing only what is right and believing only what is true from that time forward. Then the blood of Jesus will purify us from all sin, and we will be brought back into the light where we can have fellowship with God.[376]

One common thing that separates us from God is wandering down the path of discontentment. When we find ourselves wanting to complain about something, we should arrest the thought, change our minds to align our expectations with reality, and choose to thank God for it, knowing He will work things out for our good.[377]

God does not move away from us, but we often wander away from Him.[378] Since He never does anything wrong, He always remains in the light. As we consistently do what is right, we will remain close to Him where there is light and fullness of joy and we can more easily hear His voice.[379]

Therefore, whenever we feel like the troubles of this world are bringing us down, let us take steps to do what is right so we can move closer toward the light of God where joy and peace abound.

---

[376] 1 John 1:7
[377] Psalm 50:14-15, 23
[378] 2 Chronicles 15:2, Isaiah 53:6
[379] Psalm 16:11, John 15:9-11

Do Right

The story of Cain and Abel presents a good lesson in honoring God and doing right. According to the Biblical account, Abel did the right thing by presenting God with the best meat of the firstborn of his livestock while Cain gave God "some" of the produce that he had harvested from his garden. He did not give his best.[380]

When God showed favor toward Abel and his sacrifice instead of to Cain, Cain became very upset. He may have thought that his offering should have been just as acceptable since he was the oldest, or maybe his offerings had always been acceptable in the past. The exact reason doesn't matter because God does not show favoritism,[381] and He doesn't reward us when we do wrong, no matter how good our deeds were in the past.[382]

When Cain's offering was not looked upon with favor by God, he felt rejected. Instead of humbly admitting that he was wrong and committing to do better, he became angry and decided that it was his brother's fault for making him look bad.

Then God spoke with Cain and said,

> "Why are you angry? Why is your face downcast? If you do what is right, will you not be accepted? But if you do not do what is right, sin is crouching at your door; it desires to have you, but you must rule over it."[383]

---

[380] Genesis 4:2-5
[381] Acts 10:34, Romans 2:11, Galatians 2:6, Ephesians 6:9, Colossians 3:25
[382] Ezekiel 18:21-32
[383] Genesis 4:6-7

In other words, God told Cain that in order to be accepted, he must do what is right and refuse to give in to his own selfish sinful tendencies. Of course, that's true for all of us.

Notice that God didn't say, "if you do what is wrong." That's because anything that we do that is not right is not acceptable to God.[384] Riding on the fence is not doing right. There are right ways that God wants us to live, so if you want to be accepted by God and enjoy His favor and blessings in your life, then you must do what is right from God's perspective.

It's not easy to always do what is right; in fact, without God's help, it is impossible. That's why God gives us His Spirit who helps us and empowers us to do what is right.[385]

That's also why when we are not fully committed to doing only what is right, and we let our own pride and self-ishness guide our behavior, we encounter more trouble and opposition from God.[386] Yet when we humble ourselves and are determined to do only what is right, God empowers us to resist the temptations to do wrong.

Also notice that sin crouches at the door when we are willing to do anything other than what is right, so we have to take steps to guard ourselves. When we reject God or the servants that He sends to help us, we set ourselves up for trouble because we step out from under God's protecting influence.

When we are willing to compromise and not walk in the truth, it's like sin and Satan acquire holding power over us. Yet, if we are fully committed to walking in truth and doing only what is right, like Jesus did, then Satan will find no door of access and no place to have a hold on us.[387] He can still tempt us to do wrong, but his capacity to influence us will be diminished.

---

[384] James 4:17
[385] John 14:15-25, Acts 1:8
[386] James 4:4-10
[387] John 5:19, 8:28, 8:38, 12:49, 14:30

Many times we purposefully continue down a path of doing wrong hoping that no one finds out. We often live with the fear of being caught and facing consequences for many years. If we walk in the truth and do what is right, however, we won't have to live with that fear and anxiety.

Committing to always doing what is right is a simple exercise, but actually doing what is right is not always so simple. Have you ever been frustrated because you wanted to do what is right, but you kept missing the mark? The Apostle Paul wrote what I consider to be encouraging remarks to the believers in Rome about his struggles with always doing right and his frustrations with himself when he did wrong.[388]

Like Paul, we all struggle against our own sinful tendencies, which are often fueled by agents of darkness, and thankfully, Paul was bold enough to admit it. The battle is not against other people, and the battle is not always against some dark agent of Satan. Sometimes, our struggle is against our own selfish nature.[389]

We are all born with a sinful selfish nature, and in order to walk in fellowship with God, we have to first receive Jesus and commit to follow Him while denying our selfish nature daily.[390] God loves everyone equally, but in God's eyes our acceptability is linked to our righteousness because He cannot abide with us if we are walking in sin. Thankfully, when we repent, receive Jesus, and humbly walk with Him, God sees the righteousness of Jesus in us.

When we open the door of our hearts to receive Jesus, we also receive His grace or power to resist temptation.[391] The struggle against doing wrong is made much less intense

[388] Romans 7:15-25
[389] Ephesians 4:22-24
[390] Matthew 16:24, Mark 8:34, Luke 9:23, Ephesians 2:1-10, Colossians 3:5-10, 2 Peter 1-11
[391] Acts 1:8, 2 Corinthians 12:9

when we are standing with Jesus, for He has already overcome the challenges of this world.[392] When we stay focused upon Him, He empowers us to overcome them too.

Jesus said that Satan has no holds on Him,[393] and He walks continuously in the presence of the Father. If you are committed to doing only what is right, and you refuse to give in to temptation, then there will be no holding or access points around you onto which the devil can grab and hold you back. Yet, if you are willing to occasionally compromise and not do what is right in a certain area, then the devil will find out, and he will send his agents to tempt you to stumble in that area.

Making mistakes over and over can open the door to discouragement unless we are quick to confess, repent, and ask for help. No matter how many times we stumble and make the same mistake doing the wrong thing, however, we can always confess to God and choose to earnestly turn away and take a step back in the right direction.

If you are tired and weary from constantly battling against the same tempting voices and feeling empty and guilty every time you stumble and give in, then perhaps it's time for you to change your mind, make the decision that you will no longer compromise in that area, and turn to Jesus for help.

The battle may feel especially intense for a while, but over time through consistent resistance and perseverance, the challenges faced in your areas of weakness will diminish. Victory will be achieved one choice at a time, and the fullness of joy and blessings of God will sooner or later return to your life as you learn to trust Him and turn to Him for help every step of the way.

Sin always crouches at the doors to our hearts and disrespectfully tries to sneak in while our Righteousness stands

---

[392] John 16:33
[393] John 14:30

at the door and respectfully knocks and waits for us to let Him in.[394] To whom will you choose to allow access into your heart?

Making Things Right

When we are made right with God and the dividing walls of sin are demolished, open lines of communication are established so that God hears our prayers and we hear His voice.[395] It's important that we remain right with God because in this troublesome and polluted world we frequently need His help.[396]

In order to remain in fellowship with God, we must learn to control our actions, our words, and even our thoughts.[397] As Christians, when we begin to feel distant from God, we should stop and humbly ask God to search our hearts and reveal what we did to create the separation. Then we can confess, repent, and return to having fellowship with God.[398]

Recognizing our mistakes and making things right with God can be challenging at times because of our own pride and selfish tendencies, but God is always gracious when we humbly ask for help. Making things right with the people that we offend, however, is much more challenging because other people can also be prideful and selfish, and they can misinterpret our actions and misunderstand us.

A good example of a misunderstanding happened to me one Friday several years ago. I was on my way to a business lunch meeting and I was uncharacteristically early, so I

---

[394] Revelation 3:20
[395] Isaiah 59:1-2
[396] John 10:1-18
[397] 2 Corinthians 10:5
[398] Psalm 139:23-24

decided to stop by the company credit union to deposit my work expense reimbursement check.

I was well prepared for my meeting, and I had plenty of time to get there, so I was in a good mood.

Since it was lunchtime on payday, I expected to find a line at the credit union, and sure enough the line stretched to the door. It took longer than usual because there was only one teller serving walk-ins, but I was fine with the wait.

The teller was an older woman, and I noticed that she appeared stressed. When it was my turn, I greeted her cordially, gave her my deposit, and kindly commented about how busy she was. She didn't say anything, so I kept silent so she could concentrate on her work. As she gave me my receipt, I wished her well and sympathetically said, "I hope your afternoon gets better."

As I turned and approached the door, I heard her blurt out, "Smart ass!"

Who me? Ouch! I'm sure she was talking about me, but I didn't do anything to deserve that! What did I do? I was being nice to her! She obviously misunderstood me, I thought to myself. I was still stunned as I got into my car and drove away. I felt shook up and assaulted.

Before the remark, I had been in a good mood. I wasn't even upset about having to wait in the long line, but now I was becoming quite bitter and weighed down.

I soon realized I needed to forgive her and give the pain and burden of her offensive comment to Jesus. So I pulled the car over and prayed, and I released the offense. "Lord," I prayed. "I release this insult to you, and I ask you to bless that lady."

I expected to feel better and less burdened right away as was usually the case when I forgave an offense, but this time was different. I still felt weighed down and troubled, and I was puzzled. So I asked God, "What's wrong? Why don't I feel better?"

His answer surprised me. He spoke to my heart saying, "You offended that lady with your comment. Now you need to go back and apologize to her in order to make things right so your burden will be lifted."

"What?!" I replied. "Me, offend her? Really? How? I didn't say anything to offend her." As I thought about it, I soon realized that the Holy Spirit was obviously right. What I said must have offended her in some way for her to respond like she did.

Something must have already been bothering her before I came along and she must have thought I was being sarcastic. Maybe my tone was offensive. I didn't know, but it didn't matter. I knew I had to go back, and the sooner I got it over with, the better.

It wasn't easy. In fact, it was downright hard to turn back and face her again, but I knew God was right, and I had to do it. So I drove back and stepped to the back of the line again. Thankfully, there was a tall man in front of me so I could hide.

I didn't look up to make eye contact with her until it was my turn. Then I looked at her and explained, "I came in a few minutes ago and made some remarks that apparently came across offensive. I just want to tell you that I'm sorry I offended you."

Immediately, tears welled up in her eyes and she told me that she had been having a terrible day. I responded compassionately, "Well, I'm sorry for making it worse." Then she smiled and sincerely thanked me, and I turned and walked out.

My burden was lifted, and by the time I reached my car, I too was in tears as I thanked God for prompting me to go back and make it right with that precious, hard-working lady.

I learned a valuable lesson that day about the need to always be careful with what I say and to stop and pray whenever I'm feeling burdened or weighed down by something. I also learned how important it is for me to always make things right with God and others whenever I find out that something I said or did caused someone to feel offended.

Maybe one of Satan's messengers tried to stir up trouble or maybe it was all an innocent misunderstanding. I don't know. All I know is that something I said somehow contributed to another person feeling hurt, and I had to do my part and try to make it right.

Sometimes words come out wrong, and we hurt people without even realizing it. When we find ourselves feeling burdened or troubled, we need to stop, ask God why we are feeling troubled, and wait for His reply. Then we should do what He says. Otherwise, we will continually walk around in the dark and wonder why we are having so much trouble in life.

Sometimes, like in this case, we can apologize only once to make things right, but other times we have to apologize over and over for the same offense and work to reestablish trust in order to convince the offended person to soften their heart and forgive the offense.

Either way, as soon as we find out that someone took offense to something we said or did, it's then our responsibility to go to the person and do what we can to make things right.[399]

It's often necessary for us to take the time to listen to those we unintentionally offend to understand why our actions caused them to be offended. We must take to heart their words and earnestly repent so that trust can be reestablished.

Occasionally, however, even with heartfelt apologies and sincere repentance, there's nothing we can do to persuade a person whom we offended to release our offenses and forgive us. Forgiveness is a choice that each person must make for themselves. In these cases, we have to be careful not to

---

[399] Matthew 5:23-24

hold their unforgiving or untrusting attitude against them so that we can maintain an attitude of love toward them and remain in right standing with God.

Oddly enough, some of the most challenging people to convince to let go of offenses are ourselves. We sometimes get so down on ourselves for the mistakes we make that we struggle for years to break free. This is unfortunate, but as we will discuss later, God has a plan for us to walk in freedom in this area as well.

The restoration process is necessary to go through whenever we slip up and offend God or others or even ourselves. And we need to act quickly because the farther we walk into the darkness by compromising our determination to do what is right and make things right, the more difficult it is to recognize the truth and to find the motivation to change directions.

By the way, my lunch meeting went extremely well that day, and not long afterward, I was given a raise and offered a management position with the company. Were those blessings a direct result of my obedience in making things right with that teller? I don't know, but I do know that God promises to bless us in many ways when we earnestly seek Him and follow His guiding voice.[400]

Can you think of anyone whom you may have accidentally hurt that you should contact to try to make things right? Has someone hurt you whom you need to forgive?

We should remember that it's easy for us to say or do something that unintentionally hurts another person's feelings, and it's just as easy for other people to do innocent things that we mistakenly perceive as offensive. Therefore, we should practice being quick in making things right and slow in taking offense. Let's not wait. Life is too short to weigh ourselves down with regrets.

---

[400] Deuteronomy 28:1-14, Luke 11:28

Stop, Look, and Listen

The process of forgiving offenses, judgments, and other burdens from our hearts and making things right when we're in the wrong often takes much humility and effort. The most challenging part for me is denying my selfish and prideful tendencies while convincing myself that I can trust God to work everything out for me as I do the right thing and let go of whatever it is that's weighing me down. In the end, however, working through the process is always worth the effort.

When we think we are being tempted to do something that is not right, the first thing we should do is stop and ask God what He wants us to do. Then we must remain still, look for His guiding hand, and listen for His words of encouragement or instruction.

It's like being a butler or other servant waiting in the presence of their Lord or master to obtain directions or an assignment. If we serve faithfully, then our Lord will bless us, protect us, and empower us to succeed. If we fail to stop and listen or disobey His directions after we hear them, however, we will certainly stumble and fall outside of the Lord's protection.

We must learn to stop, look, and listen to our Lord.

Unfortunately, sometimes we get in a hurry and don't take the time to stop and listen. I have a bad habit of going and going and constantly juggling to keep all the balls of my life in the air. Then, finally, when everything becomes chaotic, my emotional state of mind is frazzled, and my life feels out of control, I finally give up and stop to ask God for help.

During these challenging times, I simply let go of trying to control everything in my life and let the balls fall. I retreat into the arms of the Father and rest for a while. When I feel better, I ask Him what He wants me to do, and He tells me to do something simple. When I follow His instructions, He works everything out and fills my heart with peace, hope, and encouragement.

Sometimes I am quick to listen and hear God's encouraging words, but other times my mind is so disturbed and distracted that I have to repeatedly and persistently work to disengage from my stressful life to be still long enough to hear God's words of life. We have to let go of every burden, confess, and turn from everything in our lives that is not right in order to enter into God's presence.

An example of my struggles occurred about a year after Angel and I were reunited. I had fallen into despair over several circumstances that occurred one week. First, I was frustrated because I was trying unsuccessfully to get out of debt. I had also recently gotten behind in my work, so money wasn't coming in as much as usual. I felt hopeless.

That week I was also bitten by a dog, which hurt my feelings; the children had brought home a cat with three kittens, so the house began to smell bad; Angel was being harassed by grumpy customers at work, which troubled me; and we were scheduled to move back in to our old house in two weeks, but I first needed to refinish the wood floors.

I was weighed down and felt like I had to juggle too many issues at once. I finally felt so overwhelmed that I gave up. I stopped trying to figure out and fix my complicated life, and I asked God to help me and rescue me from my misery.

Two days later, my truck's clutch went out. *Was God listening? Did He even care?* These were the thoughts I had, but I had already learned that God cares, and He listens when we humble ourselves and turn to Him for help.

Since I couldn't afford to pay a mechanic, I decided to take two days off of work so I could replace the clutch myself. As I drove the thirty-mile round trip to pick up the new clutch, which included facing approximately thirty stoplights, I recall not even once having to come to a complete stop. That seemed like a miracle!

I had been praying all the way because it's not easy to stop and go in a manual drive vehicle without a clutch to change into and out of first gear. Maybe God *was* listening.

On the morning of the second day of the clutch replacement, I woke up hearing, "Endure hardship as discipline." As I thought about those words, I realized that through all of the mess I had gotten myself into, God was treating me as a son and training me to slow down, depend on Him for everything, and not let my work, family issues, or pursuit of money push Him out. [401]

I realized I needed to change the focus of my thoughts, turn to the Lord, thank Him for the good things in my life, and trust Him to work everything out, so I did. Soon I found myself feeling encouraged, and the Lord lifted me out of my pit of despair.

During the two days I spent with grease and dirt all over me, I surprisingly found rest from all of my troubles. It turned out to be a great diversion.

Although it never occurred to me that the cure for my problems was to trust God, stop worrying about everything, and take two days off of work to replace my clutch, it turned out to be the best thing that could have happened at that time. God knew that I needed to take a break and take my focus off of my circumstances in order for me to let go of my troubles so He could lift me up out of my mess.

Soon after my attitude was aligned properly, God took care of everything and all of my troubles faded away. God had been caring and listening all along. I just needed to change my mind to stop complaining, be thankful, and align my thoughts with what was right and true from God's perspective.

It can be easy to fall into self-pity, fear, and depression when the trials of life come along, but we must practice

---

[401] Hebrews 12:7

giving our burdens over to Christ daily. If you have carried so much pain or burdens that you've felt paralyzed as I have at times, then ask God to do whatever it takes to break through the shell of self-preservation that surrounds your heart. Stop and let go of everything that is hindering you and cry out to the Lord and listen.

Trust God and do what He says, and He will set you free and bring you times of refreshing.[402] You don't have to wait until you're stressed out before you turn. You can change directions and turn to Him anytime.

David and Nabal

One of my favorite Biblical examples of how having a change of heart can lead to great results is the account of David's dealings with Nabal.

David was committed to walking in obedience to God, and David and his friends had taken it upon themselves to protect the shepherds and livestock of a wealthy neighbor named Nabal. Consequently, at sheep-shearing time David had no hesitation in asking Nabal to share some food with him and his friends.[403]

David selected ten of his companions and told them to greet Nabal in his name, explain how they had protected his property, and ask if he would share some of his food with them. So the ten men obediently left under David's authority and delivered the message in David's name and waited for the reply.

Somewhat surprisingly, Nabal, who was later reported to be "surly and mean in his dealings," insulted David and his messengers and sent them away empty-handed.

---

[402] Acts 3:19
[403] 1 Samuel 25

Since the ten men had obediently followed David's orders speaking and acting in David's name with his authority, the men did not take personal offense. It was David who effectively had been insulted.

Naturally, when David's men told him what had happened, he quickly took offense to Nabal's cruel response, and he replied, "It's been useless—all my watching over this fellow's property in the desert so that nothing of his was missing. He has paid me back evil for good!"[404]

So David quickly came up with a plan to get revenge which included killing every male in Nabal's household. He then recruited four hundred of his companions to join him in avenging himself.

Of course, Nabal and every male in his household would have been destroyed by David and his small army, but when Nabal's wife, Abigail, heard what her husband had done, she immediately gathered lots of food and provisions and departed to intercept David.

When she met up with David, she gave him and his men plenty of food and provisions. Then she tried to persuade David to change his mind and trust in God's judgment instead of taking revenge against her husband and family.

David listened carefully to Abigail, and after some consideration he realized she was right, and he changed his mind. He released the insults and his judgment against Nabal and decided to trust God to judge between the two of them as Abigail had encouraged him to do.

He realized how hastily he had reacted to Nabal's cruelty, and he thanked her and said,

> "Praise be to the Lord, the God of Israel, who
> has sent you today to meet me. May you
> be blessed for your good judgment and for

---

[404] 1 Samuel 25:21

keeping me from bloodshed this day and
from avenging myself with my own hands."[405]

Since David had forgiven Nabal and released the matter
into God's hands, God faithfully took up the task to judge
between them, and He promptly weighed the evidence and
executed justice. David was blessed for his good deeds, and
Nabal was repaid for his hateful actions.[406]

I find it interesting that the ten men who obediently
delivered David's message in his name did not take personal
offense. They simply relayed Nabal's response to David and
trusted him to work things out. David, however, decided to
take offense and avenge himself. Thankfully, after Abigail's
intervention, he changed his mind and decided to release
the offenses and trust God to work things out.

Whenever we are speaking or acting at the direction of
someone else, we are acting in their name. Consequently,
we have no right to hold on to any corresponding offenses
or take credit for anything good or bad.

When we are reborn into God's family, we become citi-
zens of God's kingdom and His ambassadors here on earth.
We should, therefore, always try to serve God and speak
and act in His name as He directs us and refuse to hold on
to anything.

David's choices were similar to the choices that we face
whenever we are insulted. We can either choose to take
offense, become angry, and plan to get revenge, or we can
choose to release the offending evidence to God and trust
Him to judge between our offenders and us.

We never know exactly what others are going through,
so we should learn to be more understanding and tolerant
of others who frequently seem mean-spirited or hateful.

---

[405] 1 Samuel 25:32-33
[406] 1 Samuel 25:38

Sometimes we need to pay attention to a wise person like Abigail who can help convince us to put aside our own selfish desires to avenge ourselves and, instead, change our minds to release the evidence and trust God to execute justice.

Therefore, whenever we feel insulted and want to avenge ourselves, we should always take time to calm down, humble ourselves, and align our thoughts and actions with what is right so that we maintain a right standing with God and not do something that we will regret. The choice is always ours, but if we make a choice that's not working well for us, it's never too late to change our minds and turn.

Naaman's Change of Heart

The Bible is full of examples of people who had a change of heart due to the influence of someone else. Some worked out for the better, and some for the worse. Another one of my favorite for-the-better stories is when one of Naaman's servants helped him change his mind to make a decision that brought about a miracle.

Naaman was the king of Syria's right-hand man, but he had a big problem: He had leprosy. One day he was told that the God of Israel could cure him. So he went to Israel, full of hope, with his horses and chariots and valuable gifts and was told to see Elisha.

When he got to Elisha's house, Elisha didn't greet Naaman personally, but sent his servant to greet him and say to him, "Go, wash yourself seven times in the Jordan, and your flesh will be restored and you will be cleansed."[407]

That sounded like a fairly easy prescription to fill, but Naaman felt insulted that Elisha didn't personally greet him, and he went away angry saying:

---

[407] 2 King 5:10

> "I thought that he would surely come out to
> me and stand and call on the name of the
> Lord his God, wave his hand over the spot,
> and cure me of my leprosy. Are not Abana
> and Pharpar, the rivers of Damascus, better
> than all the waters of Israel? Couldn't I wash
> in them and be cleansed?"[408]

He turned and went off in a rage. It seems that Naaman may have been influenced by a spirit of pride for him to react so harshly.

Thankfully, one of his servants bravely and humbly went to him and said, "My father, if the prophet had told you to do some great thing, would you not have done it? How much more, then, when he tells you, 'Wash and be cleansed'!"[409]

So after thinking it over, Naaman decided that his servant was right, and he changed his mind and had a change of heart. He humbled himself, released his judgment and offense against Elisha, and went down and dipped himself in the Jordan seven times as he had been instructed.

Then his leprosy was cured and his flesh was restored and became clean like that of a young boy.[410] Of course, Naaman was now overcome with joy and gratitude. He was glad that he had changed his mind, and he went back to thank Elisha and give him gifts.

Sometimes when we face challenges in life, God asks us to do something simple that may not make sense to test our willingness to trust Him before He works everything out for us. He also sometimes employs our friends, family, or co-workers to help motivate us to make better choices. It's quite amazing how people can change their minds so

---

[408] 2 Kings 5:11-12
[409] 2 Kings 5:13
[410] 2 Kings 5:14

quickly simply because a different perspective is presented by a trusted source.

As we seek God, we should be aware that He may employ caring family members or friends who often help us see from different perspectives to help us make better choices. God may also employ us to help convince others to make better choices.

If we learn to listen to God and follow His simple instructions, then He will miraculously work out everything for us – sometimes sooner and sometimes later. So let's be careful not to let our emotions guide us to make hasty wrong choices and miss out on the great things that God has in store for us. When we initially make a bad choice, we should not be too prideful to change our minds and change directions.

To Change or Not to Change

In order for God's strength to empower us to fight and overcome the troubles we face in this world, we must remain humbly dependent upon God.

When we make choices that dishonor God, we create trouble for others and ourselves. That's one reason why God promised to send us a helper, the Holy Spirit, who is the Spirit of Jesus, to teach us and guide us in the right direction.[411]

We certainly need help to always do what is right, so when Jesus knocks at the door of our hearts and says,

> "Here I am! I stand at the door and knock. If anyone hears my voice and opens the door, I will come in and eat with that person, and they with me,"[412]

---

[411] John 14:26
[412] Revelation 3:20

we should humble ourselves, accept that we need help, open the door, and welcome Him in.

The truth that we hold the keys that unlock the doors to our hearts is important for us to understand. For in order to experience fellowship with God and obtain His help, we must invite Him into our hearts and listen to what He says. The door is opened only from the inside, and we alone have the keys.

A good example that demonstrates the contrast between humbly depending on God versus pridefully depending on our own resources is found in the lives of two kings of Israel: Hezekiah and Asa. During most of their reigns, both of these kings of Judah trusted and depended upon God who protected them and delivered them from their enemies over and over again.

Eventually, however, both of these kings became proud of their accomplishments, and they began to depend upon their own understanding and abilities. They no longer depended on God, and then they both became ill.

When King Hezekiah was sick and was told that he didn't have long to live, he humbly turned back to the Lord in tears, repented, and begged Him to let him live longer. God heard his humble prayer and gave Isaiah instructions of what to do to bring about his healing. King Hezekiah lived fifteen more years. [413]

King Asa, on the other hand, refused to humble himself, and he didn't turn to the Lord during his illness. He relied only upon his doctors, and he died within two years. [414]

When we humble ourselves depending upon God and do things His way, then He works with us and enables us to accomplish great things in life. When we pridefully depend upon our own strength and understanding, however, we face

---

[413] 2 Kings 18-20, 2 Chronicles 29-32, Isaiah 36-38
[414] 2 Chronicles 14-16

life's challenges alone, which can be overwhelming at times. As long as we are still breathing on this earth, we can choose to turn and change course.[415]

Trust in His Name

We all have choices to make, and we all have to decide where to place our trust. If we put our trust in things that are fallible or perishable, we will certainly face disappointment at some point. If, however, we put our trust in the name of the Lord our God and align our expectations with the truth, we will never be disappointed.[416]

Trusting in the name of someone else is like trusting in their reputation, character, or the attributes of their position or title. Trusting in the name of the Lord our God is like placing our trust in God's faithfulness, loving kindness, mercy, righteousness, power, authority, ability to judge rightly and execute justice, ability to heal, protect, provide for, and rescue His people, or some other attribute of God. To trust in the name of God is equivalent to trusting in God Himself.

When we find ourselves in trouble, we need to be careful not to fall into the trap of turning to the things of this world for help instead of God because when we do, we effectively demonstrate that we do not truly believe and trust Him.[417] If we place our trust in God's name, however, then we can rest knowing that God will help us just as the Psalmist wrote:

> "Because he loves me," says the Lord, "I will rescue him; I will protect him, for he acknowledges my name. He will call on me, and I will answer him; I will be with him in trouble, I will

---

[415] 1Peter 5:5, Proverbs 16:18
[416] Psalm 20:7, 25:3
[417] Isaiah 31:1

deliver him and honor him. With long life I
will satisfy him and show him my salvation."[418]

Now that is an encouraging promise. We need to fully
understand that as long as we acknowledge who God is, and
we follow His directions, we honor Him by acting in His name,
and we remain under His protection.

Sometimes, within our hearts, we hear the voice of God
speaking to us and giving us specific instructions,[419] and at
other times we simply recognize the peace of God within our
hearts guiding us one way or another.[420] Either way, whenever we either follow the specific instructions of Jesus or act
according to what we know He would have us do, we walk in
His name under His authority and remain under His protection.

As we walk in obedience to God and carry out His instructions, we are sometimes received by others and sometimes
not. When others receive us and the messages we bring,
they are effectively receiving the King of Kings and His messages. If others reject us or insult us, and we refuse to take
offense, then they are effectively rejecting the King of Kings
and the insults fall on Him.[421]

Let's remember that we don't have to wonder or worry
about how we will protect or provide for ourselves, for as
we trust God and act in His Name, He will protect us and
provide for us.

Forgive Yourself

I find it interesting that in order to walk in joy and peace,
not only do we have to forgive the offenses of others and

[418] Psalm 91:14-16
[419] John 10:1-16
[420] John 14:27, Colossians 3:15
[421] Psalm 69:9

refuse to condemn them, but we also have to forgive ourselves for our own mistakes and shortcomings.

When we make mistakes, we sometimes condemn ourselves and think things like, "I always have trouble with that," or "I'll never learn," or "I always make stupid mistakes," or some other judgmental thoughts.

This way of thinking is self-condemning and self-destructive. We should be careful to think about and speak only that which is true, right, and praiseworthy about others and ourselves.[422] We also need to humble ourselves, learn to forgive our mistakes, and accept we stumble and need God's help just like everyone else.

It's a good thing to learn from our past mistakes, but too many people hold on to regrets for choices they made in the past. Today they find themselves bitter, short-tempered, frustrated, and frequently depressed, and they wonder why they feel so downtrodden.

Sometimes I get so frustrated with myself because I keep making the same mistakes over and over again. Thankfully, Jesus knows that our flesh is weak,[423] and He does not condemn us.[424] He can relate to how challenging it can be for us because He also faced and overcame many temptations when He walked on the earth.[425]

Some of us are quite good at forgiving others for their mistakes, for we understand that they're only human and occasionally stumble and give in to the influences of emotional baggage or the forces of darkness. Yet, we often tend to pridefully hold ourselves to a higher standard and think we should have more self-control than others.

---

[422] Philippians 4:8
[423] Matthew 26:41, Mark 14:38
[424] John 8:10-12, John 3:17
[425] Hebrews 2:18, 4:14-18

One of the things that I like about Paul the Apostle is that he was honest and exposed his challenges and weaknesses in his writings. We sometimes get frustrated when we repeatedly find ourselves doing things that we don't want to do just like Paul wrote about in his letter to the Romans:

> "For I have the desire to do what is good, but I cannot carry it out. For I do not do the good I want to do, but the evil I do not want to do—this I keep on doing...What a wretched man I am!"[426]

When we feel frustrated with ourselves like Paul described, it's important we understand that it is common for followers of Christ to face struggles like these. We all have a selfish nature, and we all must practice taking time to be still, taking our eyes off of ourselves, submit ourselves to God's judgment, and remember that Jesus suffered and gave His life for the benefit of everyone, including us.

When we struggle with falling into the same traps repeatedly, we need to commit ourselves to doing only the right thing and saying, "no" to tempting or condemning thoughts as they come to mind moment by moment. We also have to learn to trust God to judge our words and actions and bring conviction to us only when He finds it necessary. Otherwise, if we continue to judge and condemn ourselves, we can easily fall into self-hatred and depression.

As long as we inhabit these bodies that are weak and prone to stumbling, we need to purposefully deny ourselves, work to master over our sinful tendencies, and guard ourselves against the dark forces that hide and constantly try to sneak in through the doors of our hearts.

---

[426] Romans 7:18-19, 24

We should humbly ask God to search our hearts and reveal all areas where we've made mistakes that we haven't yet released. Once we release any self-inflicted offenses, they fall onto Jesus just like all other offenses. Then He will mercifully consider the evidence and bring beauty out of ashes.[427]

Remember that there is no condemnation for those who are in Christ Jesus,[428] so let's not beat ourselves down.

Satan knows our weaknesses, and he entices us to judge and condemn ourselves so we feel defeated and worthless. We must not give in to Satan's deceptive schemes or believe the lies that he whispers to us.

Don't believe anyone who lies to you or tells you that you are not worth anything. God sent His only Son to conquer sin and death, and He sacrificed Himself to save you. You are worth fighting for and you are worth dying for!

God sees beyond the surface, and He knows exactly why we do what we do, but we are often running on autopilot and blindly acting out of habit. Therefore, we should slow down, resolve to do only the right thing, and trust God to be our judge. Paul explained this practice well when he wrote: "I care very little if I am judged by you or by any human court; indeed, I do not even judge myself. My conscience is clear, but that does not make me innocent. It is the Lord who judges me.[429]

Therefore, let us remember to confess and release our failures to God, and let Him be our judge. God is undoubtedly much more forgiving and merciful than we are, and He is always right.[430] So If God doesn't condemn us, and He is always right, then why do we fight against God to hold on to self-imposed condemnation?

---

[427] Psalm 69:9, Isaiah 61:3

[428] Romans 8:1

[429] 1 Corinthians. 4:3-5

[430] Jeremiah 12:1

We all make mistakes, and through Jesus all of our mistakes are forgiven. Consequently, we have no right to continue to hold them against ourselves and punish ourselves. Let us forgive our own mistakes and accept that Jesus already willingly and completely took our punishment for those mistakes like He did for all other mistakes.[431]

When we feel like judging ourselves, let's also turn the evidence over to God and trust Him to consider it and execute justice or show mercy. Whether someone else offends us or we offend ourselves, extending mercy always triumphs over judgment.[432]

Not Always Our Fault

Sometimes someone close to us makes a costly mistake that we think we could have prevented by doing or saying something different. Thankfully however, the problems and painful events that we witness in the world are usually not our fault. Even if we hesitated to help or passively sat by and let a friend or loved one hurt themselves or someone else, we should humbly trust God to judge.

For example, when God noticed that Cain was upset, and He admonished him to do right and to control himself instead of giving in to his emotions, Cain didn't listen.[433] Instead, he gave in to his emotions, confronted Abel, and killed him anyway.[434]

I'm sure God didn't blame Himself for Cain's actions. It seems that if anyone could have convinced Cain to change his mind and do right, God certainly could have. Yet, even

---

[431] Isaiah 53:4-5

[432] James 2:13

[433] Genesis 4:6-7

[434] Genesis 4:8

after God said all the right things, He continued to allow Cain to freely make his own choices, and Cain chose to do wrong.

God does not force us to do what He wants us to do. Instead, He instructs us in the way that is best for us and makes convincing arguments to persuade us to move in the right direction, but we always remain free to make our own decisions.

God loved Abel, but He also knew that the physical death of Abel was not the end of him.[435] God sees the bigger picture. Since Abel did what was right and honored God, he certainly found rest and peace as he passed on from the troubles of this world.[436]

God knows our thoughts and what we will choose to do even before we do. And even when we slip up and make mistakes, He has a plan to work out things for our good. God can reverse the effects of any ill treatment—even death—when it's right for Him to do so. We just need to place our trust in Him.

Therefore, when you feel regret and remorse for your mistakes or even just perceived mistakes, do what you can to make things right and release the matters over to your Creator. Don't condemn yourself. Even if you know you did wrong and made a mess of things, you can still trust God to help you make things right and work everything out.

If you are going through intense suffering right now, or you can't get past some seemingly senseless suffering that you endured in the past, then humbly ask God to help you. Pour out your heart to Him and be willing to yield to His directions as you listen and trust Him to work everything out.

Ask Him to give you strength and guidance as you acknowledge that you need His help and let Him turn your life around. Remember to clear your mind and look and

---

[435] Hebrews 11:4
[436] Matthew 23:35, Isaiah 57:1-2

listen for God to answer. You may have to wait a while and be persistent, but please don't give up. You will sooner or later hear a voice behind you saying, "This is the way; walk in it."[437]

While you're waiting, remain humble, keep praying, and trust God to work everything out and to create something good and great out of your difficult circumstances just as He promised He would always do.[438] The sooner you humble yourself and give thanks for your situation in life and ask God for help, the sooner your breakthrough will occur.

We should turn to our Creator and believe what He says about us – that we are loved and have been invited to join Him to accomplish great things on this earth.[439]

God created each of us for a specific important purpose, and we are all valuable to Him. We must choose to let God be our judge and accept that we are valuable and respectable because God sees us that way, and He is always right.

Also, He is never disappointed in us because He knows every choice we will ever make, and He loves us anyway. Since God doesn't condemn us,[440] let's not condemn ourselves.

If God is for you, then who can prevail against you—no one, not even yourself. So why not release yourself from the weight of your mistakes today? Life on this earth is too short to unnecessarily weigh yourself down by dragging around the baggage of regrets.

If you confess your faults and let go of all of the mistakes that you have committed against yourself and others, then God will forgive you and direct you toward a path to lighten your load and bring joyful results.[441]

---

[437] Isaiah 30:21
[438] Romans 8:28
[439] Isaiah 41:10-11, John 3:16
[440] John 3:17, 8:11
[441] Romans 8:28, 1 John 1:9

Guard Against the Victim Spirit

Whenever we experience painful situations, we should turn to God for help and trust that He will do what is needed to heal our hearts. Oftentimes, God directs friends, family members, or even strangers to help us. It's important that those close to the victim make themselves available and do what they can to help them find relief from their pain and recovery from their losses.

Although there are many people who try to exploit others by taking advantage of their sympathies, most people who claim to be victims have truly been hurt, and they are simply trying to survive and cope with their pain the best they can. Certainly, many victims have been unjustifiably mistreated and deserve to be shown compassion.

Initially, a victim legitimately requires extra attention. That extra attention usually is quite helpful and restorative. Over time, however, forgiveness and healing should take place so that the extra attention is no longer needed. Unfortunately, many people simply don't know how to find healing and relief from their emotional pain, so they remain in their victimized state of mind.

Other people selfishly enjoy the extra attention so much that they wallow in their pitiful state and continue to solicit attention. Some also take advantage of the sympathy and generosity of others and exploit their roles as legitimate victims in order to manipulate the feelings of others so they can obtain charity or get their own way in something.

They often think that because they have been a victim of some mistreatment or tragedy, they have the right or feel entitled to continue to take advantage of the sympathies of others without taking steps toward their own recovery. That entitlement mentality is not good, and it's selfish. The spirit behind this way of thinking is usually what is called the victim spirit, the spirit of self-pity, or the spirit of entitlement.

Following the influence of the victim spirit usually leads to more misery and emptiness because it eventually drives good people away while attracting those who are caught in the same trap. Satan and his messengers love to motivate people to isolate themselves or surround themselves with people who are also walking in darkness so they can more easily and completely destroy their lives.

Instead of passively giving in to dark influences, we should do what we can to spend time with people of the light who are uplifting and encouraging as we guard ourselves against the spirit of self-pity. We may have been victims of some physical or emotional mistreatment, but when we rely on God and His Spirit to help, we are empowered to become more than conquerors.[442]

The Spirit of Rejection

We obviously need to guard ourselves against the spirit of entitlement, but we also need to stand against the spirit of rejection. The spirit of rejection is often mislabeled as a victim spirit, but it is not the same spirit. Although the two feelings often occur simultaneously, feeling rejected is not the same as feeling sorry for oneself and entitled to compensation for being violated or mistreated. It's important that we distinguish between the two, and take action to guard ourselves against both.

Many people battle with feelings of rejection because they fall into the trap of believing they are unlovable or not capable of being acceptable in some area. Unkind people may have filled their head with lies about themselves at some time in the past.

The truth is that God loves everyone, and He does not reject us, as it is written:

---

[442] Acts 1:8, Romans 8:31-39

"I took you from the ends of the earth, from its farthest corners I called you. I said, 'You are my servant'; I have chosen you and have not rejected you. So do not fear, for I am with you; do not be dismayed, for I am your God. I will strengthen you and help you; I will uphold you with my righteous right hand."[443]

When we receive and follow Jesus who was a direct descendant of Jacob (Israel),[444] we become adopted into His family, so this promise is for us.

God wants to help us and strengthen us. He does not reject us, but He cannot accept our sinful ways. He forgives us and cleanses us, however, when we humbly turn to Him in confession and repentance and receive the righteousness that comes through Jesus.[445]

Afterward, if we want to remain acceptable to God, then we have to continue to honor Him and do what is right in His eyes.[446] We cannot remain in His presence when we choose to walk in sin. God has not rejected us, but He does reject our sinful ways.

So let's not believe the lying voices that we hear from ourselves or others who are trying to bring us down. God has a perfect plan for victims to follow to bring healing and restoration to our lives. We simply have to turn to God, believe the truth, and let go of the rocks in our hearts that bring us down.

---

[443] Isaiah 41:9-10
[444] Genesis 32:28, Matthew 1:1-17, Luke 3:23-38
[445] 1 John 1:9
[446] Genesis 4:7

Digging Through the Rocks

Several years ago, I saw a dramatized account of the following true story: In Armenia, on the morning of December 7, 1988, just after 11:40 AM, while most people were working or in school, two devastating earthquakes measuring 6.9 and 5.8 on the Richter scale shook the area within minutes of each other.

With the exception of their son Armand who was at school, the members of one particular family were at home. During the quake, the dad gathered his wife and young daughter underneath a doorway and covered them as the building shook, everything rattled, and things fell all around them. Thankfully, they were not harmed, but they were understandably shaken up.

Following the earthquake, Dad looked out the windows and saw collapsed buildings and devastation all around, so they turned on the radio to listen to news reports. Soon they heard a report that some of the schools had collapsed. Immediately they thought of Armand, and Dad rushed out of the house to check on him.

Upon arriving at the school, Dad found that Armand's school had indeed collapsed. Dad frantically made his way over to where his son's classroom had been, and he began crying out for his son and weeping as he started digging through the debris. He heaved aside heavy chunks of concrete and steel as he called out desperately for his son. Unfortunately, there were no answers and no indications that there were any survivors.

Other parents came by, surveyed the destruction, and tearfully concluded that their children were gone. When they saw the pile of rubble, they lost any hope that their children could have survived the school's collapse. Still, Armand's dad refused to give up hope.

After digging for several hours, he found his son's coat, and he wept and hugged it as he longed to embrace his son once again. Then he started digging again. Several more hours went by as Dad continued to dig through heavy chunks of steel and concrete in search of his son. Many other parents came by during this time to grieve the losses of their children.

The afternoon hours passed into evening, and the daylight faded into darkness, but Dad kept on digging. After dark, a rescue workman came by on his way home and suggested he go home and let the rescue workers handle it later, but Dad refused to leave and continued digging through the night.

As the sun rose, the same rescue workman passed by again and urged him to go home and get some rest, but he would not give up. By now, his hands and knees were cut and bleeding from all of the sharp edges of steel and concrete.

After continuously digging for more than thirty-eight hours, however, Dad heard voices crying out, "Help! We're down here!" With renewed energy, he carefully cleared away more heavy chunks of concrete, and a path was cleared for one of Armand's classmates to slowly but joyfully climb out. Then another child came out, then another, and another, but where was Armand?

Finally, after fourteen children had carefully worked their way out from under the rubble, Armand came out last and Dad tearfully engulfed him in his arms. The two wept together.

Then Armand told Dad how everyone was so frightened, and how he had assured them, "I know I can always count on my dad. So if he's still alive, I know he will not stop searching until he finds me, and all of you with me will be rescued too."

When he heard his dad's voice, he was overcome with joy and so glad that he had not lost faith in him. His dad had truly rescued him!

As many as 60,000 lives were reported lost as a result of those two catastrophic earthquakes. Yet, on that terrible December day in 1988, one boy's hero became a hero to many others because he persevered and refused to give up.

When I consider this story, I am reminded of at least three interesting points:

First, in the same way that Armand chose to trust his dad to find him and rescue him, we can choose to trust our Father to always help us in our times of need. Even when we feel desperate and trapped in a dark place, we can rest knowing that God will never let us down.[447]

Secondly, the dad didn't have to try to save his son. For whatever reason, the other parents had chosen to give up and not to dig through the rubble. Armand's dad could have joined them and passively accepted and grieved his losses. Instead, he chose to actively search and not give up, and his hard work and perseverance resulted in saving the lives of his son and many others.

Similarly, God doesn't give up on us, and we should not give up on each other. As long as God is directing us to accomplish certain tasks, we should persevere and trust Him to help us. Just as Jesus passed through walls to help His friends understand that He had risen,[448] He will pass through or move walls to help us too.

Finally, after the dad had provided a way of escape, the children had to choose to come out. How foolish it sounds to even consider that maybe the reason it took so long for the children to be rescued is that while they were calling for help, they were simultaneously holding on to the debris that entrapped them and refusing to step out to safety.

Too often that seems like what some people do as they repeatedly say they are struggling and need help, but they

[447] Psalm 25:3, Isaiah 28:16, Romans 9:33, 10:11, 1 Peter 2:6
[448] John 20:26

quietly hold on to fear, anxiety, offenses, and judgments. It's no wonder that they don't feel relief.

We are all born into bondage, and we all need to be rescued. Thankfully, God has provided a way of escape for all of us. But not everyone chooses to accept His rescue plan, and some don't even want to admit they need help.

Some of us fail to walk on water and rise above all of our troubles because we won't let go of our boatload of heartaches, doubts, and fears. We allow fear of the unfamiliar to outweigh our faith and trust in God. If we want to be free, we have to trust God enough to let go of the familiar ways that have held us back.

The children were trapped under physical debris, so anyone should have seen that they needed help. Unfortunately, we often find ourselves trapped under emotional and spiritual burdens and debris that we cannot see. In these instances, we need to call for someone who sees beyond the surface to help us identify and release the burdens that keep us in bondage and to guide us to safety and freedom.

Thankfully, God will dig through all of the rocks that surround our hearts in order to expose areas that need healing even when we don't realize it. We simply have to choose to soften our hearts, turn to God for help, let go of the lies, heartaches, fears, offenses, and judgments that weigh us down, and keep our eyes fixed on Jesus so that we can follow Him along the path to freedom.

God took the first step to share His perfect life with us. Now we just have to take steps to accept God's plan of rescue and share our broken lives with Him.

Letting Go of the Rocks

For most of my life, I didn't understand what Jesus did for me, and I held on to everything. Finally, when my burdens became so great, I was forced to either learn how to get rid of them or be crushed to death under their weight.

When I consider the burdens of life that I carry, I sometimes picture a sack of rocks on my back. Those rocks are either wounds or worries by which I allow myself to be weighed down.

Many people I've met know that they carry these unwanted burdens as well, but they do not know how to get rid of them. Either they do not have a clear understanding of what God has done and continues to do for us, or they know that Jesus carried the burdens and suffered so they wouldn't have to, but they can't convince themselves to release them.

Sometimes when we let go of invisible things like offenses and disappointments, we question the validity of the exercise. In these cases it often helps to perform a physical act while simultaneously taking action in our hearts to reinforce the validity of the exercise. I think this is one reason that a bride and groom give each other rings that symbolize the unending love that they have pledged to one another during a wedding ceremony.

The act of water baptism also physically symbolizes and serves to reinforce the decision to spiritually put to death and bury our sinful nature in order to be reborn and clothed in the righteousness of Jesus,[449] it often helps to perform symbolic physical acts to reinforce the truth of other spiritual realities.

In a similar way, when I recognize that I have hurts and worrisome thoughts that I need to release to God, I've often found it helpful to take time to gather some rocks and find a creek, pond, or other body of water to throw the rocks into as I verbally identify and release each of my burdens. It also works with sticks or rocks thrown off of a cliff, shells tossed in the ocean, or something similar.

---

[449] 1 Peter 3:19-22

Taking physical action validates the spiritual reality and marks the point in time that the decision was made. It can also demonstrate evidence of a faithful heart.[450]

Remember, God is always faithful, and He will dig through the rocky places that cover up the pain that lingers in your heart. You simply have to choose to go to Him, soften your heart, and pay attention to what He tells or shows you.

When God points out the rocks in our hearts, we need to understand that we have to do our part to let them go because we have the power to bind and to loosen – to retain and to release.[451]

The things we retain or release impact our hearts as well as the spiritual atmosphere around us. In order to be free from the things that weigh us down emotional and spiritually, we have to make conscious decisions to let them go.

Trying to ignore or cover up our pain is never a good long-term response. We may be able to temporarily forget it, but it will remain and come back to the surface later if we don't release it.

Furthermore, when we are not grounded in the truth, and we believe lies or we hold onto disappointments, offenses, and judgments, then we give the devil a foothold or door of access into our lives. That's not good because Satan's goal is to steal, kill, and destroy your life,[452] and all he needs is one foot in the door of your heart to have access to cause you trouble.

You may not be able to identify exactly where you have granted access, but God knows what you are doing that separates you from Him and gives the devil access to your life. So why not soften your heart and ask God what it is? Open

---

[450] James 2:14-26
[451] Matthew 18:18
[452] John 10:10

the eyes and ears of your heart and let God guide you back to Him and help you close off the doors of access to Satan.

He may show us that we are carrying offenses, hurts, and judgments, or that we are worrying and fearful about finances, work, relationships, or something that we need to let go. Once we recognize the burdens that we are carrying, then we can take them to Jesus and release them to the One who already bore our grief and carried our sorrows.[453]

The sooner you let them go, the sooner you can start living again. As long as you can breathe, it's not too late.

Turn and Look for Jesus

As Jesus traveled throughout the various towns and villages, he met many people tormented by the effects of living in this sinful world, and He had compassion on them. As they came to Him for help, He healed them.[454]

Today, the same compassionate Jesus still lives and heals us when we go to Him for help. Time and space does not limit God, and He wants to help us reconcile our past painful events even if many years may have passed.

Anytime we are reminded of a past hurt, we can revisit and walk through the emotional pain again while understanding the truth that Jesus, who is present throughout all space and time, was also present and wanted to help us in the past.[455]

Think of a specific time when you were hurt. Can you remember who it was that hurt you? Now recall what it was that he or she did that caused you to feel hurt. Do you remember what happened that hurt you? Do you remember the specific feelings that you felt?

---

[453] Isaiah 53:4
[454] Matthew 9:35-36
[455] Psalm 139

If you can stay focused, you probably can remember most of the details and can even feel the same feelings as you re-enact the painful event in your mind.

At the time you were hurt, you may not have realized it, but Jesus was there to hold you and comfort you and take away your pain. If you still feel the pain today, however, then you obviously didn't notice Him there and haven't yet let go of the pain.

I lived through the first thirty-five years of my life not knowing that Jesus had been with me all along. The perception I gathered from my physical senses was my only reality. I'm sure dark spirits have always influenced me, but for most of my life, I was not aware of the spiritual reality beyond the physical dimension.

In the past, you may not have known Jesus was there with you to carry the pain when you were hurting, so you didn't realize you could give the pain and sorrows over to Him. Today, however, you know that God is everywhere and for Him, time and space have no limits. As you now recall the hurtful event, remember that Jesus was actually there with you to help you and to carry your pain.[456]

Jesus hated to see you experience the pain you endured, and He wants you to give all the pain to Him so He can carry it and apply it to His finished work at the cross and you can rest.[457]

Through the eyes of your imagination, as you remember the painful event, look for Jesus, and you will see Him there with you. Turn to Him, give Him your pain, share your feelings, and He will give you comfort, love, and a sense of worth and acceptance. Just close your eyes and recall the painful circumstances surrounding your afflictions.

---

[456] Psalm 69:9, Isaiah 53:4, Matthew 11:28
[457] Deuteronomy 4:29, 2 Chronicles 15:2, Matthew 7:7

As feelings of rejection, abandonment, disappointment, assault, disrespect or other painful feelings come to the surface, find Jesus, go to Him, and release all of the pain to Him. Let Him hold you, melt away your pain, and give you comfort and rest.

Take time to identify each painful memory, loosen the ties that bind the pain to your heart, and give each hurt to Jesus. Then ask God to give you His heart for the person who hurt you so you can understand their situation, which will help you also let go of any judgments you made against them. You'll probably be surprised as your heart feels lighter and fills with compassion for each person who hurt you.

You cannot change the physical events of the past, but you can redirect your emotional and spiritual response to those events.

The emotional pain may resurface, and you may feel intimidated and hesitate to go through the emotional trauma again, but remember that you survived the event the first time, and you will survive the memory as well. Just bravely revisit the event in your mind and give the sorrow and the pain to Jesus. He will bring healing to your heart and take care of you.[458]

If you still find it difficult to release the pain, and you hesitate to forgive, then ask the Lord to show you why your offender mistreated you as he or she did. Many times, your offender was mistreated in a similar way by a relative or someone else, and their own emotional pain was influencing their actions.

With this knowledge, your heart may be filled with compassion so that you are more willing to release the offense. Also, if you judged them or made a vow not to be like them or do what they've done, then you should renounce the judgment, repent, and ask God to forgive you for judging them.

---

[458] Luke 10:19

God sees your heart, and He will forgive you and bring about healing.

Our enemy wants us to believe that the events that took place in the past cannot be changed. This is certainly true from a physical perspective where time and space constrains us, but in the spiritual dimension time and space have no limits.

At any time and any place, we can prayerfully revisit past events in our minds and ask God to reveal Himself and help us change the outcome from a spiritual perspective. As our spiritual perspective improves, and we choose to turn our hearts in a direction that honors God, He will bring about healing so that our emotional state will improve as well.

Therefore, whenever something triggers memories that bring pain, ask God to open the eyes of your heart and take you back to revisit events of the past through the vision of your imagination. At the same time listen for His instructions, and Jesus will meet with you there.

God delights in helping and blessing those who place their trust in Him.[459] It may be a challenge to trust in someone you cannot see, but the next time you're weighed down and burdened, instead of turning to some temporary pleasure or escape, turn to Jesus, let go of your pain, and let God demonstrate His goodness and love for you.

---

[459] 2 Chronicles 16:9, Psalm 37:4, Ephesians 3:20

9

YOUR FAITH HAS HEALED YOU

The road to healing can seem impossible to find at times, but it only seems that way. We must choose to believe God and earnestly trust Him before we can see the path.

When Jesus walked the earth, many who saw what He did and heard what He said believed Him and put their faith in Him, and He healed those who came to Him at that time. [460] He didn't tell people to wait until they get to heaven to be set free.

Similarly, when we believe and trust God today, He works things out for us today. Have you ever noticed how often Jesus told the people He had healed that their healings were a result of their own faith? He said things like:

> "Take heart, daughter. Your faith has healed you."[461]

---

[460] Matthew 4:23-24, 8:16, 12:15, 14:36, Mark 6:56, Luke 4:40
[461] Matthew 9:22

"Your faith has healed you. Go in peace and
be freed from your suffering."[462]
"Your faith has saved you. Go in peace."[463]
"Rise and go. Your faith has made you well."[464]
"According to your faith will it be done to
you."[465]
"Everything is possible for him who believes."[466]

When Jesus walked the earth, He was confined to our space and time, and people would physically go to Him for help. Everyone who believed and trusted in Jesus and came to Him for help was healed of their various afflictions.[467]

When Jesus ascended back to the Father, He was released from the confines of space and time, and His Spirit was released upon the earth into the hearts of His followers who also performed miracles and healed people who believed and trusted in Him.[468]

Today, the Spirit of Jesus still lives in the hearts of believers, and He is still at work healing people who put their faith in Him. If we understand who Jesus is, believe all that He did and still does for us, trust Him, and listen to and follow His directions just like His first disciples, then we too will experience healing and carry God's authority to help others.

---

[462] Mark 5:34
[463] Luke 7:50, 8:48
[464] Luke 17:19
[465] Matthew 9:29
[466] Mark 9:23
[467] Matthew 4:23, 9:35
[468] Acts 2:1-4, 2:43, 5:16

Fervent Prayer

Today, instead of communicating with God through Jesus in the flesh,[469] we communicate with Him directly through prayer in the spirit.[470]

The Apostle James once wrote,

> "The effective, fervent prayer of a righteous man avails much."[471]

When we turn from our sinful ways and receive Jesus, who is called the Righteous One,[472] God covers us with His righteousness and adopts us as His children. This adoption comes with great privileges such as unlimited access to spend time with God through prayer.[473]

God accepts us when we do what is right and approach Him with a humble and contrite spirit and a repentant heart,[474] and He hears our prayers when we walk according to His will as it is written,

> "We know that God does not listen to sinners. He listens to the godly person who does his will."[475]

---

[469] John 14:9
[470] John 14:23-24
[471] James 5:16 NKJV
[472] Acts 3:14, 7:52, 22:14, 1 John 2:1
[473] Ephesians 2:11-22, 3:8-12
[474] Genesis 4:7, Psalm 51:17, Isaiah 57:15, 66:2
[475] John 9:31

Also:

> "Surely the arm of the Lord is not too short to save, nor His ear too dull to hear. But your iniquities have separated you from your God; your sins have hidden His face from you, so that He will not hear."[476]

The psalmist wrote,

> "If I had cherished sin in my heart, the Lord would not have listened, but God has surely listened and has heard my prayer."[477]

Also:

> "The eyes of the Lord are on the righteous, and his ears are attentive to their prayer, but the face of the Lord is against those who do evil."[478]

Therefore, in order for God to hear our prayers, we must humble ourselves and do what is right.[479] When we feel distant from God due to our own misdeeds, and we repent, God is faithful to forgive our sins and cleanse us from our unrighteousness so we can re-enter His presence where He can hear our prayers.[480]

It's also important to remember that just because we have turned away from our sinful behavior and God hears

---

[476] Isaiah 59:1-2
[477] Psalm 66:18-19
[478] Psalm 34:15-16, 1 Peter 3:12
[479] Romans 1:17, 3:22
[480] 1 John 1:9

us does not mean He will always do what we ask because we don't always ask with right motives.[481] We sometimes ask in our own name by asking for what we want instead of listening to the Spirit of Jesus and aligning our prayers with what He wants.

Effective prayers are born out of faith. According to the Bible, faith begins with hearing the words of God.[482] When we choose to listen and believe His words, and we deliver them as directed by Him, He will deliver the results.

In other words, in order for God's will to be done on earth as it is in heaven, we must listen to His voice, see what He wants to show us, speak out His words on earth, and do what He tells us to do. In this way, we act in God's name whereby we participate with Him in accomplishing His supernatural purposes here on earth.

Just because we spend time with God and faithfully proclaim His words, however, doesn't guarantee that our requests will always be granted when we expect them to. Certainly Jesus was full of faith, but on one occasion, Jesus had to pray twice for a man to be completely healed of blindness. The first time the man's sight was only partially restored, so Jesus prayed again. Then his sight was fully restored.[483]

Why did Jesus need to pray more than once for the man to be completely healed? Was it due to a shortcoming of Jesus? Certainly not. I believe the lack was in the blind man because in another place it was written that Jesus didn't do many miracles in some places because of the people's lack of faith.[484]

Perhaps the man was holding on to his familiar condition of blindness because he was afraid of what his life would

[481] James 4:1-3
[482] Romans 10:17
[483] Mark 8:22-26
[484] Matthew 13:58

be like if he could see. Maybe he hesitated to fully let go because he didn't fully trust that what God wanted to give him was better than what he had known all his life. Who knows? Regardless of the reason, we must remember that in order for us to receive God's blessings, we must learn to trust Him enough to let go of our burdens, doubts, and fears.

If Jesus sometimes prayed more than once to accomplish something, then we should not be surprised if we have to pray repeatedly to accomplish something good in our own lives or in the lives of those for whom we are praying. We sometimes have to convince those for whom we are praying to let go of the familiar things that are holding them back before healing can take place.

Unlike a baby tooth being uncontrollably pushed out of the way by the new stronger permanent tooth, old habits usually don't easily yield and move out of the way. We can choose to stubbornly hold on to them and refuse to let them go. Unfortunately, that's too often the choice we make.

In holding on to the old familiar ways, we miss out on the healing, joy, rest, and the new life that God wants to give to us. It's like trying to keep new wine in old wineskins. It doesn't work.[485] We have to learn to fast by letting go of our old, familiar, and selfish ways.

When Jesus first walked on the earth, many people heard about the healings and miracles so they believed that God was working through Him, and they trusted Him and went to Him for help. Many people came to Jesus and were freed from demons or healed of various issues after He prayed or spoke only a few words.[486]

Not everyone who lived at the time of Jesus or heard about Him was healed, but only those who actually put their

---

[485] Matthew 9:14-17

[486] Matthew 4:23-24, 8:13, 16, 9:22, 29, 12:15, 14:36, 15:28, Mark 5:34, 6:56, 9:23, 10:52 Luke 4:40, 7:50, 8:48, 17:19

faith in Him. Obviously, the people had also been convinced that they needed to let go of whatever was causing their trouble, and they had enough faith in Jesus to go to Him, ask for help, let go of their burdens, and receive healing.

At another time, in Lystra while Paul was teaching, he saw a lame man who appeared to have "faith to be healed," so he told the man to stand to his feet. The man believed and responded to Paul. He was healed as he stood up.[487]

At other times, no words were needed at all. Once a faithful woman simply touched the hem of Jesus' garment to obtain healing.[488] Also, people were healed when Peter's shadow passed by them,[489] and handkerchiefs and aprons that Paul had touched were taken to sick people and God healed them as well.[490] The key to their healing was their faith in God.

Today, the key to our healing is also our faith. If we ask God for guidance, listen for His words, and truly believe the words that God speaks, then when we pray to God using His own words, our prayers will be effective. We have to choose to let go of the lies that we have believed and put all of our trust in God and believe the truth that He reveals to us.

We also must pray fervently, which is to pray with enthusiasm, passion, or intensity of spirit.[491] This requires that we stay focused, so it's good to go somewhere quiet and private where we can minimize distractions.

---

[487] Acts 14:8-10
[488] Mark 5:25-29, Luke 8: 43-44
[489] Acts 5:15
[490] Acts 19:11-12
[491] http://www.dictionary.com/browse/fervent

Jesus would get up early and go somewhere private and quiet to pray,[492] and He instructed His followers to do the same.[493]

In a quiet and private place, we can more easily envision ourselves in God's presence where we can focus and freely pour out our hearts to Him. While in His presence, we must also pay attention to what He wants to tell us. We should not stop wrestling in prayer until we connect with the heart of God and receive His answer or whatever He has for us.[494]

Whenever we need help, as believers in Jesus, we should humble ourselves and turn to our Father who wants to give us exactly what we need for any situation we face. We must truly trust God, fervently pray, actively wait on Him, patiently listen, and follow His instructions in order to achieve victory.

Angels to the Rescue

Sometimes when we ask God for help, He sends angels. For example, on the night that Jesus was betrayed, He prayed three distinct times for the Father to "take this cup" from Him. He was apparently dreading the pain of being physically tortured and spiritually separated from the Father, and He asked for help.[495]

Instead of removing the task set before Him, our Father sent an angel to comfort and strengthen Him so He could make it through the incredible challenges He faced and carry out the great plan of our redemption.[496]

I find it interesting that the Father helped Jesus by sending an angel to help Him that night. Angels had also been sent

---

[492] Mark 1:35
[493] Matthew 6:6
[494] Luke 18:1-8
[495] Psalm 22, Luke 22:42
[496] Luke 22:43

to help Him earlier after fasting and being tempted in the wilderness.[497] At another time, Jesus explained that if He wanted, He could ask the Father who would send more than "twelve legions of angels" to help Him.[498]

If Jesus welcomed the help of angels while He faced challenges on earth, then we too should welcome their help. We can always ask our Father to send angels to help us. We just have to be careful not to worship them or elevate them to a higher position than God gives them.[499] Our position as children of God is higher than the angels.[500]

Jesus told His followers that if we publicly acknowledge Him before others, then He would make us known among the angels.[501] Have you ever been helped by an angel? Have you heard stories of how a person like an angel came along at a desperate time and rescued someone and then disappeared?

A good example of angels rescuing a Christian happened on one occasion after the apostles had been publicly speaking to crowds about Jesus and the good news about the life found in Him, and they were arrested and put in jail. During the night, an angel came and let them out and told them to continue publicly proclaiming the good news.[502]

At another time, after Peter had continued publicly proclaiming the good news concerning Jesus and was arrested and imprisoned, God sent an angel to rescue him while his friends were praying for him.[503] Therefore, when we or

---

[497] Matthew 4:11, Mark 1:13

[498] Matthew 26:53

[499] Revelation 19:10, 22:8-9

[500] Hebrews 1-2

[501] Luke 12:8

[502] Acts 5:17-24

[503] Acts 12:5-11

someone we care about need help with something, it's perfectly acceptable to ask God to send angels to help.

Also, let's remember that God often answers our prayers in ways that we don't expect because He has a better plan than what we might have in mind. Instead of removing the challenges that we face, He may strengthen us to go right through them to accomplish a greater purpose like He did with Jesus, Paul, and others.

Whenever you face a difficult decision, the most reassuring thing for you might just be to hear His comforting voice saying something like, "Do not fear for I am with you, and I will help you" as He told His people through Isaiah[504] and to Paul through a vision while he was in Corinth.[505] God helps us and guides us through His Spirit,[506] but don't be surprised if He also chooses to dispatch an angel to help you.

Be More Than You Can Be

Do you remember the U.S. Army slogan used during the 1980's and 1990's that said, "Join the U.S. Army and be all you can be"? I like that slogan, and it probably motivated many people to join the Army. After all, most people want to reach their potential and get all they can out of life, and that slogan certainly promoted the achievement of that goal.

Many times, however, we work hard, earn degrees, land great jobs, make lots of money, or accomplish certain goals only to discover that we still feel empty and unfulfilled. A limiting factor to personal greatness is our own pride and self-reliance, which inherently limits how far we can go and how successful we can be on our own.

---

[504] Isaiah 41:10
[505] Acts 18:9-11
[506] John 14:26

When we stand with God, however, all things are possible.[507] With His guidance we can effectively be more than we can be and obtain higher levels of success and fulfillment than we could ever achieve on our own.

We must take action. Just reading about God and His plan for mankind is not enough. [508] In order to exceed our own abilities and obtain abundant life, we must choose to believe God and follow His specific plan for each of our lives.

God recognized that people were harassed and seemingly helpless back then, and He knows we are often mistreated and harassed today. He also knows that there are far too many victims on this planet, but He is willing and able to help and heal everyone who believes in Him and humbly comes to Him for help. We simply have to let go of our old ways and bravely step out into the new ways that God has established for us.

Like the greatest superhero, Jesus cannot be defeated, and when we stand with Him, we cannot be defeated either.[509] So let's humble ourselves, believe and follow Jesus, and trust God to work everything out. Let's realize that we need help and cannot help ourselves. Let's accept His gift and provision and stop tugging on our pain and wrestling with everything that weighs us down.

We should remember that through the work of Jesus Christ we are more than conquerors[510] and that God loves us and has a great plan for our lives. He may be waiting for us to open the doors of our hearts and put all our trust in Him so we can personally experience His great love and break free from our victimization today.

---

[507] Matthew 19:26, Mark 10:27
[508] John 5:39
[509] John 16:33
[510] Romans 8:37

We can't change the events of the past or how we arrived at where we are today, but we can change how we view the past, how we respond to life's challenges going forward, and how we will finish. It's time to reconcile the events of the past with the truth and press forward toward the finish line.

Humbly reading and accepting God's instructions in the Bible can equip us with the knowledge that can lead us to salvation,[511] but we must make the conscious decision to receive and follow the instructions of Jesus daily like the early disciples did in order to be set free and walk the path of salvation where God's supernatural powers are available to us.[512]

Since many physical events are influenced by activities in the spiritual realm, we need to learn the proper use of supernatural tools and weapons like forgiveness to effectively make a positive impact on the physical world in which we live.

The tools and weapons of God are not physical; they are supernatural and capable of demolishing our supernatural enemy's strongholds at the foundational level. Doing things God's way is much more effective than using physical or logical tools and techniques.[513]

Why do we limit ourselves to thinking and doing only what our minds can conceive and figure out? Why don't we choose to believe God and learn from Him who created us, loves us, and empowers us to be more then we can be?

Today some people claim the miracles that were witnessed and recorded in the Bible by the early disciples occurred only at that time, and we should not expect to witness similar miracles today. They choose to believe that God no longer performs miracles through His followers,

---

[511] 2 Timothy 3:15
[512] John 3:16, Romans 10:9
[513] 2 Corinthians 10:4

and consequently, they are not able to observe them. Their unbelief becomes self-fulfilling.

When we depend on the familiar things in our lives and refuse to let go of our old habits and patterns of thinking, we limit ourselves. When believers let go of what's familiar, however, like when they travel to foreign or unfamiliar places, they more often witness healings and other supernatural events because they choose to place more of their dependence on God to guide them during those times.

When we humble ourselves and choose to wholeheartedly believe and depend on God, He changes our hearts, strengthens us, exalts us, and empowers us to do His will, overcome the enemy, impact lives, and change the broken world around us in miraculously ways. [514] The supernatural act of forgiveness is just one of the many ways we can participate in miracles on earth.

Therefore, let's stop limiting ourselves by depending on our own understanding and abilities to figure things out. Instead, let's surrender everything to our Creator and fill our thoughts and minds with His encouraging words and be the men and women that He created us to be.

Let us live up to His vision of who we are, and let's remind ourselves daily that it is only by depending upon God and following the Spirit of Jesus that we will experience real and lasting victory! With God, we can truly be more than we can be.

Joseph's Faith

The Biblical account of Joseph demonstrates how we can be more than we can be when we choose to turn from our prideful ways, humble ourselves, and put our faith in God.

---

[514] Luke 10:19, Acts 1:8

Joseph was his father's favorite son, and his eleven brothers hated him because of the special treatment he received and because he would report back to his dad whenever they did something wrong.[515]

Joseph had two dreams that suggested he would one day rise above his mom, dad, and brothers. These dreams fueled his already puffed up and prideful view of himself, and he boasted about how special he was. Eventually, his brothers became so full of hatred toward him that they bound him and sold him as a slave to some traveling merchants.[516]

Joseph had no choice but to accept his challenging circumstances and hope for better things. He became a good worker and a faithful servant to an Egyptian official. Unfortunately, his troubles continued, and one day, he was falsely accused of making advances toward the official's wife. He was sentenced to prison where he remained for a long time.

Based upon what Joseph said later, I expect that while in prison, he cried out to God for help. Most likely, God comforted him, reminded him of the dreams that were yet to be fulfilled, and convinced him to let go of the offenses and disappointments and place his trust in Him.

Sometime afterwards, through a series of providential events, Joseph was released and appointed to a very powerful government position. God supplied Joseph with great wisdom, and as Governor, he issued decrees to store up grain in preparation for an upcoming time of drought and famine.

During the famine, his brothers came to him seeking assistance. After Joseph had given aid to his brothers and their families, they asked him to forgive their offenses which he had apparently already done because he made the following statement to them,

---

[515] Genesis 37:1-4 NKJV
[516] Genesis 37:5-28

"You intended to harm me, but God intended
it for good to accomplish what is now being
done, the saving of many lives."[517]

God had turned everything around for good, Joseph's
dreams had indeed come to pass, and he humbly realized
it. He blessed his brothers and their families, and they were
honored in Egypt.

One thing we can learn from Joseph's life is that even
though other people choose to hurt us, when we humble
ourselves, release the offenses, judgments, and disappointments, and choose to let God be Judge and Healer, we can
rest knowing that He will always lift us up, bring healing to
our hearts, and execute justice against our offenders at the
right time.[518]

Another point to consider is that God often opposes us
when we are acting in arrogant and prideful ways in order to
redirect our lives toward a better end. No matter how dark
our life circumstances appear to be, we should remember
that we can always turn to God and trust Him to turn our
lives around and bring us to a place of blessing and light.

The Wounded Heart is Healed

As we discussed earlier, the cry of the victim's heart is
to be heard and understood, and to find healing from the
pain they carry in their hearts. The afflictions of the heart
are invisible, but they often weigh a person down more
than visible physical afflictions. When physical issues are

---

[517] Genesis 50:20

[518] Deuteronomy 28:1-6, 15-19, 1 Samuel 26:23, Psalms 62:11-12,
Proverbs 14:14, 19:17, Jeremiah 17:10, Matthew 16:27, Ephesians
6:8, James 4:10, 1Peter 5:6, Revelation 22:12

accompanied by spiritual and emotional afflictions, the results can be devastating.

That's why healing the invisible issues of the heart is so essential to maintaining a healthy life of joy and fulfillment. Fortunately, the Spirit of Jesus who is invisible is willing and eager to heal our hearts.

Our afflictions are often brought about because we have hardened our hearts so that we can neither see with our eyes, hear with our ears, nor understand what we should do. So our path to healing begins when we soften our calloused hearts and choose to believe God. After our eyes and ears are opened, and we discover the truth, obtain understanding, and purposefully turn in the right direction, God will heal us.[519]

Regardless of whether or not you can readily identify the actions or words that caused the pain in your heart, Jesus can still accomplish the task of healing you from the inside out. He knows your pain. He feels your pain, and He has compassion for you. Even today, even now, He longs to comfort you and heal your heart, but you must tear down the walls that you have built and let Him help you.

No matter what challenges we go through in this life, we always have choices to make. Even if we cannot change our circumstances, we can change our perception of the challenges that we face. When we consider that God will work all things out for our good as we trust in Him and follow His instructions, we can rejoice knowing that as we humble ourselves before Him, He will help us overcome all of life's challenges.

Sometimes our biggest challenges in life come as a result of our own calloused heart and lack of understanding. Therefore, we've previously identified the five "Open and SHUT" steps that can be taken in order for us obtain freedom

---

[519] Isaiah 6:9-10, Matthew 13:14-15, Acts 28:26-27

and healing from the weight of offenses, judgments, and disappointments. These steps are:

STEP 1. Open Our Hearts: We must soften and open any areas of our hearts that we have hardened for protection so we can receive love, instruction and encouragement. We must humble ourselves and admit we need help.

STEP 2. See With Our Eyes: We must open our eyes and recognize we have blind spots and issues that we need help to overcome. We must focus on the Truth so that we can identify and reject lies that have misguided our hearts and minds and use the eyes of our imagination to see what God wants to show us.

STEP 3. Hear With Our Ears: We must open our ears to gather information and listen to instruction from someone who speaks the truth with love. As we read God's written words, we must listen for Him to instruct us and enlighten our minds and remember that He can and will do exactly as He promises.

STEP 4. Understand With Our Hearts: We must seriously consider the truth of what we see and hear to develop an understanding of the truth as it pertains to our situations.

STEP 5. Turn: We must change our minds to align our thoughts and expectations with what God allows for us, ask Him to change our hearts when necessary, and actively turn toward the path of life that God directs each of us to take. We must choose to turn from our old habits and release every offense, judgment, and disappointment that has weighed us down, stolen our joy, and hindered our relationships.

Depending on our levels of understanding and trust and how much enemy opposition we are facing at the time, sometimes these steps can be made quickly and effortlessly, while at other times, these steps must be made through deliberate efforts over several hours or days.

While taking these steps, we should remember that our enemy tries to cause us to fail, but Jesus has given us His authority to overcome all the powers of the enemy,[520] and He promises that we will be safe as long as we remain with Him.[521] We must, therefore, not try to work alone or get ahead of Him because the battle belongs to our God.[522] It is not by our might or power but by His Spirit that we will experience healing and victory one step at a time.[523]

There is a time for humility, a time to ask for help, a time for seeing, a time for hearing, a time for understanding, a time for turning, and a time to be healed. For you, the time could be right now. If you haven't done so already, why not put this book down, turn to Jesus, let Him have your junk, and let Him set you free? Ready...set...go! May God's abundant blessings flow freely to you as you take these steps and walk with Him.

---

[520] Luke 10:18
[521] Matthew 10:22
[522] 1 Samuel 17:47
[523] Zechariah 4:6

10

WHY ME? (APPENDIX)

I placed this chapter at the end of this book because some readers may find it unnecessary because they already know why they're having troubles, or they don't care to know why. However, for those of us who find it helpful to know why we may be having so much trouble in this world, I have included the results of my research here.

Are you convinced that God cares about you? Have you ever wondered why if God is all-powerful, all-knowing, loving, and compassionate,[524] then why does He allow people to be hurt so much?

People suffer for different reasons in different ways at different times. Suffering is never pleasant at the time, but that doesn't mean it's not beneficial. Much of our suffering is caused by our own actions or the actions of others. Some afflictions can be attributed to the hand of Providence, some to the hand of Satan, and some challenges come as a result of living in this fallen world.

As we read through the Bible, we encounter many godly men and women who suffered and asked the question, "Why

---

[524] Psalm 116:5, James 5:11

me?" One of the most memorable was Job, but we also find that others also questioned God about their circumstances, and God often answered them.[525] Sometimes He gave them a better understanding of the purposes behind what was happening as they faced challenges, but many times the purposes were not revealed at all or at least not until much later.

Even while Jesus was suffering on the Cross, He cried out asking the Father, "Why have you forsaken me?"[526] Of course Jesus already knew the answer to His question: He felt forsaken because our sins that were placed upon Him created a barrier of separation between Him and the Father.[527] The same thing happens to us when we have wrongdoing on our account.

It's completely acceptable to ask God why we are going through difficulties in life as long as we are not accusing Him of doing something wrong. In fact, God welcomes us when we humbly come to Him with our sincere questions.[528] Sometimes God answers us in ways that we completely understand right away, and other times He helps us by sending us on a journey of discovery.

Thankfully, for followers of Jesus, all of the suffering that we experience on this earth is temporary. When we consider that we will spend eternity in paradise where there is no pain or suffering, but only everlasting joy and rest in the unobstructed presence of our loving God, our current sufferings will certainly appear trivial by comparison.[529]

---

[525] Exodus 5:22-23

[526] Matthew 27:46, Mark 15:34

[527] Isaiah 59:1-2

[528] James 1:5

[529] Romans 8:18

Freedom to Hurt Each Other

No one deserves to be mistreated, and God doesn't want you or anyone else to be hurt by the hateful actions of others. He loves you and me and wants us to love each other too.[530] Nevertheless, one of the primary reasons that we get hurt is that people are free to make their own choices, and sometimes they choose to do unkind things or act carelessly which results in us getting hurt.

God is good, and since we are created in His image, each of us has the capacity to do good things. Unfortunately, we were also born with a selfish nature, so we often exercise our free will to intentionally hurt others, or we carelessly hurt others by selfishly trying to meet our own needs without considering how our actions might affect others. In either case, it's important to realize that God hates it when the offensive actions of us or others cause trouble and pain.[531]

Our choices always trigger consequences. The choices we make now will have either temporary consequences that we experience only while living on the earth, eternal consequences that we will have to endure forever,[532] or some combination of both.

Since we are created in God's image,[533] and He is the creator of everything, we too can create things. We all have choices of whether or not we use our creative abilities for good and loving purposes or for evil and hateful purposes. Certainly, many people use their creative gifts to help others, but many also use their creative gifts to manipulate others for selfish gain or to inflict pain.

---

[530] Leviticus 19:18, John 15:12
[531] Psalm 5:1-6, 11:4-7, Proverbs 6:16-19, Zechariah 8:17
[532] John 3:18
[533] Genesis 1:26-27

Some people are deliberately mean and hateful, and others are just careless. When people are not careful, accidents happen that usually hurt other people. In fact, people are frequently careless with their actions and even more careless with their words.

Whenever people have a careless attitude about hurting others, it's often because they themselves have been hurt, and they are acting out of a bitter and calloused heart. They may have been abused, and consequently, they hardened their hearts in order to cope. Now, they routinely hurt others out of habit.

If the sources of the pain are not identified and released, then those hurts will continue to trigger bitterness, anger, and hateful thoughts and actions toward others. They then become open targets for the father of lies and master of deception, the devil, to work more diligently to motivate them to hurt others.[534]

People also do careless things that hurt us when they are influenced and misguided by the invisible evil spirits and messengers of Satan who constantly cause trouble and try to break up relationships to hinder God's good work in this world. Like the Jews who wanted Jesus to be crucified, these people probably don't realize the full extent of what they are doing.[535]

They may not know they are being influenced by demons, but they will still have to give account to God for their actions.[536] When we understand that offensive people often don't realize what they are doing, it becomes easier to forgive their offenses and avoid passing judgment against them.

Of course, convincing ourselves that our offenders are simply acting ignorantly out of their own hurts and knowing

---

[534] James 1:9-25
[535] Luke 23:34
[536] Romans 14:12, Hebrews 4:13

that no misdeed will go unpunished can motivate us to release their offenses more easily, but forgiveness doesn't always immediately eliminate the sting of the offenses. In time, however, after the offensive stinger is removed, the pain will subside. We should learn to rule over our thought life and commit to treating others right even when others treat us wrong.

The Biblical account of the life of Joseph demonstrates an excellent example of how God can restore our lives when we forgive those who do us wrong and trust God to work things out. After God had sustained Joseph through slavery, imprisonment, and restoration, and Joseph had chosen to forgive his brothers for selling him into slavery, he told them, "You intended to harm me, but God intended it for good to accomplish what is now being done, the saving of many lives."[537]

From the events of Joseph's life, we can learn that even though other people choose to mistreat us, we can always trust God to work everything out as long as we maintain our integrity and honor God with our own choices.

People who are misguided by Satan or their own selfish desires can certainly cause harm to us emotionally and physically, but not spiritually. Of course, this pain can be intense at times, but in the grand scheme of things it is still temporary.[538]

Pain is never pleasant, but it helps to be reminded that when we endure suffering while following Jesus and doing the right thing, we will reap eternal rewards, the benefits of which will far outweigh the costs. Or as Jesus explained: "Blessed are you when people insult you, persecute you and falsely say all kinds of evil against you because of me. Rejoice and be glad, because great is your reward in heaven,

---

[537] Genesis 50:20
[538] Luke 12:4-5

for in the same way they persecuted the prophets who were before you."[539]

Knowing we will be rewarded in the heaven when we are mistreated for doing the right thing offers some consolation, but someone might ask, "Since God is good, and He wants us all to love each other and not hurt each other, and He is all powerful, then wouldn't it seem that the easiest way to solve most of the world's problems would be for God to force people to be nice to each other?"

Well, that might sound like the easiest thing for God to do, but I'm sure that would not be the best plan. If it were the best plan, then God would certainly do it.

Think about it: If God forced us to do His will, then that would totally nullify the liberty and freedom that He already freely gave to each of us. That would not be good because it would be contrary to His loving character. God does not treat us like puppets or act as a dictator in our lives.

We need to remember, however, that with freedom comes responsibility. Every word spoken and action committed will be judged, and each person will have to give an account for what he or she has said and done.[540] God is faithful, and He will always execute justice at the proper time.[541] That's good news.

And there's even better news: He also loves us so much that He provides healing for all who have been hurt by the misdeeds of others.[542] God not only gives us freedom to make choices, but He also provides healing and restoration for all people who are hurt by the bad choices of others. We simply have to trust Him and follow His instructions to obtain that healing.

---

[539] Matthew 5:11-12
[540] Matthew 12:36-37, 25:31-46
[541] Psalm 33
[542] Psalm 10:14-18

In fact, even when our own bad choices and mistakes cause us emotional pain, God loves us so much that He offers us the same healing and restoration. All we have to do is turn to Him, confess our mistakes, release our burdens, and follow His instructions.[543] He will gladly carry our burdens, give us rest, and restore what we have lost or had stolen from us.

God's Loving Opposition

Sometimes we suffer because other people carelessly or intentionally hurt us. However, not every feeling of hurt, disappointment, or frustration originates with the careless or hateful actions of others.

Another reason we feel hurt or suffer hardship is that God lovingly opposes us by setting up frustrating or even painful roadblocks whenever we independently wander down a dangerous path that will eventually lead us to more pain or our own destruction.[544] When we wander, God often moves to get our attention and help us realize we need to change directions to protect us and prevent greater pain and suffering.

I used to think God opposed the proud to show them that He's the boss. I thought that God would occasionally or randomly wreck independent-minded and arrogant people's lives to teach them a lesson. However, after reading the Bible, I learned I was completely mistaken.

God doesn't do anything randomly or by accident, and He does nothing out of unkindness or hatred. If God is directly responsible for your opposition, then you can find comfort knowing that He doesn't oppose us without a good purpose. God has a good reason and purpose behind everything that He chooses to do or allows to be done.

---

[543] Matthew 11:28
[544] James 4:6, 1 Peter 5:5

Sometimes it seems like God is against us, but it only seems that way.[545] He always works in our lives to do what's best for us to accomplish His great plans, and sometimes that requires training and opposition.[546]

The account of Balaam in the Bible demonstrates this type of discipline. Balaam was a decent man for the most part, but he was motivated by greed and self-ambition when he decided to disregard God's directions and help Balak. He was going in a dangerous direction and almost got himself killed, but God used his donkey to help get his attention while an angel opposed him. The angel of the Lord told him, "I have come here to oppose you because your path is a reckless one before me."[547]

It took three opposing maneuvers plus speaking through a donkey for God to finally get Balaam's attention so he would be persuaded to change directions. Just like Balaam, one of our problems is that we often fail to exercise the self-control to resist selfish motivators like greed, which always leads us to trouble and pain.

God wants us to live joyful and abundant lives, and He doesn't want any of us to perish,[548] so He often steps in to oppose us when we pridefully go in the wrong direction. He also prunes out the unproductive or self-destructive parts of our lives to help us reach our potential.[549] Of course, this pruning is always uncomfortable, but our lives become much more fruitful and more fulfilling in the long run.

A good father would not just let his young child carelessly run across busy streets. He would train him or her to watch and be careful before crossing. If his child recklessly

[545] Romans 8:31
[546] Romans 8:28
[547] Numbers 22:32
[548] Matthew 18:14
[549] John 15:1-8

ran toward a busy street, he would run after him or her and abruptly stop them before they were hit.

Similarly, God works in our lives and sometimes stops us to prevent us from getting hurt or to teach us to depend on Him more so that we can accomplish greater things. This is what happened before Paul became an apostle.

Luke reported how the Apostle Paul, called Saul at the time, was on his way to Damascus to capture and imprison any Christians he could find. He was convinced he was doing the right thing. Then Jesus suddenly appeared in a bright light and opposed him along the road. Paul became blind as a result, and he was understandably shaken up. [550]

Within three days, Paul had made a complete change of heart and accepted Jesus as the Messiah. Then God sent a man named Ananias to pray for him to restore his sight. After Paul was healed, he was eager to share his experience and newfound faith in God with everyone he met.[551] He later expressed how glad he was that God had opposed him and rescued him like He did.[552]

It's interesting that it took the clear and direct opposition and discipline of God to motivate Paul to radically change the course of his life from hating and killing Christians to fervently promoting Christianity.

Paul's "thorn in the flesh" is another great teaching example of how sometimes God allows us to face challenging circumstances in order to motivate us to change course so we can reach higher levels of fulfillment and accomplish His good plans on the earth.

Many people have opinions of what Paul's "thorn in the flesh" may have been. If you read through the book of Acts and Paul's letters, you may conclude like I did that the

---

[550] Acts 9:1-19, 22:7-16

[551] Acts 9:18-30

[552] 2 Corinthians 12:10

"thorn" was a fear-provoking spirit that God allowed for good reasons. [553]

After Paul understood what was going on, here's how he described the situation in his second letter to the Corinthians:

> "Therefore, in order to keep me from becoming conceited, I was given a thorn in my flesh, a messenger of Satan, to torment me. Three times I pleaded with the Lord to take it away from me. But He said to me, "My grace is sufficient for you, for my power is made perfect in weakness." Therefore I will boast all the more gladly about my weaknesses, so that Christ's power may rest on me. That is why, for Christ's sake, I delight in weaknesses, in insults, in hardships, in persecutions, in difficulties. For when I am weak, then I am strong."[554]

At first, Paul was frustrated by the spirit, but by the time he wrote this letter, he had concluded that God had allowed a "messenger of Satan" to torment him to keep him "from becoming conceited" and ultimately strengthen his ministry.

Paul may have earlier become so proud of his accomplishments that he began to depend upon his own ability to figure things out rather than on God, so God allowed him to be tormented by a spirit of fear to keep him humbly dependent on Him. That would certainly make sense based upon what he wrote, but there may have been another good reason for him to alter his course.

---

[553] Acts 9:1-31, 13:50, 14:9-12, 14:19, 16:19-24, 18:9-10, 19:11, 21:30-36, 22:24-25, 23:10-13, 28:8, 1 Corinthians 2:3, 2 Corinthians 11:23-33, 12:1-9, Ephesians 6:19-20, 2 Timothy 3:10-11
[554] 2 Corinthians 12:7-10

Instead of speaking to and teaching relatively small groups of people and risk being physically attacked, Paul began writing letters, which have been copied and read over and over by many, many more people. Later, when he was imprisoned, his letters were even more useful.

I'm sure that Paul could not have known at that time how huge an impact his letters would have in encouraging others and advancing God's kingdom on the earth. We, however, know now that God has used Paul's letters to teach possibly billions of people about His power and goodness.

If Paul had not suffered and been "tormented" by that "messenger of Satan," then he might not have been as motivated to write so many letters. We all owe Paul a debt of gratitude for not giving up and for changing the course of his ministry in the midst of the challenges he faced. We can also learn from Paul's example to be patient and prayerful whenever we face opposition.

We often pridefully and blindly make decisions without regard for doing what is best from God's perspective, and we eventually find ourselves traveling down paths that are not always best for us. This process can be gradual like floating down a seemingly peaceful river not realizing that a huge waterfall is just around the next bend.

That's the way I felt in my marriage as I blindly floated along, thinking that my hateful actions toward my wife were justified because she wasn't doing what I thought she should do. Her refusing to continue to live with me and moving out were exactly the opposition I needed for me to wake up and get serious about changing directions.

If we are not prayerful and careful to listen to God, we won't even realize we are heading down a path toward more trouble. That's another reason that we are admonished to stay alert because Satan and his messengers are always trying to keep us distracted so we won't see disaster coming.[555]

Furthermore, we sometimes get so attached to someone or something that we place a higher priority on the person or thing than we give to God. If we're not careful we may find ourselves making idols out of the people or things in our lives. I idolized my wife for a long time, which is one reason why I used to react so harshly whenever she let me down.

Obviously, placing more importance on any person or thing above God demonstrates either ignorance about who God is or willful rebellion against Him. He eventually opposes us and removes those idols from our lives.

I haven't always appreciated God's loving opposition, but over time I've learned to be grateful that God allows challenges and obstacles to come along to redirect me toward a better and safer path. This demonstrates to me that God loves me, and He is faithful to keep His promises.

God knows what lies ahead just beyond the next turn in the path. Our perspective is limited, but His is infinite. So when God steps in and opposes us, we should gratefully yield because it's always a good thing. If we're stubbornly depending upon only what we see from our perspective, however, then we may fall into the trap of concluding that the opposition is for no good reason and try to maneuver around it.

Naturally, God's loving hand of opposition doesn't usually fit our agenda, and He will oppose us causing varying levels of inconvenience, discomfort, or pain depending upon whether we yield to Him or resist Him. Sometimes God's loving hand of opposition is mistakenly taken as an enemy attack. That's also why it's important that we are prayerful and seek the Lord continuously.

---

[555] John 10:10, 1 Peter 5:8

It's encouraging when we remind ourselves that God loves everyone, and He doesn't want anyone to perish and go through eternity separated from Him. Some people know about God, but they live almost their entire lives pridefully trusting in their own understanding instead of depending on their Creator. In doing this, they separate themselves from God.

If these people continue to maintain their independence from God, then they will remain separated from Him and His goodness during their life on earth as well as for all eternity. We should never stop praying for the people we know who fall into this category because a last minute change of heart is always possible.

God sometimes mercifully allows stubborn and self-reliant people like these to go through disease or suffering in order to motivate them to finally give up on themselves or their idols and turn to God before it is too late. As long as a person is still breathing, it's not too late to turn to God.

I've known several self-reliant people who have died of cancer. During their final weeks of life on earth, however, several displayed changes of heart with renewed trust in God. If their cancer battle caused them to finally turn to Jesus and wholeheartedly put their trust in God before passing away, then we should be thankful that God brought the opposition.

Our perspectives are limited. We see only what we see, and that's not usually all that much. While in this world we may not always immediately recognize when God is using the hardships in our lives to motivate us to change directions and move in step with His better plans, so we need to make time to pray about everything.

If you keep feeling like you're running into frustrating obstacles and roadblocks, then consider that God may be opposing you in order to protect you from serious heartache and long-term misery because He loves you. Don't be so blind or shortsighted that you blame something or someone else for your troubles.

God may be allowing the troubles to refine your character, another person's character, or both so that He can release greater good into your lives and change the world for the better.

No Fear of God

Another reason we have troubles is that we don't walk in the fear of the Lord. If we don't fear God, then we won't be careful to follow His instructions, and we will carelessly or purposefully do things that dishonor God, which results in trouble for us.[556]

The fear of the Lord is the beginning of knowledge and wisdom,[557] and a right relationship with God starts here. Unfortunately, the concept of fearing God has often been misunderstood, and many people are suffering because they have been misled about what it means to fear God.

Some people think that because the Bible says "God is love"[558] and He loves everyone, He should not be feared. Or they say that since Jesus took our punishment and satisfied the wrath of God[559], we no longer need to fear Him, but we should still give Him the honor and respect that He deserves.

There is some truth in both of these viewpoints, but there is also some misunderstanding. We honor and respect kings, presidents, military heroes, and other respectable people. Fearing God is more about having great concern for how God will respond to us if we act in ways that displease Him. God will not let the guilty go unpunished, but He takes care

---

[556] Deuteronomy 28
[557] Psalm 111:10, Proverbs 1:7, 9:10
[558] 1 John 4:8, 16
[559] Romans 5:1-11

of those who trust in Him.[560] Understanding these truths is where the path to wisdom and salvation begins. [561]

Jesus taught His followers about the importance of fearing God when He said:

> "I tell you, my friends, do not be afraid of those who kill the body and after that can do no more. But I will show you whom you should fear: Fear him who, after your body has been killed, has authority to throw you into hell. Yes, I tell you, fear him."[562]

Therefore, Jesus taught that we should fear God and remember to always place more emphasis on pleasing Him than pleasing ourselves or others.

It is also written that God said,

> "These are the ones I look on with favor: those who are humble and contrite in spirit, and who tremble at my word."[563]

If you've been leaning on your own understanding or more concerned about what other people say instead of what God says, then you may be causing much of your own troubles. Throughout the Scriptures, God teaches us that if we follow the ways of men and worry about what others think instead of considering what God thinks, then we will have trouble.[564]

---

[560] Nahum 1

[561] Luke 1:50

[562] Luke 12:4-5

[563] Isaiah 66:2

[564] Deuteronomy 29:18-28, Jeremiah 17:5-8

When God displayed His power at Mount Sinai and the people were afraid, Moses told them:

"Do not be afraid. God has come to test you, so that the fear of God will be with you to keep you from sinning."[565]

The primary purpose of fearing God, therefore, is to motivate us to avoid doing wrong. Since Moses told the people to not be afraid, he knew God was only demonstrating His power to the people to help them understand He was serious. They were not doing anything wrong, so they did not need to be afraid of any punishment at that time.

Fear motivates us in the beginning. Love motivates us in the end. Zechariah, the father of John the Baptist, said that God has come to

"rescue us from the hand of our enemies and to enable us to serve Him without fear in holiness and righteousness before Him all our days."[566]

Also Mary, the mother of Jesus, said that God is holy and

"His mercy extends to those who fear him, from generation to generation."[567]

As you may recall, John the Baptist came to prepare the way of the Lord. [568] The purpose of many of John's messages was to remind people of their sin, which separated them

---

[565] Exodus 20:20
[566] Luke 1:74-75
[567] Luke 1:50
[568] Matthew 3:3, Mark 1:1-3, Luke 1:76, 3:1-4

from God and of the upcoming wrath of God, which would be poured out against all who refused to repent.[569] John's messages worked to instill the fear of God in the hearts of all who received his words and prepared them to receive the good news about God's love poured out through Jesus Christ.[570]

When people combine the fear of God with an understanding of His justice, mercy, faithfulness, and sovereignty, they are motivated to repent of their sinful ways and turn to God where they discover and receive His love.

I find it interesting that those who listened to John the Baptist and feared God enough to turn and receive the baptism of repentance by him were able to hear and understand the truth that Jesus presented, but those who had not repented at the teaching of John could not understand the teachings of Jesus. [571]

One reason that people often stumble over the truth about God's love for us is that we are taught about the love of God before we have a proper understanding about the fear of God.

It is usually our fear of God that leads us to repentance, and it's our genuine repentance that opens the door for Jesus to come into our hearts where we receive His holiness and are covered in His righteousness. This enables us to walk with God so that we can personally get to know Him and experience His love that motivates us to follow Him and empowers us to love others while eliminating all of our fears.[572]

---

[569] Matthew 3:1-12, Luke 3:1-18, John 3:36
[570] John 3:27-36
[571] Luke 7:29-30
[572] Isaiah 30:15, Matthew 3:7-9, Luke 3:7-9, Romans 2:4, Ephesians 2

One of the truths about Jesus is that He came to reveal and demonstrate the loving nature of God to those of us who fear Him so that we could learn to serve Him without fear.[573]

God wants us to commit ourselves to doing what is right and avoiding doing what is wrong.[574] If we choose to care about what God cares about, then we honor God and He blesses us. If we choose not to care about what God cares about, then we can easily be misled into believing lies and act upon those lies which leads to our own misery and self-destruction.

God always keeps His promises and does what He says He will do. So don't be misled into thinking that God doesn't see or care about you just because you may not recognize His active involvement right now. If you truly want an abundant and joyful life, then you must first choose to believe God, fear Him, and do what He says is right. Then your eyes will be opened to see God.

The fear of God prepares our hearts and enables us to hear and receive the words of God. When we repent of our selfish ways and accept Jesus, we become right with God and can enter into His presence.[575] As we do right and abide in His presence, we experience God's love with fullness of joy without fear because fear has to do with punishment for doing wrong.[576]

God's love is perfected or made complete when we walk in obedience to God, receive His love, and spread that love to others.[577] True love comes from God, and through His Spirit we receive His love into our hearts for the purpose of giving it to others. In this way His love is perfected through

---

[573] Luke 1:74
[574] Genesis 4:7
[575] Hebrews 4:14-16
[576] 1 John 4:18
[577] 1 John 5:1-3

us which glorifies Him, as the Apostle Paul explained, "For from Him and through Him and for Him are all things."[578]

When we love others as Jesus instructed,[579] we effectively love God and complete the cycle because whatever we do for others, we do for God.[580]

In other words, the fear of God motivates us to obey God, and when we obey Him by loving others, His love is perfected through us and we remain in His presence where there is no fear.

One way that our enemy tries to lure us away from God is by distorting our perception of fear. Another way he accomplishes this mission is by desensitizing us to our natural fear reflex by making normally fear-provoking events appear fun like certain Halloween activities, telling or listening to scary stories, or watching horror movies.

When we repeatedly activate the fear response through so-called fun entertainment, we desensitize ourselves to the positive influence that fear should have in motivating us to honor and obey God.

The fear of the Lord is the beginning of knowledge and wisdom, for the mysteries of God are revealed only to those who fear Him.[581] We simply cannot understand and experience the mysterious love of God until we first choose to make pleasing Him our top priority.

When we are not walking in ways that please God, we should not be surprised when we have trouble and can't hear from God or obtain His help because He doesn't listen to the prayers of prideful people who don't fear Him enough to follow His instructions. [582]

---

[578] Romans 11:36
[579] John 15:9-17
[580] Matthew 25:40
[581] Psalm 25:14
[582] Psalm 34:15-16, Proverbs 28:9, John 9:31, 1 John 5:14

Furthermore, when we purposefully depend on ourselves or other people for help before we turn to God, we
dishonor God because we demonstrate that we don't really
believe or trust Him. So let's stop worrying about what others
say or think about us and pay attention to what God says.

Only God can be fully trusted to always lead us in a good
direction and guide us safely through the challenges of living
in this world. And if we learn to fear God so that we desire
to please Him more than others, then we will be motivated
to do right and God's blessings will follow.

Sowing and Reaping

Another reason that we experience pain and frustration
in our lives is that we have deliberately dishonored God with
our choices, and we are simply reaping the painful consequences of our own wrongful actions, as it is written, "God
will repay each person according to what they have done."[583]

Whether we fear God or not, there's no way around it:
We reap what we sow.[584]

Not only will we be repaid with the same kind of treatment that we give others, but it will also be multiplied back
to us. Some people call it karma, but Jesus spoke of this prin-
ciple when He instructed the people, saying:

"Do not judge, and you will not be judged.
Do not condemn, and you will not be condemned. Forgive, and you will be forgiven.
Give, and it will be given to you. A good measure, pressed down, shaken together and
running over, will be poured into your lap.

---

[583] Romans 2:6
[584] Job 4:8, Galatians 6:7

For with the measure you use, it will be measured to you."[585]

An interesting aspect of God's economy is that He multiplies the fruits of our attitudes and actions. In whatever measure we sow, we will reap more by that same measure. If we treat others with respect and kindness, then we will more often be treated with respect and kindness.

If we treat others with hatred and disrespect, then more often we will be treated with hatred and disrespect as well. When we speak or act in a way that brings pain to God and others, sooner or later we will reap for ourselves painful consequences.[586] When we sin, we always reap painful consequences for ourselves.[587]

Of course, not everyone will choose to respond to us in the way we treat them, but a majority will. When we are not kind, and others mistreat us, God will still hold them accountable for their unkind treatment of us just as He will hold us accountable for the unkindness we show others.[588]

There are many examples in the Bible where a person did something wrong and reaped the consequences of those actions. It was commonly accepted that most afflictions were a direct result of some earlier sinful action. This understanding was reflected in a conversation that Jesus once had with His disciples, who asked, "Rabbi, who sinned, this man or his parents, that he was born blind?"[589]

Jesus did not rebuke him for asking such a question because He understood that much of the time our troubles are brought about by our own choices.

---

[585] Luke 6:37-38
[586] Proverbs 22:8, Galatians 6:7
[587] John 5:14
[588] Romans 2: 7-11
[589] John 9:2

On at least two occasions, Jesus also provided a direct correlation between sin and physical infirmities. Once after Jesus had healed a man who had been lame for thirty-eight years, He encountered him at the temple and told him, "See you are well again. Stop sinning or something worse may happen to you."[590]

Jesus clearly indicated that the man's physical condition was directly related to whether he chose to do right or wrong. As it is written in the book of Deuteronomy, obedience to God leads to physical and emotional blessing and disobedience to God results in physical and emotional cursing.[591]

At another time a man who was paralyzed was lowered through the roof next to Jesus, and in order to bring healing, Jesus told the man, "Friend, your sins are forgiven."[592]

Then He told the skeptical Pharisees and teachers of the law, "Which is easier: to say, 'Your sins are forgiven,' or to say, 'Get up and walk'?"[593]

Here, Jesus equated the healing of the man's physical ailments with the forgiveness of his sins, thereby again indicating that his physical paralysis was a direct result of sins that he had committed.

We know we cannot assume that all physical ailments are caused by our own sins,[594] but according to the Scriptures, many of our problems are caused by our own offensive behavior.[595] In these cases, if the sins are forgiven, then the curse causing the infirmity is removed and physical healing can take place. In the Bible, Elihu once explained it this way,

---

[590] John 5:14
[591] Deuteronomy 28
[592] Luke 5:20
[593] Luke 5:23-24
[594] John 9:3
[595] Deuteronomy 28:15-68

"But if people are bound in chains, held fast by cords of affliction, He tells them what they have done—that they have sinned arrogantly. He makes them listen to correction and commands them to repent of their evil. If they obey and serve Him, they will spend the rest of their days in prosperity and their years in contentment. But if they do not listen, they will perish by the sword and die without knowledge."[596]

Whenever we are having troubles, therefore, it's a good idea to ask God to search our hearts and reveal what's going on because we may have turned away from God and done something wrong for which we are reaping those troubles.

Many times throughout Scripture, God chose to make covenants with His people. God's love is unconditional, but experiencing many of the blessings of God depends upon our fulfilling certain commitments.

For example, in Deuteronomy 28, Moses recorded that God promised to bless the people *if* they obeyed His voice. In 2 Chronicles 7, it is recorded that God promised to forgive the sin and heal the land *if* His people would humble themselves, pray, seek His face, and turn from their wicked ways.

Later Jesus taught,

"If you forgive men their trespasses, your heavenly Father will also forgive you. But if you do not forgive men their trespasses, neither will your Father forgive your trespasses."[597]

---

[596] Job 36:8-12
[597] Matthew 6:14-15 NKJV

Therefore, we must understand that if we choose to go our own way and break covenant with God by not performing our end of the deal, then we should not expect God to follow through with His side of the deal, which includes blessings. We should not be surprised to find ourselves facing troubles.

God promised over and over that He would never leave or forsake people who are faithful to Him, and He is always faithful to hold up His end of the deal. We on the other hand, are not always good at keeping our end of the bargain, and we often go astray.

Many people have been led to believe that God promised never to leave or forsake anyone, but that's certainly not what the Scriptures say. God promised never to leave or forsake people like Moses, Joshua, and the people who crossed the Jordan into the Promised Land because they remained faithful to Him.[598] He didn't make that promise to people who He knew would not always be faithful.

God loves each of us unconditionally, but in order to walk with God and enjoy the blessings that are promised, we must trust Him, turn from evil, and faithfully do what pleases Him. King David wrote,

> "Those who know your name trust in you, for you, Lord, have never forsaken those who seek you."[599]

He also said,

> "Turn from evil and do good; then you will dwell in the land forever. For the Lord loves the just and will not forsake his faithful ones."[600]

---

[598] Deuteronomy 31:6,8
[599] Psalm 9:10
[600] Psalm 37:27-28

Elsewhere it is written,

> "The Lord is with you when you are with him.
> If you seek him, he will be found by you, but
> if you forsake him, he will forsake you."[601]

There are dozens of accounts in the Bible where God's people turned away from Him and forsook Him by following other gods and the corrupt customs of other people. God told Moses that this would happen and that if the people of Israel broke covenant with Him, then He would forsake them and let them face the consequences of their rebellion.[602]

As foretold, Jacob's descendants broke covenant and followed after other gods and participated in the detestable practices of the neighboring peoples. Therefore, God removed His blessing from them and allowed them to face the consequences of their rejection of Him.[603]

After they endured many troubles, they repented and turned back to God. Then He rescued them. This pattern of turning away from God, getting into trouble, turning back to God, and being rescued happened repeatedly over the years. [604]

We serve a merciful God who forgives our rebellion when we turn from our wicked ways and humbly depend on Him for help.[605] When we understand and believe who God is and all that He has lovingly done and promises to do for us, then we are motivated to turn to Him and seek to please Him. As

---

[601] 2 Chronicles 15:2

[602] Deuteronomy 31:16-17

[603] Judges 10:6-14

[604] Judges 10:1, 1 Samuel 12:10, 1 Kings 9:9, 11:33, 2 Kings 22:17, 2 Chronicles 24:24

[605] Isaiah 55:7, 2 Chronicles 7:14

long as we listen to Him and follow His instructions, we will remain in His presence and experience good things.[606]

When we act in ways that are not right, however, our wrong actions create a barrier that separates us from God.[607] When we carelessly do wrong, we effectively forsake Him as we remove ourselves from His protective covering, and we find ourselves alone and in trouble.

Here's what King David once prayed when he was facing many troubles,

> "Do not withhold your mercy from me, Lord; may your love and faithfulness always protect me. For troubles without number surround me; my sins have overtaken me, and I cannot see. They are more than the hairs of my head, and my heart fails within me. Be pleased to save me, Lord; come quickly, Lord, to help me."[608]

In this Psalm, David clearly connected his many troubles with his sins. He recognized that his own sinful actions brought about the trouble that he was going through. He didn't blame someone else. He took responsibility for his own actions, and he accepted the truth that he deserved the trouble he faced. Nevertheless, David did not hesitate to ask God for mercy and for help to be saved from those troubles.

We should all do likewise. Even if we walk in the fear of God most of the time, we will still sometimes find ourselves acting selfishly and doing the wrong thing which results in bringing trouble down upon ourselves. And like David, we should accept that we deserve to face uncomfortable

---

[606] John 8:29
[607] Isaiah 59: 1-2
[608] Psalm 30:11-13

consequences for our mistakes. Nevertheless, we should not hesitate to ask for mercy.

The Apostle Paul also understood that we reap what we sow. He once explained to the believers in Corinth that one of the reasons that many of them were weak and troubled by sickness or had died was that they had dishonored Jesus.[609]

Just because we have chosen to believe God and accept that Jesus carried our sins doesn't mean we should not concern ourselves with doing what is right and honoring to God. Anytime we dishonor God with our choices, we should expect to reap painful consequences.

The law of sowing and reaping is a spiritual law that God established to work for every person. Like gravity, the law of sowing and reaping either works to contribute to our well-being, like when we obey God by loving others and we reap blessings, or it works to bring about suffering in our lives such as when we disobey God and fall into sin and reap painful consequences.

Just as surely as jumping off a cliff will bring painful consequences, lying, cheating, and stealing will also inevitably bring painful consequences. God gives us instructions and boundaries because He loves us and knows what's good for us. His instructions may not always make sense to us now, but God will always work things out for our good when we maintain our commitment to honor Him.

If you know you deserve the troubles that you're facing, and you are simply reaping what you've sown, then confess the truth and repent. Turn from your misguided ways and make restitution where you have wronged other people. Confess your sin, ask God for mercy, and remember that He is faithful to forgive you and to cleanse you from all unrighteousness.[610]

---

[609] 1 Corinthians 11:27-32
[610] 1 John 1:9

Living in a Fallen World

Another main reason that we encounter troubling issues and challenges is that we live in a world that has been polluted by man's sin and is currently under the manipulating influence of Satan and his agents of darkness. Too many people have chosen to either reject God or choose to believe that God doesn't exist, so they walk in darkness where Satan rules, and they pollute their own lives as well as the world around them.

Originally, this world was perfectly wonderful, beautiful, and full of light and life.[611] When Adam and Eve chose to rebel against God, however, and they introduced sin into the world, they allowed darkness to creep into their lives and separated themselves from the safety and joy that comes with walking in the light with God.[612]

Before long, darkness began spreading and bringing deception, unrest, pain, suffering, death, and destruction to the inhabitants of the earth.[613] After Cain killed Abel, God said that the blood of Abel, which was soaked up by the ground, cried out to Him seeking justice.[614]

Unfortunately, as the population increased, so did the wickedness. Some people choose to walk in darkness instead of light for various reasons,[615] and they try to motivate others to join them there so they won't feel so alone. The polluted and defiled condition of the world reflects man's darkened state.

Some people blame fossil fuel air pollution for climate changes and certain weather patterns, but according to the

---

[611] Genesis 1

[612] Genesis 3

[613] Matthew 8:12, 22:13, 25:30

[614] Genesis 4:10, Matthew 23:35, Luke 11:51

[615] John 3:19-20

Bible, the root cause of global pollution is our own sinful rebellion against our Creator which has brought about curses on the earth, as it is written:

> "The earth dries up and withers, the world languishes and withers, the heavens languish with the earth. The earth is defiled by its people; they have disobeyed the laws, violated the statutes and broken the everlasting covenant. Therefore a curse consumes the earth; its people must bear their guilt."[616]

So it's not surprising that as populations increase and sin and selfishness continue to spread across the globe, we would also see increases in natural disasters like earthquakes, typhoons, tsunamis, tornados, hurricanes, floods, diseases, and other natural calamities.

God gave mankind dominion over the earth, and we have polluted it with our sinful ways.[617] Satan wants to distract us and direct us away from this truth so he can convince us to blame God and turn away from Him, which causes us even more trouble.

Therefore, when we suffer due to some natural disaster or disease, let's not give in to the temptation to blame God for it because we will only cause ourselves more trouble. God loves us and wants to help us, so He repeatedly calms storms and rescues those who honor Him and humbly cry out to Him for help.[618]

When Jesus walked the earth, He helped many people, and He healed all the sick who were brought to Him for

---

[616] Isaiah 24:4-6
[617] Genesis 1:26-28, Isaiah 24:4-6
[618] Psalm 107

help.[619] At least once He also calmed a storm to rescue those in distress.[620]

We do well to remember that Jesus still lives today, and when we humbly ask Him to help us, He often calms the storms and eliminates the suffering in our lives too. God may not always choose to eliminate the circumstances causing our distress, but He always provides refuge and restoration for those who choose to walk with Him.[621]

Living in a War Zone

Not only are we negatively impacted by the darkness and sinful pollution currently in the world, but we also sometimes get hurt either directly or indirectly by our enemy who works against God and His people to steal, kill, and destroy the good things that God has given us.

When Adam and Eve agreed to give in to the manipulating tactics of Satan, they effectively gave the devil the authority that God had previously given to them to rule over the earth.[622] So we now live in a world that is currently under the dominating and deceptive influences of Satan, who tries to lead us into darkness toward destruction as the Apostle John explained, "We know that we are children of God, and that the whole world is under the control of the evil one."[623]

Since we live in a world that is currently under the influence and rule of Satan,[624] temptations and offensive words and actions fly all around us like bullets on a battlefield. Of

---

[619] Matthew 4:24, 8:16, 12:15, Luke 4:40, 5:15

[620] Mark 4:39

[621] 2 Samuel 22:3, 31, Psalm 5:11, 9:9, 34:22, 62:8, Proverbs 10:29, Isaiah 57:13, Jeremiah 16:19, Nahum 1:7, John 16:33, Romans 8:28

[622] Genesis 1:26-28, 3, Luke 4:5-6, Romans 6:16

[623] 1 John 5:19

[624] John 8:44, 1 Peter 5:8, 1 John 5:19, Revelation 12:9

course, Satan's goal is to deceive and destroy the lives of as many people as possible, so he diligently works to entice us to reject God's ways, to hurt each other, and to blame each other. Satan doesn't care who he hurts.

It's like constantly living in a war zone. Sin has infested the world and invisible battles frequently take place around us because our enemy wants to maintain dominion over us or recapture us if we've been set free. His ultimate goal is to completely destroy our lives, and he employs anything that works to accomplish this goal.

He especially likes to deploy his agents to entice us to do wrong when we are tired, weak, or puffed up with pride. When we are walking in darkness and doing wrong, we also become targets for the devil and his agents to afflict us with disease, sickness, and other troubles.[625]

God created each of us to fulfill an important purpose in this world. Our enemy knows this, and he wants to wreck our lives in order to hinder God's plan.[626] And as long as we try to walk in the light, we will be targeted for attack.

Therefore, we should remember that many times the motivating influences behind the selfish or hateful actions of others originated with Satan himself, [627] and often the person whom we blame for our pain and suffering most likely did not work alone, as it is written: "Our struggle is not against flesh and blood, but against the rulers, against the authorities, against the powers of this dark world and against the spiritual forces of evil in the heavenly realms."[628]

Consequently, much of our suffering comes either directly or indirectly from Satan's efforts. This is common to everyone, so there is no shame in admitting that you

---

[625] Job 2:4-7, Luke 13:11, 16, Acts 10:37-38
[626] Ephesians 6:12
[627] Matthew 13:37-39, Ephesians 6:12, Luke 13:16, 22:31
[628] Ephesians 6:12

have been a victim of attack from the powers of darkness. Even Jesus was tempted by the devil in the same way that we are.[629]

Satan also influenced other people to try to wreck the life of Jesus,[630] and he thought he had been victorious when Jesus was tortured and executed. Thankfully, His physical death was not the end of the story, and Jesus was raised from the dead back to life, never to die again.[631]

We should remember that no force of evil can stand against the power of God,[632] and God's ultimate purpose for you will also prevail if you wholeheartedly trust Him and yield to the leading of the Holy Spirit, just as Jesus did.

There are invisible battles between light and darkness and good and evil taking place all around us. So as long as we live upon the earth, we will have to deal with offenses that are launched in our direction – some specifically directed against us that are meant to hurt us and others randomly dispersed, which we foolishly take and hold.

We should remember that in a similar way that the ultimate source of physical energy on earth is the sun, the ultimate source of spiritual energy throughout the universe is God. The way through which we have access to this energy is established by Jesus, the Light of the world. When we receive Jesus, we are given the light of life, which is eternal and even more powerful than the sun or Satan.[633]

As followers of Jesus, we have been given authority to overcome all the powers of our spiritual enemies, so nothing that Satan's forces can do to us will cause harm to

---

[629] Matthew 4:1-11, Mark 1:13, Luke 4:2-14

[630] Matthew 16:23, Mark 8:33, John 13:2, 27

[631] Romans 6:9

[632] Luke 10:19, Romans 16:20

[633] Matthew 5:14, John 8:12

us spiritually.[634] All agents of darkness have to submit to the authority that we carry as obedient children of God.

Of course, the agents of darkness will lie and try to convince us that we are powerless against them. They will try to intimidate us with their deceptive tactics, but if we believe the truth and put our trust in God, then we will be empowered to stand and overcome.

Hard-hearted people gravitate toward the darkness because they believe lies and do wrong, and they try to hide in the dark because they mistakenly think they won't get caught.[635] As followers of Jesus, since our lives reflect the light of God, we naturally and supernaturally expose the deeds of darkness, and the light that we carry irritates those who walk around in the dark. We then attract the attention of Satan's messengers and often become targeted for attack.

As followers of Jesus, we will have to suffer through various trials while living in this world. So we shouldn't be surprised when we have troubles, and we should remind ourselves that God is always faithful.

We should also remember that there is no disaster or abuse that is so destructive that God isn't able to bring about complete healing and restoration in our lives. We may be left with scars that remind us of the trials we have faced, but we must remember that God is always faithful to help us and heal our hearts when we wholeheartedly depend on Him.

Family Patterns of Destruction

Another reason that people face troubles is many people grow up in families where certain patterns of destructive behavior are passed from generation to generation. These patterns of iniquity become so ingrained in a family culture

---

[634] Luke 10:19
[635] John 3:19-21

that to the family members they often appear perfectly normal and acceptable as if they were genetically instilled in them.

Some of these patterns of iniquity include things like viewing pornography or engaging in other sexual perversions, speaking with vulgarity, profanity, sarcasm, or coarse joking, giving in to phobias, having prejudiced or chauvinistic attitudes, practicing idolatry, over-indulging in alcohol or using drugs, being lazy or passive, or engaging in other wrong behaviors.

When people grow up in homes where these or other destructive patterns of behavior are routinely carried out or considered normal, then they often become blind to their true destructive nature, and they carelessly adopt the same bad habits and continue the same patterns of destruction.

Oftentimes we don't recognize these destructive patterns in our own lives until we have children and we realize we are treating our children in harmful ways like we were mistreated.

It's important that we reject the temptation to accept the lie that we have to continue living with these destructive patterns of behavior or that we can't change just because we haven't yet learned a better way. With God's help, we can identify these patterns of iniquity and break free from their destructive influences.

Dysfunctional patterns like sexual immorality, alcohol and drug dependency, mental disorders, eating disorders, or other destructive patterns often pass from generation to generation. I believe that much of this destructive behavior is motivated or influenced by agents of darkness that become so familiar to us that within certain families they largely go unnoticed. These familiar spirits are given access to our lives when we choose to believe and embrace their lies, which are often passed from generation to generation.

Many people are lied to and abused physically and emotionally as part of Satan's plan to bind them up in misery so they will harden their hearts and turn against God.[636] Unfortunately, there are plenty of people who mistakenly blame God for their troubles and are often unknowingly being used by Satan to try to destroy the lives of others.[637] Please don't fall in to this trap.

Just like our own selfish tendencies trip us up sometimes, the devil also crouches at the door of our hearts looking for the right time to sneak in. We must stay alert and resist him so that he doesn't gain access to our lives and steal everything of value to us.

Like I mentioned earlier in the section titled, "Sticks and Stones," a few of the more common lies that the agents of darkness motivate people to tell us as children are "You're a bad boy," "You're a bad girl," "You're ugly," "You deserve to get hurt," "You're stupid," "You're fat," "You'll never amount to anything," and "You're good for nothing."

We must identify and reject these and other lies and replace them with truth. Of course, we also should continue to resist the tempting spirits who try to influence us to believe anything that isn't true or entice us to fall back into old patterns of thinking and behaving. Unfortunately, many times those tempting spirits are so familiar and sneaky that we don't have a clue that they are even there.

This is an excellent reason to spend time in fellowship with God and with people who truly care about us. We all need close friends or relatives around us with whom we can freely conduct ourselves and expose our true feelings so that they can observe us and point out our blind spots, polluted thinking, and the rough places in our behavior.

---

[636] Luke 13:16

[637] Acts 13:10, 2 Timothy 2:26

With God's help, we can identify the origins of our wrong patterns of thinking and the root causes of our bitterness and take steps to change and move toward healing and freedom.

To Display God's Power and Goodness

Another reason some people are afflicted with various issues is that God planned it that way so His power and goodness would be displayed on the earth.

This is what Jesus said about the man who was born blind and was healed after he was over forty years old. John recorded:

> "As he [Jesus] went along, he saw a man blind from birth. His disciples asked him, 'Rabbi, who sinned, this man or his parents, that he was born blind?' 'Neither this man nor his parents sinned,' said Jesus, 'but this happened so that the works of God might be displayed in him.'"[638]

Notice that according to Jesus, this man's lifelong affliction had been given to him for the purpose of displaying God's power and good works on the earth. The man's blindness was not a consequence of anyone's sin or some pollution in the world.

I find it interesting that Jesus instructed the blind man to make his way to the pool of Siloam and wash the spit mud off of his eyes in order to be healed. The man was obviously humble enough to resist arguing about how he would get there since he was blind, and after he carefully took those steps, he was healed.

---

[638] John 9:1-3

Thus, some trials and painful circumstances come to us through no fault of our own in order to display God's power and goodness on the earth to strengthen our faith in Him. Sometimes, the purpose of enduring these trials is to strengthen our dependence upon God and to keep us from getting prideful, which is always a good thing.

At other times, God's goodness is displayed through our healing like in the case of this blind man. Also, sometimes we experience healing only after we obediently take just a few prescribed steps. Therefore, let's persevere and trust that God will bring about good in our lives in whatever way He sees fit.

To Be Spared From Evil

Often we ask God, "Why?" when someone we know dies unexpectedly or at a young age. One of the most emotionally painful events that we face on this earth is the tragic death of a loved one. No matter what others say to us or what we know about God's goodness and faithfulness, the losses we experience can feel devastating.

If our friends and family who have passed away were believers, then we can find consolation in the hope that God may have arranged for them to be taken away to be spared from having to endure more of the evil influences of this world, as the following Scripture explains: "The righteous perish, and no one takes it to heart; the devout are taken away, and no one understands that the righteous are taken away to be spared from evil. Those who walk uprightly enter into peace; they find rest as they lie in death."[639]

This is good news that has brought me comfort whenever I grieve the loss of a fellow believer in Christ. After they

---

[639] Isaiah 57:1-2

have accomplished the purposes for which they were created, they are taken away to rest in peace.

It's like the person simply fell asleep and is now resting. Their physical body has died, but their soul and spirit lives on. At some point in time, they will be given a new body and awakened to experience the pure goodness of God face to face and forever.[640]

So sometimes when we ask, "Why do bad things happen to good people?" or "Why do good people die young?", one answer is that this world is currently full of pain and wickedness and God takes some of the righteous ones away to enter rest and to spare them from having to continue to face the evil and painful aspects of this world.

We can always trust God to accomplish what is best – even when we don't yet fully understand. When we encounter troubling events in life, it's helpful to consider what things look like from God's perspective. From His viewpoint, He sees death as simply a transition like falling asleep.[641] Their spirit lives on apart from their bodies, and this is certainly not a tragedy from God's perspective.

If you have lost a loved one who followed Jesus, then you can choose to believe God and live at peace, knowing that your loved one will truly never die and is now "asleep" and will rise again when Jesus returns. [642] The person is able to rest and is free from physical pain, temptations, and struggles with this sinful world.

Knowing your loved one trusted Jesus and is resting in peace is comforting, but it may not help much to diminish the pain of the personal loss of living out the rest of your days on the earth without them. We, who are left behind, always have to go through a grieving process whenever we lose a

---

[640] 1 Corinthians 15:42-54
[641] Luke 8:49-56, John 11:11-27
[642] John 3:16, 11:23-26, 1 Corinthians 15:51-56, 1 Thessalonians 5:10

close friend or family member, and it's good and proper for us to weep and mourn for a season.

We will certainly have to make life adjustments, so let's cry out to the Lord for help. He wants us to give the pain that we carry over to Him.

This reminds me of the day after my mother died of cancer. As I sat at my dining table lamenting over how much I would miss her, I became overwhelmed with grief and started sobbing.

Then to my surprise, while sobbing, I heard in my heart a voice saying, "What about Me? I'm still here."

I recognized that Jesus had just spoken to me, and I quickly and thankfully agreed with Him. "Yes Lord; You are still here."

I instantly felt His real and comforting presence. He reminded me that my mom was at rest with Him. I let go of my pain, and my tears of grief were amazingly transformed into tears of joy, and I began laughing. I was amazed and overjoyed with the remarkable transformation within my heart. Of course, there were other times when I grieved the loss of my Mom on this earth, but I am comforted knowing that she was a believer, and I will see her again.

God is always on time. He may not find it best to heal and restore the physical lives of the people we care about during their time on earth, but we can always trust Him to do what is best and to restore the heartfelt losses that we have endured.

Don't Blame God

Whenever we or people we care about experience tragedy and there's no person to blame, we are often tempted to blame God.

It's certainly a good thing to ask God for answers, but we have to be careful. Sometimes, God allows hardships to come upon us for some good reason, so attributing unpleasant events to the hand of Providence can be appropriate, but we must not fall into the trap of blaming God in a way that's critical or judgmental of Him or His motives.

To blame is to "assign responsibility for a fault or wrong."[643] So to blame someone for something is to find fault with their actions and implies there was some unfair or wrong action that either mistakenly or purposefully occurred.

We can certainly blame each other for things because we often make mistakes and do the wrong thing. Nothing, however, that God does is ever unfair, wrong, or a mistake. We may not always understand why God does what He does, but His ways are higher than our ways, and He always does what is right.[644] So to use the word "blame" is never appropriate with God.

A great example of a person who blamed God for his trouble and was rebuked was Job. God allowed Satan to test Job by causing him to suffer several painful losses over a short period of time.[645] Job lost his all of his children to a tornado, and he lost his livelihood, but he still maintained his integrity and honored God. Then he got terribly sick,[646] and after a while, he began to question God's righteousness and justice.[647]

He couldn't understand why, if God loves righteousness and justice, then how could God allow him to suffer so much since he had done so many good things and not any bad things. He finally blamed God for his troubles and complained that God wasn't treating him fairly.[648]

---

[643] Google.com/blame
[644] Isaiah 55:9, Jeremiah 12:1
[645] Job 1
[646] Job 2
[647] Job 32: 1-2
[648] Job 27:2, 31:1-28

How many of us are like Job and tempted to justify ourselves before God as we consider all of the good things we've done? We have to be careful not to fall into this trap of justifying our selfish actions or prideful attitudes.

We also have to be careful not to fall into the trap of questioning God's goodness by comparing our lives with others. It's easy to think that God has treated them or us unfairly. However, we must not entertain those lies.

After God rebuked Job, he humbled himself, repented, acknowledged that God's ways are always right, and admitted that he had no right to conclude he deserved better than what he had been given. Then God blessed the rest of his life, giving him twice as much as He had before the hardships had come upon him.[649]

Reviewing this chapter in Job's life should remind us that God's ways are right and just, and that all of our good deeds can never justify us before God. God speaks to us in various ways and warns us about doing wrong, but we all at least occasionally do wrong. Ultimately, we deserve death because by ourselves we will never live up to God's standard of perfection.[650] Thank God for sending His Son to save us!

When we experience suffering, we should humble ourselves and acknowledge that we have not always done what is right and accept whatever uncomfortable circumstances we face. We should also rejoice and praise God as we remember that Jesus experienced the death and separation that our deeds deserve.[651]

Anything seemingly good or bad that we have experienced while living on this polluted earth will eventually get much better if we humbly maintain our trust in God. All bad things will be eliminated, and all of the best things that

---

[649] Job 42:10-17
[650] Job 33-37
[651] Job 33:27-30

we experience or can imagine doing here on earth will be immeasurably better after Jesus returns and eliminates all evil and restores perfection to the earth. [652]

If you are facing painful trials in your life right now, and you think you did nothing to deserve the hardships, then remember what happened to Job and humbly accept whatever God has allowed to happen in your life. Consider that God may be refining your character, and ask Him to reveal any areas of your life that might need refining.

Also, instead of complaining about our circumstances, we accomplish much more and pass through our suffering much more quickly when we give thanks to God in the midst of our challenges. One of the most effective ways to activate God's blessings in our lives is to give praise and thanks to God when we don't feel like it because it's a sacrifice to do so.

The world will let you down. Other people will let you down. Even you will let yourself down, but God will never let you down, so don't blame Him for anything. He is loving and perfect in all His ways,[653] and He is always right.

Regardless of whether we completely understand all the "whys" of our suffering, God can still be completely trusted to help bring about what's best for us.

God leads us down different paths during different seasons of life, and we may not always fully understand why God does what He does. We can rest in hope, however, knowing that He always honors us when we honor Him,[654] and He works things out for good at the right time as we persevere and continue to trust in Him.[655]

---

[652] Revelation 22:1-5

[653] Matthew 5:48

[654] 1 Samuel 2:30

[655] Romans 8:28

May The LORD bless you and keep you;
May the LORD make His face shine upon you
and be gracious to you;
May the LORD lift up His countenance upon
you, and give you peace.

(Numbers 6:24-26 NKJV)

S.D.G.